Integrating Sustainability and ESG in Private Equity

AF761668

This book reveals how sustainability and ESG principles can be implemented towards a competitive advantage through compelling real-world case studies and proven frameworks. Following Alex Morgan's evolution from sceptical analyst to sustainability advocate, this book demonstrates how systematic ESG integration delivers superior financial returns while creating stakeholder value.

The book provides comprehensive guidance for implementing sustainable practices throughout the private equity life cycle, from enhanced due diligence that uncovers hidden risks and opportunities, to operational excellence frameworks that drive performance improvements, to exit strategies that capture ESG premiums. Through various case studies, readers discover practical methodologies for value creation across environmental, social, and governance dimensions. Essential frameworks include materiality assessment, stakeholder engagement, regulatory compliance, and measurement systems that transform sustainability from administrative burden to strategic intelligence.

This essential guide serves students, private equity professionals, institutional investors, portfolio company executives, and sustainability practitioners seeking to implement ESG strategies that bring about true value creation. With detailed implementation playbooks, sector-specific approaches, and proven methodologies, this book positions readers to build resilient, high-performing businesses that benefit all stakeholders while meeting evolving investor and regulatory expectations.

Esohe Denise Odaro is a sustainability executive with extensive experience in private equity, having overseen ESG strategy for portfolios exceeding €26 billion and participated in investment committees at firm and portfolio company levels. She has served on the Responsible Investment Advisory Group of UK Private Capital, the ESG Working Group of Invest Europe, and the Private Equity Task Force under the Sustainable Markets Initiative. Previously, she served as Global Head of Investor Relations and Sustainable Finance at the World Bank Group's International Finance Corporation (IFC), where she spearheaded development of innovative sustainable finance products as part of a $17 billion annual funding programme during which she chaired the Executive Committee of the Green, Social and Sustainability Linked Bond Principles administered by ICMA. She holds an MBA in Finance from Cornell University and an MSt in Sustainability Leadership from the University of Cambridge.

Sasja Beslik is a Swedish financial expert promoting sustainability worldwide. He is currently working in Japan as Chief Investment Strategy Officer for SDG Impact Japan. He has held senior roles at ABN Amro, Nordea (as CEO of Nordea Investment Funds Sweden and Head of Responsible Investments), PFA Danish commercial Pension Company, and J. Safra Sarasin. Awarded a medal from His Majesty the King of Sweden for outstanding environmental contribution (2016) and recognized as a Young Global Leader at the World Economic Forum (2011), Sasja is author of several books and weekly newsletter "ESG on Sunday".

Routledge Research in Sustainability and Business

Circular Economy in the European Union
Organisational Practice and Future Directions in Germany, Poland and Spain
Dagmara Lewicka, Joanna Zarębska, Roman Batko, Maciej Woźniak, Dariusz Cichoń, Beata Tarczydło, Monika Pec

Degrowth, Depth and Hope in Sustainable Business
Reflections from Denmark, Finland and Sweden
Iana Nesterova

Green Innovation in Central and Eastern Europe
Iryna Bashynska, Dagmara Lewicka, Svitlana Filyppova and Olha Prokopenko

Sustainability Reporting in Central and Eastern Europe Countries
Marzena Remlein and Ana Rep

Explainable Artificial Intelligence for Sustainable Development
Advancing Social and Economic Transformations
Edited by Ewa Wanda Ziemba, Wioletta Grzenda and Michal Ramsza

Integrating Sustainability and ESG in Private Equity
A Playbook for Generating Long-Term Value from Sustainable Practices
Esohe Denise Odaro and Sasja Beslik

The Purpose-Driven Organisation in Times of Climate Crisis
Edited by Katie Bailey and Katie Manning

The Informal Business Sector in BRICS+ Countries
Sustainable Economic Development in the Global South
Edited by Brian Ngwako Mokgatetswa Mahosi, Fulufhelo (Fulu) Netswera, Ayanda Sibiya, Elton Fernandes, Sergei Smirnov and SHEN YI

An Organisational Guide to Skills for Green Workforce Transformation
Edited by Karen Cripps and Candy Ho

For more information about this series, please visit: www.routledge.com/Routledge-Research-in-Sustainability-and-Business/book-series/RRSB

"An essential guide to the next phase of sustainability in private markets. The authors take an intellectually grounded but practical and coherent approach. An excellent read"

– **Alison Taylor**, *Clinical Professor, NYU Stern School of Business, Author of Higher Ground, HBR Press*

"A new standard for sustainable investing"

– **Chrissa Pagitsas**, *CEO Pagitsas Advisors*

"Essential reading for anyone who believes that business, like art, has the power to shape a better future"

– **Marine Tanguy** - *Founder & CEO, MTArt Agency*

"Finally—a playbook that transforms ESG from compliance burden to competitive advantage. Every PE professional and MBA student needs this roadmap to unlock real value creation."

– **Carlos Reyes**, *Head of Sustainability, Palladium Equity Partners*

"A masterfully crafted must-read to navigate the globally complex landscape of ESG integration in private equity"

– **Arunma Oteh**, *Academic, University of Oxford, former Treasurer World Bank*

"This comprehensive book bridges the much needed gap between academic foundations and practical implementation. Students and practitioners alike will find actionable tools for integrating ESG into private equity and the theoretical underpinnings highly useful."

– **Emre Usmenez**, *Associate Professor and Director of Master's in Sustainability Leadership, University of Cambridge*

"This book masterfully translates academic research into actionable frameworks, showing that rigorous ESG integration is not only principled but also smart investing backed by measurable returns"

– **Evan Greenfield**, *Managing Director, Head of ESG, Private Equity at British Columbia Investment Management Corporation (BCI)*

Integrating Sustainability and ESG in Private Equity

A Playbook for Generating Long-Term Value from Sustainable Practices

Esohe Denise Odaro and Sasja Beslik

Routledge
Taylor & Francis Group
LONDON AND NEW YORK

Designed cover image: Getty Images

First published 2026
by Routledge
4 Park Square, Milton Park, Abingdon, Oxon OX14 4RN

and by Routledge
605 Third Avenue, New York, NY 10158

Routledge is an imprint of the Taylor & Francis Group, an informa business

© 2026 Esohe Denise Odaro and Sasja Beslik

The right of Esohe Denise Odaro and Sasja Beslik to be identified as authors of this work has been asserted in accordance with sections 77 and 78 of the Copyright, Designs and Patents Act 1988.

All rights reserved. No part of this book may be reprinted or reproduced or utilized in any form or by any electronic, mechanical, or other means, now known or hereafter invented, including photocopying and recording, or in any information storage or retrieval system, without permission in writing from the publishers.

Trademark notice: Product or corporate names may be trademarks or registered trademarks, and are used only for identification and explanation without intent to infringe.

British Library Cataloguing-in-Publication Data
A catalogue record for this book is available from the British Library

Library of Congress Cataloging-in-Publication Data
A catalog record has been requested for this book

ISBN: 978-1-041-03838-2 (hbk)
ISBN: 978-1-041-03837-5 (pbk)
ISBN: 978-1-003-62563-6 (ebk)

DOI: 10.4324/9781003625636

Typeset in Sabon
by Taylor & Francis Books

We do not inherit the earth from our ancestors; we borrow it from our children and so this is for the next generation—Penelope, Kenyon, Otas Jr, Efe, Ivie, Imade, Azuwa, Iwinosa and Isaiah, you are the future, and the world will be a better place because of you

—Esohe

To my wonderful children, my greatest achievement in life. Always remember that the choices you make shape your lives. Stay humble and support one another, for that's what truly matters. Believe in yourselves, and know you have the power to create your own paths in life.

—Sasja

Contents

List of Illustrations xi
Disclaimer xiii
Foreword xiv
Preface xvi
Acknowledgements xviii
Acronyms and Abbreviations xx

PART I
Foundations 1

1 Private Equity Uncovered: From Wall Street to the World 3

2 ESG Fundamentals for Investors: Building the Foundation 17

3 Building ESG Advantage: From Compliance to Competitive Edge 34

PART II
Implementation Excellence 55

4 ESG Integration in Practice: The Systematic Approach 57

5 Due Diligence that Delivers: Finding Gold and Avoiding Landmines 75

6 Value Creation Playbook: The First 100 Days and Beyond 98

7 Metrics that Matter: Measuring What Drives Value 118

8 The Exit Advantage: How Sustainability Boosts Your Multiple 137

PART III
Navigating Complexity 155

9 Regulation Without Tears: Making Compliance Work for You 157

10 Portfolio-Level Optimization: Scaling ESG Excellence 174

11 Technology and Digital Transformation for ESG Excellence 192

12 The Sustainable PE Playbook: Lessons from the Field 209

13 Conclusion: The Future of Sustainable Private Equity 228

Glossary 232

Additional Reading Resources 238

Subject Index 243

Author Index 254

Illustrations

Tables

1.1 Global private equity market overview (2024). *Market size, activity levels, and regional distribution* 5
2.1 Evolution of ESG investment approaches (1970–2025). *From ethical screens to integrated value creation* 20
3.1 Eccles et al.'s (2014) sustainability performance study. *18-year longitudinal analysis of 90 high sustainability companies vs 90 matched controls showing systematic outperformance across multiple financial metrics* 36
3.2 Seven value creation mechanisms framework 40
4.1 Value creation evolution 59
5.1 Four-dimensional assessment matrix. *Due diligence framework for ESG risk and opportunity assessment* 78
5.2 Technology-enhanced assessment tools 80
5.3 Climate scenario analysis framework. Network for Greening the Financial System (NGFS) scenarios 87
5.4 Data quality scoring framework 88
6.1 Four foundation elements 99
6.2 ESG Quick Start Programme timeline (90 days) 102
6.3 Stakeholder mapping matrix (influence/interest) 104
6.4 Stakeholder engagement protocol 105
6.5 Stakeholder engagement methods by group 108
7.1 Material ESG metrics by industry sector 121
7.2 Data collection hierarchy 124
8.1 ESG-driven exit value enhancement 138
8.2 Exit preparation timeline (12–18 months) 141
9.1 SFDR article classifications and requirements 160
9.2 Integrated regulatory compliance framework 164
9.3 Compliance efficiency strategies 165
9.4 CSRD implementation timeline (2024–2028) 167
10.1 Stakeholder mapping matrix, portfolio level 186
11.1 ESG technology maturity framework by company size 193

11.2 AI applications in ESG management 195
12.1 Comprehensive assessment and baseline establishment 210
12.2 Phased implementation roadmap 214

Boxes

Chapter 1: Common Questions Alex Fields 12
Chapter 2: Common Questions Alex Fields 21
Chapter 2: Common Questions Alex Fields 29
Chapter 3: Common Questions Alex Fields 37
Chapter 3: Common Questions Alex Fields 44
Chapter 4: Common Questions Alex Fields 66
Chapter 5: Common Questions Alex Fields 82
Chapter 5: Common Questions Alex Fields 93
Chapter 6: Common Questions Alex Fields 103
Chapter 7: Common Questions Alex Fields 121
Chapter 7: Common Questions Alex Fields 128
Chapter 8: Common Questions Alex Fields 141
Chapter 8: Common Questions Alex Fields 147
Chapter 9: Common Questions Alex Fields 159
Chapter 9: Common Questions Alex Fields 166
Chapter 10: Common Questions Alex Fields 177
Chapter 10: Common Questions Alex Fields 183
Chapter 11: Common Questions Alex Fields 194
Chapter 11: Common Questions Alex Fields 199
Chapter 11: Common Questions Alex Fields 204
Chapter 12: Common Questions Alex Fields 213
Chapter 12: Common Questions Alex Fields 219

Disclaimer

This educational textbook employs entirely fictional case studies for pedagogical purposes. Kerring Capital Partners and all portfolio companies described herein—including Solid Hej Components, Summit Peak Facility Services, Alpine Foods, Ridgeline Solutions, Riviera Specialty, Helix Chemicals, Precision Peak Manufacturing, and Apex Industries—are hypothetical entities created solely for educational illustration.

All companies, financial data, operational metrics, ESG outcomes, and business scenarios are fictional examples designed to demonstrate key principles of sustainable private equity. They do not reflect actual company performance or real-world transactions.

All characters, including Alex Morgan, Jim Kerring, Ivie Chen, Kenyon Iken, Maria Santos, Imade Zala, Penelope Day, Hans Mueller, Marcus Weber, and Efe Iwinosa, are fictional composites developed from synthesized industry experience and academic research. Any resemblance to actual persons, companies (living, defunct, or operating), or specific business transactions is purely coincidental and unintended.

The case studies presented combine publicly available academic research with fictional narratives to create accessible learning tools for MBA and executive education programmes.

Foreword

There is something clarifying about a backlash. It cuts through euphemisms, tests conviction, and reveals who was committed and who was merely compliant. The recent politicization of ESG—especially in the United States—has exposed the fragility of much of the earlier consensus. But it has also created an opportunity to establish a deeper, more grounded form of sustainability practice that prioritizes operational insight over branding, pragmatism over performance.

This is precisely where *Integrating Sustainability and ESG in Private Equity* makes its timely and important contribution. Rather than positioning ESG as a moral ideal, the authors move ESG from theory to decision-making, focusing squarely on its practical implementation within private equity. Private equity, after all, offers fertile ground for sustainability practices: it thrives on patient capital, concentrated ownership, and the capacity to effect strategic change at scale. In other words, private equity has a unique ability to harness sustainability as a driver of genuine operational improvement and long-term value creation.

At the centre of this narrative is Alex Morgan—a nuanced, carefully constructed protagonist whose career trajectory mirrors the industry's own journey. Alex is neither a sustainability evangelist nor a sceptic. He embodies something much more realistic and relatable: an experienced private equity professional grappling with how sustainability fits practically within the rigorous demands of investment performance. This authenticity sets the book apart. By grounding sustainability decisions in Alex's real-world challenges and successes, the authors demonstrate clearly what ESG integration looks like in practice, moving decisively from theory to decision-making.

The book does more than discuss ESG at a conceptual level. It is highly specific in outlining exactly how private equity professionals can translate ESG principles into actionable strategies. Through Alex's experiences, we gain direct insight into the nuances of materiality assessments, effective board oversight structures, and how to meaningfully link management incentives to sustainability metrics. Moreover, we see first-hand how sustainability initiatives can drive operational efficiencies, mitigate risk, and enhance market positioning.

The timing of this book couldn't be more appropriate. As regulatory requirements expand globally and stakeholder expectations intensify, private equity firms face mounting pressure to develop genuine sustainability capabilities. Those who master this integration early will gain significant competitive advantages; those who delay will find themselves playing catch-up in an increasingly demanding environment.

Most fundamentally, this book embodies an idea that has guided my own professional journey: dedicating our careers to business gives us a unique opportunity—and, indeed, a responsibility—to actively contribute to making the world better. In *Integrating Sustainability and ESG in Private Equity*, we see clearly how private equity professionals can step forward, integrating sustainability deeply and strategically, enhancing not only their firms' resilience and returns but also their meaningful impact on society and the planet.

Prof. Ioannis Ioannou
Associate Professor of Strategy and Entrepreneurship
London Business School

Preface

That November morning in 2017, Ivanka Trump shared her views on sexual harassment and women's empowerment in front of a half-empty venue in Tokyo at the World Assembly for Women. We were across town addressing something far more consequential: how institutional capital could reshape the global economy. The sustainable finance conference in Minato Roppongi was standing room only—over 500 registrations from investors who understood that something fundamental was shifting.

After Tokyo's governor spoke about the city's green finance programme, we took the stage with a simple proposition: superior returns and positive impact aren't mutually exclusive. They're mutually reinforcing.

Six years later, we were both in a conference room at a leading bank's office in London hosting similar conversations with private capital investors, the landscape had transformed completely. Sustainability wasn't a nice-to-have anymore, it had become table stakes for serious institutional capital. We began writing this book to support those who like us believe in the power of finance and business to create lasting change.

This book uses narrative case studies featuring fictional companies to make complex ESG concepts accessible and memorable. Kerring Capital Partners and its portfolio companies are composites drawing on publicly available research, industry best practices, and our combined decades of experience across multiple organizations and geographies.

We chose this approach for three reasons. First, it allows us to demonstrate principles without confidentiality constraints. Second, it enables us to construct perfect teaching examples that might not exist in a single real-world case. Third, it protects proprietary information while sharing valuable insights.

Readers seeking real-world validation will find extensive academic citations throughout each chapter, including longitudinal studies from Harvard Business School, research from London Business School, and frameworks from NYU Stern and Oxford.

Whether you are preparing for private equity careers or are an investment professional looking to understand sustainability or are conducting your first or 100th ESG due diligence, this book meets you where you are and shows you where the industry is heading.

Now, as we complete this book, we are operating in a dramatically different political environment. While public markets navigate ideological battles, private equity can quietly implement what works. The firms that master this integration will build competitive advantages their peers cannot replicate.

As Eric Hoffer observed, “In times of change, learners inherit the earth, while the learned find themselves beautifully equipped to deal with a world that no longer exists.” Today’s learners are those who look beyond politics to understand what actually drives lasting business value.

The sustainability revolution in private equity is not coming, it is here. The question isn’t whether ESG or sustainability will become important, but whether you or your firm will be part of leading this transformation or struggle to catch up while others capture the value.

Welcome to the future of private equity where sustainability isn’t a political position, but a proven path to superior returns.

Esohe Denise Odaro, Paris
Sasja Beslik, Stockholm
January 2026

Acknowledgements

We owe a profound debt to our former colleagues, peers and friends who comprise the sustainable finance pioneers with whom we both worked with decades ago. The work done led to "mainstreaming" of ESG within institutional investing at scale and it built the infrastructure that made this book possible.

The green bond market creators—who transformed a €0.8 billion experiment in 2007 into a €500+ billion annual market by 2024—didn't just create new financial instruments; they established the analytical frameworks, impact measurement methodologies, and institutional investor appetite that enabled ESG integration across all asset classes.

Their insistence on rigorous use-of-proceeds tracking, transparent impact reporting, and independent verification created the operational discipline that private equity and credit markets now demand. When pension funds and insurance companies learned to evaluate climate risk through green bond frameworks, they naturally began applying the same analytical rigor to their private market allocations.

The International Capital Market Association's principles, the Climate Bonds Initiative's taxonomy work, and countless hours spent educating institutional investors about sustainability metrics created the intellectual foundation upon which modern ESG integration in private markets stands.

To the private equity professionals who embraced sustainability integration despite initial scepticism: your willingness to experiment and learn enabled the development of methodologies that now benefit the entire industry.

To the limited partners who pushed their general partners towards better ESG practices: your advocacy created the market incentives that drove industry transformation.

To the portfolio company management teams who implemented ESG initiatives with enthusiasm and rigour: your operational excellence created the performance data that validates sustainable private equity approaches.

To the academic researchers who provided intellectual foundation for sustainable finance: your rigorous analysis enabled evidence-based implementation rather than good intentions alone.

And to the next generation of private equity professionals who will inherit and improve upon the frameworks presented in this book: the future of sustainable capitalism depends on your commitment to excellence in ESG integration.

The work continues.

Acronyms and Abbreviations

AI	artificial intelligence
API	application programming interface
AUM	assets under management
B2B	business-to-business
CEO	chief executive officer
CFO	chief financial officer
CHRO	Chief Human Resources Officer
COO	chief operating officer
COP	Conference of the Parties (UN Climate Change Conference)
CPO	chief procurement officer
CSR	corporate social responsibility
CSRD	Corporate Sustainability Reporting Directive
EBITDA	earnings before interest, taxes, depreciation, and amortization
ESG	environmental, social, and governance
ESRS	European Sustainability Reporting Standards
EU	European Union
GDPR	General Data Protection Regulation
GHP	Greenhouse Gas Emissions
GP	general partner
GRI	Global Reporting Initiative
HVAC	heating, ventilation, and air conditioning
ILPA	Institutional Limited Partners Association
IoT	Internet of Things
IPO	initial public offering
IRR	internal rate of return
ISSB	International Sustainability Standards Board
IT	information technology
KKR	Kohlberg Kravis Roberts (private equity firm)
KPI	key performance indicator
LED	light emitting diode

LP	limited partner
LBO	leveraged buyout
MBA	Master of Business Administration
ML	machine learning
NLP	natural language processing
NPV	net present value
OEM	original equipment manufacturer
PE	private equity
PRI	Principles for Responsible Investment
R&D	research and development
RFP	request for proposal
ROI	return on investment
SASB	Sustainability Accounting Standards Board
SDGs	sustainable development goals
SEC	Securities and Exchange Commission
SFDR	Sustainable Finance Disclosure Regulation
SOC 2	Service Organization Control 2
SRI	socially responsible investing
TCFD	Task Force on Climate-related Financial Disclosures
TCO	total cost of ownership
UK	United Kingdom
UN	United Nations
UNFCCC	United Nations Framework Convention on Climate Change
US/USA	United States of America
VC	venture capital

Part I

Foundations

1 Private Equity Uncovered

From Wall Street to the World

1.1 The Private Equity Difference

October 2011: Kerring Capital Partners'[1] Boardroom

"We need to talk about the elephant in the room."

Alex Morgan's voice cut through the usual Monday morning chatter as partners filed into Kerring Capital Partners' boardroom, coffee cups and tea mugs in hand. Three years into what had seemed like a promising career in private equity, Alex was about to challenge everything the firm thought it knew about making money.

"Precision Peak Manufacturing is haemorrhaging cash, Summit Peak Facility Services can't keep employees for more than six months, and our prized chemicals deal with the 'attractive margins...'" Alex clicked to the first slide. "We might be about to walk into a €15 million environmental disaster with that one."

Jim Kerring, the silver-haired managing partner who had hired Alex straight from Cambridge, leaned back in his leather chair with the expression of someone preparing to hear and refute whatever was coming his way.

"The numbers are telling us a story different to that we initially saw," Alex continued, feeling the familiar mixture of conviction and career anxiety that came with challenging senior partners, even though he had been tasked by the managing partner to do just that. "From our last portfolio review meeting, our three worst-performing deals have something in common that our models never captured. And our best performers? They seem to have accidentally solved problems we didn't even know we were supposed to be measuring."

This was not the conversation Alex had planned to have when joining private equity in October 2008. Back then, ESG was barely a footnote in investment committee discussions. Environmental due diligence meant checking for obvious contamination. Social factors were someone else's problem. Governance was just making sure the CEO was not stealing.

But three years of watching deals succeed and fail had taught Alex something the textbooks never mentioned: the most profitable investments shared an unexpected characteristic. They created value for everyone—employees, customers, communities—not just shareholders. And the disasters? They had systematically ignored stakeholders until those stakeholders fought back.

DOI: 10.4324/9781003625636-2

Sidebar: Private Equity Definition

Private equity firms pool money from institutional investors to buy companies, improve their operations over an average of 3–7 years, then sell them for a profit. Unlike public stock markets where anyone can buy shares, PE involves direct ownership of entire businesses with hands-on management to drive value creation.

Alex's introduction to private equity had been brutal. He had expected Kerring Capital Partners to renege on his employment offer as most firms were doing to his classmates. It was October 2008—three weeks after Lehman Brothers collapsed, credit markets frozen, and half the deals in Kerring Capital Partners' pipeline vanishing overnight. Not exactly the gentle introduction to finance that Alex had imagined when accepting the analyst position fresh from Cambridge.

"Forget everything you think you know about investing," Jim had announced during Alex's first proper meeting. The Kerring Capital Partners' Monday morning ritual: eight people crammed around a mahogany table dissecting their portfolio companies like they were performing surgery. Coffee-stained spreadsheets covered every surface, but the real decisions happened in those heated debates about whether to fire the CEO of their automotive parts business or double down on their struggling retail chain.

"Public market investors," Jim continued, jabbing his Mont Blanc pen at a chart showing Precision Peak Manufacturing's latest numbers, "they buy pieces of paper and pray the market likes them. We buy the whole business and make it better. It's the difference between hoping and knowing."

As a nervous new analyst, Alex thought Jim was being dramatic. Later on, from watching dozens of deals unfold over the next few years—some brilliant successes, others expensive disasters—the distinction became painfully clear. This was not just another asset class. It was a completely different way of thinking about business, money, and value creation.

1.1.1 *Current Market Context (2024–2025)*

By 2024, global private equity had evolved into a $6.3 trillion industry, fundamentally different from Alex's early experience during the financial crisis. The statistics tell the transformation story that as at 2024:

- **93% of PE firms** integrate ESG factors into investment decisions.
- **€2.8 trillion** in ESG-labelled private market assets globally.
- **67% of Limited Partners** require specific ESG reporting from GP partners.
- **84% of PE professionals** believe ESG creates long-term value for companies.

1.1.2 *The Anatomy of a Private Equity Transaction*

Alex's education in private equity mechanics began with the acquisition of Ridgeline Solutions, a mid-sized cardboard and packaging manufacturer serving

Table 1.1 Global private equity market overview (2024). *Market size, activity levels, and regional distribution*

Metric	*Global Total*	*YoY Change*	*Key Regions*
Assets Under Management (AUM)	$6.3 trillion	+8.2%	North America: 58% Europe: 27% Asia-Pacific: 15%
Annual Fundraising	$1.2 trillion	+3.5%	US: $680B Europe: $340B Asia: $180B
Deal Activity (Deal Count)	28,400 transactions	−12.3%	North America: 45% Europe: 32% Rest of World: 23%
Deal Value	$847 billion	−18.5%	Buyouts: $512B Growth: $218B Other: $117B
Dry Powder (Uninvested Capital)	$2.8 trillion	+15.2%	Buyout: $1.6T Growth: $710B Venture: $490B
Average Hold Period	5.8 years	+0.3 years	Trend: Longer holds IPO exits: 12% Strategic sales: 63%
ESG-Focused Funds (% of AUM)	$890 billion (14%)	+42%	Europe leads: 22% of AUM US: 11% Asia: 8%

Source: Compiled from industry reports (Preqin, Bain Capital, PitchBook, 2024). Market conditions as of Q4 2024.

e-commerce and retail clients across Northern Europe. The €38 million deal became a teaching case study within Kerring Capital Partners, revealing how private equity firms create value through a combination of strategic, operational, and financial improvements—though the reality proved more complex than the textbook version suggested.

Phase 1: Deal Sourcing and Initial Screening (Months 1–2)

Kerring Capital Partners identified Ridgeline Solutions through proprietary sourcing, i.e. direct outreach to the founding family who had quietly explored succession options. This direct approach avoided competitive auction processes that typically inflated prices and compressed due diligence timelines.

The initial screening revealed attractive characteristics: €52 million in annual revenue, 14% EBITDA margins, and dominant positions in sustainable packaging segments showing 18% annual growth. Management had underinvested in technology and process improvements, creating clear value creation opportunities for an operationally sophisticated buyer.

Phase 2: Due Diligence and Valuation (Months 3–4)

Traditional due diligence examined financial performance, competitive positioning, operational capabilities, and legal compliance. Kerring Capital Partners deployed specialist consultants for commercial due diligence (market analysis and customer interviews), operational due diligence (manufacturing efficiency and supply chain assessment), and financial due diligence (quality of earnings and working capital analysis).

However, the traditional approach largely overlooked environmental and social factors that would later prove material to business performance. A perfunctory environmental assessment checked for obvious contamination but missed systematic issues with waste management and worker safety. Customer sustainability requirements—increasingly important in packaging markets—received minimal attention. Employee engagement and turnover, critical factors for operational businesses, were addressed through standard HR data requests without deeper analysis.

This limited ESG assessment reflected industry practice in the early 2010s, as demonstrated by research from Khan, Serafeim, and Yoon (2016). Their comprehensive study would later reveal that focused attention on financially material ESG factors generated 4.2 percentage point annual outperformance, while immaterial factors showed no benefit—requiring sophisticated analysis to distinguish between the two. At Ridgeline Solutions, this lack of systematic ESG due diligence would create complications during ownership that systematic assessment could have identified and addressed from the outset, setting the stage for more comprehensive ESG due diligence which will be expanded upon in the following chapter.

Phase 3: Acquisition and Integration (Months 5–6)

Once the deal closed, Kerring Capital Partners immediately implemented their 100-day integration plan. This included installing new financial reporting systems, establishing board governance structures, and beginning operational improvements identified during due diligence.

Such speed of change often shocked portfolio company management teams. At Ridgeline Solutions, Alex watched the CEO, Tom Mitchell, struggle to adapt to monthly board meetings, detailed performance reporting, and aggressive improvement targets that demanded EBITDA (Earnings Before Interest, Taxes, Depreciation, and Amortization—a key measure of operational cash flow) growth of 15% annually.

This integration challenge would become more complex as ESG considerations became central to value creation plans. The International Finance Corporation's (2002) landmark study "Developing Value" analysed over 240 cases across 60+ developing countries, finding that improved environmental, social, and governance practices could boost sales, cut costs, and reduce risks. However, the study also revealed that success required careful attention to local context and stakeholder relationships—factors that aggressive integration timelines sometimes overlooked. Nevertheless, the implication was clear: successful ESG integration required sophisticated analysis to distinguish material from immaterial factors—exactly the kind of detailed due diligence that private equity firms were equipped to conduct.

1.2 Historical Evolution and Market Transformation

1.2.1 The Origins: Financial Engineering (1970s–1980s)

Private equity's modern form emerged from the leveraged buyout (LBO) boom of the 1980s—a financial strategy where investors use significant amounts of borrowed money to acquire companies—when pioneering financiers like Henry Kravis and George Roberts, pioneering financiers like Henry Kravis and George Roberts, discovered they could acquire large companies using minimal equity and maximum debt.

The original private equity model was elegant in its simplicity. Investment firms would identify undervalued or inefficiently managed companies, acquire them using 70–90% debt financing, implement aggressive cost reductions and operational improvements, then sell the companies at higher valuations within 3–5 years. The combination of operational improvements, financial leverage, and multiple expansion (for instance, paying six times EBITDA to buy, selling at eight times EBITDA) generated spectacular returns for successful deals.

Alex's introduction to this financial alchemy came through Kerring Capital Partners' war stories from the 1990s and early 2000s. Jim Kerring had built his reputation during this era, executing deals where the mathematical beauty of leverage amplification overshadowed concerns about long-term business sustainability or stakeholder impact.

"We were financial engineers," Jim explained during one of their regular review sessions. "Buy low, improve operations, sell high. It worked brilliantly when credit was cheap and targets were genuinely undervalued. But those days? They're gone."

1.2.2 Market Maturation and Competition (1990s–2000s)

As the private equity industry grew, increased competition drove sophisticated changes in strategy and operations. By the 2000s, simple financial engineering was no longer sufficient. Firms needed genuine operational expertise, sector specialization, and sustainable value creation capabilities to generate superior returns.

This evolution coincided with the first serious academic research on private equity performance. Davis and colleagues (2014) found that private equity-backed companies showed productivity improvements of 2% annually compared to non-PE firms, but employment effects varied significantly based on transaction characteristics and economic conditions. The research suggested that successful private equity required more than financial manipulation—it demanded real operational improvements.

Academic research also began examining the relationship between social factors and business performance. Orlitzky, Schmidt, and Rynes (2003) conducted a comprehensive meta-analysis of 52 studies exploring corporate social and financial performance, finding that companies with stronger social responsibility practices achieved modestly better financial results. While these findings were preliminary, they suggested that stakeholder relationships might affect business performance in measurable ways.

In 2005, United Nations Secretary-General Kofi Annan invited a group of the world's largest institutional investors to New York with a bold proposition: What if investing responsibly was not just morally right, but financially smart? The idea was simple yet revolutionary. Instead of treating ESG factors as nice-to-have extras, what if investors integrated them into their core investment decisions? After all, a company poisoning local water supplies faces regulatory risks. As does a business with terrible labour practices that might struggle to attract talent.

The result was the UN Principles for Responsible Investment (PRI), launched in April 2006 with 63 founding signatories representing US$4 trillion in assets. By 2024, this network would grow to over 5,000 signatories managing more than $120 trillion—representing nearly half of global professionally managed assets. The PRI's six principles articulated a framework for integrating ESG considerations into investment decision-making, active ownership, and disclosure practices.

"I remember when the PRI launched," Alex reflected years later during a training session for new analysts. "Most of us thought it was well-intentioned but irrelevant to actual investment decisions. We were spectacularly wrong. Those early adopters built capabilities and relationships that created genuine competitive advantages—advantages that late movers are still struggling to replicate a decade and a half later."

1.2.3 The ESG Integration Era (2010s–Present)

By the 2010s, ESG considerations had evolved from niche concerns to mainstream investment factors. This transformation reflected multiple converging forces: expanding regulatory requirements, growing institutional investor mandates, accumulating academic evidence, and—perhaps most importantly—recognition that ESG factors could materially affect business performance and investment returns.

"The breakthrough moment for me came in 2016," Alex explained to the investment committee during a presentation on portfolio ESG strategy. "Khan, Serafeim, and Yoon published research that changed everything. They demonstrated that companies performing well on material ESG issues—factors that actually affect their specific business model—generated 4.2 percentage point annual outperformance. Meanwhile, companies pursuing generic ESG initiatives showed no benefit whatsoever."

This research provided the analytical framework that Alex had been seeking—a way to distinguish value-creating sustainability initiatives from expensive virtue signalling. Material ESG factors for manufacturers included energy efficiency and workplace safety. For consumer brands, product quality and labour practices mattered most. Financial services needed strong governance and data security. The key insight was that effective ESG integration required sophisticated analysis, not generic checklists.

1.3 Value Creation Mechanisms in Modern Private Equity

1.3.1 The Three Pillars of PE Value Creation

Alex learned that modern private equity creates value through three primary mechanisms, each requiring different capabilities and time horizons:

Operational Improvements (EBITDA Growth)

The foundation of private equity value creation involves improving company operations to increase earnings. This includes revenue growth through market expansion, pricing optimization, and new product development, alongside cost reductions through operational efficiency, procurement optimization, and organizational restructuring.

At Ridgeline Solutions, Kerring Capital Partners identified €4.2 million in annual EBITDA improvement opportunities through better procurement, manufacturing efficiency, and customer pricing optimization. Implementation required 18 months of intensive operational work but created sustainable competitive advantages that persisted beyond ownership.

Multiple Expansion

PE firms aim to sell companies at higher valuation multiples than purchase prices. This occurs through improving business quality (growth rate, margin stability, competitive positioning), reducing risk perception (customer concentration, supply chain vulnerability, regulatory exposure), and positioning for strategic buyers who value specific capabilities or market positions.

Multiple expansion represented the most ESG-sensitive value driver. As research by Kengelbach and colleagues (2024) would demonstrate, companies with advanced ESG capabilities commanded systematically higher valuation multiples—with 77% of M&A professionals observing higher valuations for ESG-mature companies in their survey of 115 global dealmakers.

Financial Optimization

Sophisticated capital structure management amplifies operational improvements through optimal debt-equity ratios, dividend recapitalizations, and refinancing opportunities that reduce interest costs or return capital to investors.

However, Alex observed that financial optimization alone rarely created sustainable value. Deals that relied primarily on leverage and financial engineering showed significantly higher failure rates during economic downturns, while companies with genuine operational improvements demonstrated resilience.

1.3.2 ESG as Value Creation Amplifier

"Here's what changed my thinking completely," Alex told the team during a portfolio review. "I used to see ESG as a constraint—something that might limit our operational flexibility or require expensive investments. But systematic analysis of our portfolio showed the opposite."

Alex clicked to a slide showing performance data across Kerring Capital Partners' investments over the past decade:

Portfolio Analysis: ESG Integration vs Financial Performance

- **High ESG Integration** (top quartile): 25.3% IRR, 3.2× average multiple.
- **Medium ESG Integration**: 19.7% IRR, 2.6× average multiple.
- **Low ESG Integration** (bottom quartile): 16.4% IRR, 2.1× average multiple.

"The pattern was undeniable," Alex continued. "Companies where we systematically addressed material ESG factors generated superior returns across all three value creation mechanisms. They achieved better operational improvements through employee engagement and resource efficiency. They commanded higher exit multiples because buyers recognized the competitive advantages. And they handled leverage better because stakeholder relationships created operational resilience."

This pattern aligned with broader academic evidence. Eccles, Ioannou, and Serafeim (2014) conducted an 18-year longitudinal study comparing 180 US companies (90 high-sustainability firms matched against 90 controls). Their research found that high sustainability firms significantly outperformed low sustainability counterparts on both stock market and accounting measures, with the performance gap attributed to improved internal processes and stakeholder relationships.

Similarly, Friede, Busch, and Bassen (2015) conducted the most comprehensive meta-analysis of ESG research to date, aggregating results from over 2,000 empirical studies. Their findings were striking: roughly 90% of studies showed non-negative ESG-financial performance relationships, with the majority demonstrating positive correlations. The evidence overwhelmingly suggested that sustainability and profitability were complementary rather than conflicting objectives.

"The key insight," Alex emphasized, "is that ESG creates value through the same mechanisms we've always used—it just does it better. Energy efficiency reduces costs. Employee engagement improves productivity. Customer sustainability partnerships drive revenue. These aren't separate from our value creation playbook. They're enhanced versions of what we've been trying to do all along."

1.4 Industry Criticism and Controversy

1.4.1 Employment and Operational Impact

Private equity has long faced criticism regarding employment practices and operational impacts. Critics point to high-profile cases where PE-backed companies implemented significant layoffs, reduced employee benefits, or aggressively cut costs in ways that harmed workers and communities.

"The criticism isn't entirely unfair," Alex acknowledged during a university panel discussion on private equity's social impact. "Some firms have prioritized short-term financial optimization over long-term stakeholder value creation. Those deals often fail spectacularly—and they deserve the criticism they receive."

However, the systematic evidence presents a more nuanced picture. Davis and colleagues' (2014) comprehensive research on private equity and employment found that PE-backed establishments showed average job growth rates comparable to non-PE businesses, with significant variation based on transaction characteristics. Firms pursuing operational improvements rather than pure financial engineering showed better employment outcomes and superior returns.

1.4.2 Fee Structures and Value Transfer

The "2 and 20" fee structure—2% annual management fees on committed capital plus 20% of profits above a specified hurdle rate—has generated persistent debate about whether private equity transfers value from pension funds and other investors rather than creating new value.

Alex engaged with this criticism directly when presenting to potential limited partners (LPs): "The fee question is legitimate. You need to understand exactly what you're paying for and whether we're delivering value that justifies those fees. Here's how I think about it..."

Alex would then walk through Kerring Capital Partners' value creation track record, showing how their systematic ESG integration approach generated returns that more than compensated for fees even after accounting for risk. The key was demonstrating genuine competitive advantages rather than relying on financial leverage or market timing.

Research by Fancy (2021) highlighted potential misalignment between stated ESG objectives and actual investment practices, suggesting that some firms might use ESG marketing to justify premium fees without delivering corresponding performance. However, sophisticated LPs increasingly demand evidence of genuine ESG integration rather than superficial marketing—creating competitive advantages for firms with authentic capabilities.

1.4.3 Stakeholder Impact Assessment

The most fundamental criticism involves private equity's historical focus on shareholder returns, often suggested to be at the expense of broader stakeholder interests. This criticism gained urgency as ESG considerations became more central to investment evaluation, requiring firms to demonstrate systematic stakeholder value creation.

"This is where ESG integration becomes strategic rather than just defensive," Alex explained to the team. "By systematically creating value for all stakeholders—employees, customers, suppliers, communities—we generate superior financial returns because those stakeholders support rather than resist our value creation initiatives."

Research by Friede, Busch, and Bassen (2015) provided evidence that stakeholder value creation and financial performance were complementary rather than conflicting objectives. Their comprehensive analysis found that roughly 90% of studies showed non-negative ESG-financial performance relationships, suggesting that concerns about shareholder-stakeholder trade-offs were based on false dichotomies rather than systematic analysis.

Common Questions Alex Fields

Q: Doesn't ESG integration reduce returns by constraining our operational flexibility?
A: The data shows exactly the opposite. Our high-ESG integration deals generated 25.3% IRR versus 16.4% for low-integration deals. Material ESG factors create competitive advantages—they don't constrain value creation, they enable it.
Q: How do we respond to critics who say PE destroys jobs?
A: Show them the evidence. Davis and colleagues found PE-backed firms show comparable job growth to non-PE businesses—but only when firms focus on operational improvements rather than pure financial engineering. That's exactly what systematic ESG integration drives us toward.
Q: What about the fees? Aren't we just extracting value?
A: Fair question. Our answer is performance. After fees, our ESG-integrated approach generates returns that significantly exceed public market alternatives. The fees are justified when we deliver genuine competitive advantages rather than relying on leverage and market timing.

1.5 The Future of Private Equity

1.5.1 Technology and Data Integration

"The technology revolution in ESG is just beginning," Alex explained to a group of portfolio company CEOs in late 2024. "And it's going to fundamentally change how we create value."

The presentation outlined emerging capabilities that would transform private equity operations: Artificial intelligence enabling real-time sustainability monitoring and optimization. Machine learning algorithms identifying patterns in operational data that humans couldn't spot. Satellite imagery providing independent verification of environmental performance. Blockchain creating transparent and verifiable supply chain tracking.

"But here's the critical insight," Alex emphasized. "Technology amplifies capabilities—it doesn't replace judgement. The firms that will win are those combining technological sophistication with deep sector expertise and authentic stakeholder relationships. Technology makes systematic ESG integration more efficient and effective, but it doesn't eliminate the need for genuine commitment and capability."

1.5.2 Regulatory Convergence

Looking forward to 2025 and beyond, regulatory frameworks are converging towards mandatory sustainability disclosure and impact measurement. The EU's Corporate Sustainability Reporting Directive (CSRD), US SEC climate disclosure rules, and similar initiatives across Asia-Pacific markets are creating standardized data availability and accountability requirements.

"Regulatory convergence creates both opportunities and challenges," Alex noted during a limited partner meeting. "Standardized data will improve ESG due diligence efficiency and accuracy—we'll be able to compare companies more reliably and identify material risks more systematically. However, mandatory disclosure will also increase compliance costs and transparency requirements that may affect competitive dynamics."

For Kerring Capital Partners, the strategic response was clear: build advanced ESG capabilities ahead of regulatory requirements, creating competitive advantages in deal sourcing, value creation, and exit execution. Early movers would establish relationships, develop expertise, and refine processes that later entrants would struggle to replicate.

Since 2024, sustainability regulation has entered a phase characterised less by continuous expansion and more by consolidation, simplification, and enforceability. This shift is illustrated by the European Commission's November 2025 proposal to reform the Sustainable Finance Disclosure Regulation (SFDR), which explicitly acknowledged that existing disclosures had become complex, costly, and insufficiently decision-useful for investors (European Commission, 2025).

1.5.3 Stakeholder Capitalism Evolution

The broader evolution toward stakeholder capitalism—where companies systematically consider impacts on employees, customers, suppliers, communities, and the environment alongside shareholder returns—is reshaping private equity strategy and operations.

"This evolution aligns perfectly with private equity's fundamental approach," Alex reflected during a strategy session. "Unlike public market investors who rely primarily on financial analysis and market timing, we've always needed deep understanding of operational factors, competitive dynamics, and stakeholder relationships to drive value creation. ESG integration is simply the logical extension of this approach—applying systematic analysis to factors that materially affect business performance."

The integration of ESG considerations represents not just compliance or risk management, but rather a source of systematic advantages in deal sourcing, value creation, and exit execution. As research by the UN Principles for Responsible

Investment and Bain (2025) demonstrated through their Sustainability Value Creation framework—developed with input from 400 global investors—private markets offer unique opportunities to drive financial value through sustainability, precisely because of the active ownership model that characterizes private equity.

As Alex wrapped up the presentation to Jim Kerring and the partnership that October morning in 2011, the room sat in thoughtful silence. What had started as a challenge to conventional thinking had become a roadmap for transformation.

Jim leaned forward. "Alright, Alex. You've convinced me there's something here. But here's my question: if ESG is such a powerful value driver, why isn't everyone already doing this? What's our competitive advantage?"

Alex smiled, recognizing the opening to discuss the next chapter of Kerring Capital Partners' evolution. "That's exactly the right question. And the answer reveals why ESG represents one of the most significant competitive opportunities we've seen in private equity in the past two decades. Let me show you the fundamentals—the research base, the value creation mechanisms, and the practical frameworks that separate genuine ESG integration from expensive virtue signalling."

The conversation that followed would reshape Kerring Capital Partners' investment strategy and, over the following decade, establish them as leaders in sustainable private equity. But it all started with understanding the fundamentals—the research foundation and practical frameworks that distinguish value-creating sustainability initiatives from superficial approaches. That foundation is where we turn next.

For private equity, this recalibration is particularly significant. Sustainability data is increasingly assessed not only for regulatory compliance, but for its relevance to capital raising, portfolio governance, and exit preparedness. The direction of travel is therefore not deregulation, but a heightened emphasis on credibility, materiality, and operational relevance across the full investment lifecycle.

Chapter Summary

Core Insight

Private equity has evolved from 1980s financial engineering to sophisticated operational improvement, with ESG integration emerging as a systematic value creation driver. Companies in Kerring Capital Partners' portfolio with high ESG integration generated 25.3% IRR versus 16.4% for low-integration deals—demonstrating that sustainability and profitability are complementary, not conflicting.

Critical Success Factors

- **Understand the three value levers**: Operational improvements enhanced with ESG can drive higher of returns, multiple expansion, and financial optimization.

- **Focus on materiality**: Khan, Serafeim, and Yoon (2016) showed material ESG factors drive 4.2% outperformance while immaterial initiatives show no benefit.
- **Build early-mover advantages**: The 2006 PRI signatories established capabilities and relationships that created lasting competitive advantages over late entrants.
- **Leverage active ownership**: PE's concentrated ownership enables systematic ESG integration more effectively than passive public market investing.

Watch Out For

⚠ Generic ESG approaches without materiality assessment waste resources and generate no value.

⚠ Pure financial engineering without operational improvements shows higher failure rates during downturns.

⚠ Ignoring stakeholder relationships creates resistance that undermines value creation initiatives.

⚠ Technology alone does not create value, it must amplify genuine capabilities and stakeholder relationships.

Tools You Can Use Now

- **Three-pillar value creation framework**: Operational improvements + Multiple expansion + Financial optimization.
- **ESG materiality filter**: Focus only on factors that affect your specific business model.
- **Stakeholder value mapping**: Identify which stakeholder relationships drive competitive advantages.
- **Portfolio performance comparison**: Benchmark high vs low ESG integration to quantify impact.

What's Next

Chapter 2 dives deep into ESG fundamentals—the evolution of sustainability thinking, the seven mechanisms through which ESG creates value, and the critical distinction between material and immaterial factors. You'll learn to navigate rating system limitations, understand regulatory evolution, and develop frameworks for systematic ESG integration. Alex's crisis experience with Riviera Specialty provides the catalyst for transformation from scepticism to systematic advocacy.

Note

1 All companies and characters in this book are fictional. Kerring Capital Partners and its portfolio companies are hypothetical entities created for educational purposes. Financial data and outcomes are illustrative examples designed to demonstrate environmental, social, and governance (ESG) integration principles.

References

Bain & Company. (2024). *Global private equity report 2024*. Bain & Company.

Davis, S. J., Haltiwanger, J., Handley, K., Jarmin, R., Lerner, J., & Miranda, J. (2014). Private equity, jobs, and productivity. *American Economic Review*, 104 (12), 3956–3990. doi:10.1257/aer.104.12.3956.

Eccles, R. G., Ioannou, I., & Serafeim, G. (2014). The impact of corporate sustainability on organizational processes and performance. *Management Science*, 60 (11), 2835–2857. doi:10.1287/mnsc.2014.1984.

European Commission (2025). Impact Assessment Accompanying the SFDR Review.

European Commission (2025). Proposal for a Regulation amending Regulation (EU) 2019/2088 (SFDR)

Fancy, T. (2021). The secret diary of a "sustainable investor" [Essay series]. Medium.

Friede, G., Busch, T., & Bassen, A. (2015). ESG and financial performance: Aggregated evidence from more than 2000 empirical studies. *Journal of Sustainable Finance & Investment*, 5 (4), 210–233. doi:10.1080/20430795.2015.1118917.

International Finance Corporation. (2002). Developing value: The business case for sustainability in emerging markets. World Bank Group.

Kengelbach, J., Herfurth, J., Degen, D., Oberbracht, D., Fromholzer, F., & Schubert, J. (2024, April 18). The payoffs and pitfalls of ESG due diligence. Boston Consulting Group.

Khan, M., Serafeim, G., & Yoon, A. (2016). Corporate sustainability: First evidence on materiality. *The Accounting Review*, 91 (6), 1697–1724. doi:10.2308/accr-51383.

Orlitzky, M., Schmidt, F. L., & Rynes, S. L. (2003). Corporate social and financial performance: A meta-analysis. *Organization Studies*, 24 (3), 403–441. doi:10.1177/0170840603024003910.

PitchBook Data, Inc. (2024). *Global PE breakdown Q4 2024*. PitchBook.

Preqin. (2024). *Global report 2024: Private equity*. Preqin Ltd.

Principles for Responsible Investment & Bain & Company. (2025). Value creation through sustainability in private markets. PRI.' Update the in-text citation on p.13 to '(Principles for Responsible Investment & Bain & Company, 2025)'.

United Nations Global Compact. (2004). Who Cares Wins: Connecting financial markets to a changing world. UN Global Compact.

2 ESG Fundamentals for Investors

Building the Foundation

Weekend Crisis: March 2015, Riviera Specialty

The call came at 2.47 a.m. on a Saturday. Alex Morgan fumbled for the phone, recognizing the number but not expecting weekend emergencies from portfolio companies.

"Alex, we have a situation." The voice belonged to Maria Santos, the newly appointed CEO of Riviera Specialty, one of Kerring Capital Partners' more challenging investments. "The environmental regulators shut us down three hours ago. Complete operations halt and they are talking about criminal charges!"

Alex sat up in bed, instantly awake. Riviera Specialty produced industrial chemical blending and solvents for European manufacturing markets—a business that seemed straightforward during due diligence 18 months earlier. The financial models showed steady growth, strong margins, and a defensible market position. Environmental issues had not appeared as significant risks.

"What happened?" Alex asked, already reaching for laptop and car keys.

"Soil contamination. Groundwater pollution. Turns out we've been leaking industrial solvents for at least three years. The initial estimate is €47 million in clean-up costs, plus potential fines and community compensation." Maria's voice carried the strain from the long night dealing with regulators, lawyers, and increasingly hostile local officials.

By Sunday evening, Alex had spent 36 hours learning more about environmental compliance, stakeholder relations, and operational culture than the previous three years combined. The investigation revealed systematic problems that traditional due diligence had completely missed, problems that would ultimately cost Kerring Capital Partners over €36 million and fundamentally change Alex's approach to investment analysis.

This crisis marked Alex's conversion from ESG sceptic to advocate. The question was not whether environmental, social, and governance factors mattered—the wreckage of Riviera Specialty made that brutally clear. The real question was how to systematically assess and manage these factors to create value rather than merely avoiding disasters.

DOI: 10.4324/9781003625636-3

2.1 The Evolution of Sustainability Thinking

2.1.1 From Environmental Regulation to Stakeholder Capitalism (1970s–Present)

Over the following weeks, as Alex immersed in damage control at Riviera Specialty, the parallels to the industry's broader evolution became clear. Sustainability thinking had followed a predictable path from reactive compliance to strategic value creation—and Kerring Capital Partners had somehow missed the entire journey.

"It's not that we ignored sustainability," Alex explained to Jim Kerring during one of their regular debriefs. "We just treated it as a compliance checkbox rather than a business fundamental. The disconnect between our sophisticated financial analysis and our superficial environmental assessment was…embarrassing."

The evolution Alex studied traced clear phases across five decades:

Phase 1: Environmental Regulation (1970s–1980s)

Modern environmental consciousness emerged from regulation rather than voluntary corporate action. The US Clean Air Act (1970), Clean Water Act (1972), and similar legislation globally established basic environmental standards that companies needed to meet. Sustainability meant compliance—avoiding fines and operating shutdowns.

Phase 2: Corporate Responsibility (1990s)

The concept evolved beyond regulatory compliance towards broader corporate social responsibility. The 1987 Brundtland Report's definition of sustainable development— "meeting the needs of the present without compromising the ability of future generations to meet their own needs"—provided philosophical grounding that resonated beyond environmental circles.

Companies began publishing sustainability reports and establishing CSR departments. However, these efforts remained largely peripheral to core business strategy—marketing initiatives rather than operational transformations.

Phase 3: Triple Bottom Line Integration (2000s)

The early 2000s saw growing recognition that environmental and social factors had business implications beyond compliance and reputation. John Elkington's "Triple Bottom Line" framework—measuring success across financial, environmental, and social dimensions—gained traction as companies recognized that stakeholder relationships affected business performance.

As mentioned in Chapter 1, the UN Principles for Responsible Investment launched in 2006, with then Secretary-General Kofi Annan's proposition that responsible investing might be both morally right and financially smart, marked a watershed moment. The PRI's six principles articulated a framework for integrating ESG considerations into investment decision-making, moving sustainability from philanthropic concern to fiduciary responsibility.

Phase 4: ESG Integration and Materiality (2010s)

The 2010s brought sophisticated analytical frameworks that distinguished value-creating sustainability from expensive virtue signalling. Academic research by Khan, Serafeim, and Yoon (2016) revolutionized ESG investment approaches by demonstrating that material ESG factors—those financially relevant to specific business models—drove 4.2 percentage point annual outperformance while immaterial factors showed no benefit. This materiality insight transformed ESG from generic checklist to sophisticated analytical framework requiring industry expertise and business judgement.

"That materiality research changed everything for me," Alex reflected. "It meant I could approach ESG the same way I approached any other investment factor—with rigorous analysis to distinguish what actually matters from what sounds good but has no business impact."

Phase 5: Stakeholder Capitalism (2020s)

The COVID-19 pandemic accelerated evolution towards comprehensive stakeholder capitalism—systematic consideration of impacts on employees, customers, suppliers, communities, and environment alongside shareholder returns. The 2019 Business Roundtable statement, where 181 CEOs committed to stakeholder rather than shareholder primacy, marked symbolic recognition of this shift.

By 2024, stakeholder capitalism had moved from aspiration to operational reality for leading companies. Morgan Stanley's (2025) "Sustainable Signals: Corporates 2025" report found that 88% of companies now see sustainability as a long-term value creation opportunity, with over 80% believing they can measure ROI of sustainability projects. This represented fundamental evolution from compliance mindset to strategic integration.

2.1.2 The Research Foundation: Building the Evidence Base

As Alex dug deeper into sustainability research, compelling evidence base emerged.

"Listen to this," Alex told Ivie Chen, Kerring Capital Partners' head of portfolio operations, during one of their working sessions on revamping their due diligence approach. "Orlitzky and colleagues analysed 52 studies in 2003 and found modest but consistent positive relationships between corporate social performance and financial results. But that was just the beginning."

The academic evidence had accumulated steadily.

Eccles, Ioannou, and Serafeim (2014) conducted an 18-year longitudinal study of 180 US companies, comparing "high sustainability" firms that adopted ESG

Table 2.1 Evolution of ESG investment approaches (1970–2025). *From ethical screens to integrated value creation*

Era	*Period*	*Key Characteristics*	*Milestones*	*Adoption*
Ethical Screening	1970s–1990s	Exclusionary approach Moral and religious values Avoid "sin stocks" (tobacco, weapons, gambling) Negative screening dominant	• 1971: Pax World Fund • 1982: Sullivan Principles • 1990s: Apartheid divestment	<5% of AUM
SRI Integration	1990s–2000s	Socially Responsible Investing (SRI) Best-in-class selection Positive screening emerges ESG factors as risk indicators	• 1992: Rio Earth Summit • 1997: GRI founded • 2000: UN Global Compact	5–12% of AUM
ESG Mainstreaming	2006–2015	ESG integration framework Materiality focus Active ownership Fiduciary duty recognition	• 2006: PRI launched • 2011: SASB founded • 2015: Paris Agreement • 2015: SDGs adopted	15–30% of AUM
Value Creation	2015–2020	ESG as value driver Performance correlation proven Active engagement Data and analytics	• 2017: TCFD recommendations • 2019: Business Roundtable • 2020: COVID-19 accelerates focus	35–50% of AUM
Integrated Sustainability	2020–2025	Mandatory disclosure Double materiality Science-based targets Impact measurement standard	• 2021: COP26 Glasgow • 2023: ISSB standards • 2024: CSRD effective • 2025: Climate disclosure mandatory	60–75% of AUM

Key Trend: From exclusion → integration → value creation → mandatory practice
Note: Adoption rates represent percentage of global PE/investment AUM with formal ESG policies or commitments. Regional variations significant (Europe leads US by 10–15pp).

policies early against carefully matched controls. Their findings were striking: high sustainability companies significantly outperformed low sustainability counterparts on both stock market returns and accounting measures, with the performance gap attributed to improved internal processes and stakeholder relationships built over time.

Clark, Feiner, and Viehs (2015) synthesized existing research in a comprehensive meta-study for the University of Oxford, finding that 80% of studies showed positive effects of sustainability on stock price performance and 88% demonstrated operational improvements. The evidence suggested that ESG integration created value through multiple mechanisms rather than single channels.

Perhaps most comprehensively, Friede, Busch, and Bassen (2015) aggregated results from over 2,000 empirical studies that is the largest meta-analysis of ESG research ever conducted. Their findings provided overwhelming evidence: roughly 90% of studies showed non-negative ESG-financial performance relationships, with the clear majority demonstrating positive correlations. The research didn't just show that sustainability and profitability could coexist, it suggested they were mutually reinforcing.

"So why aren't we doing this already?" Ivie asked the obvious question.

"Because," Alex replied, clicking to the next slide, "the research also shows that not all ESG matters equally. That's where materiality comes in."

Khan, Serafeim, and Yoon's (2016) breakthrough research provided the analytical framework Alex had been seeking. Their study demonstrated that companies performing well on material ESG issues—factors that actually affected their specific business model and industry—generated 4.2 percentage point annual outperformance. Meanwhile, companies pursuing generic ESG initiatives across immaterial factors showed no benefit whatsoever.

Ivie said, studying the data. "So, it's about being smart about which sustainability factors actually drive your business."

Common Questions Alex Fields

Q: How do we know this research applies to private equity? Most studies focus on public companies.

A: Valid concern. But the research on material ESG factors is even more relevant for us. We have operational control and concentrated ownership—exactly the tools needed to systematically address material factors. Public market investors can only hope management does it. We can make it happen.

Q: What if the ESG-performance link is just correlation, not causation?

A: Eccles and colleagues addressed this through matched-pair analysis and 18-year timeframes—hard to explain away as spurious correlation. More importantly, the mechanisms are logical: energy efficiency reduces costs, engaged employees are more productive, good governance prevents value-destroying decisions.

Q: Aren't ESG ratings a simpler approach than this materiality analysis?

A: Berg and colleagues showed ESG rating correlations average only 0.54—compared to 0.99 for credit ratings. That divergence (with 56% of it driven by measurement differences) means we can't outsource ESG analysis to rating agencies.

2.1.3 Rating System Challenges

As ESG investing gained popularity, numerous rating agencies emerged to assess corporate sustainability performance. However, research revealed significant limitations and inconsistencies that affected investment decision-making—limitations that would prove critical for Kerring Capital Partners' approach.

Berg, Kölbel, and Rigobon (2022) documented systematic problems in their analysis of major ESG rating providers. Their research revealed that ESG rating correlations averaged only 0.54—dramatically different from the 0.99 correlation for credit ratings. This "aggregate confusion" stemmed from three sources:

- **Measurement differences (56%):** Agencies used different indicators to assess the same ESG attributes.
- **Scope variations (38%):** Agencies focused on different ESG attributes entirely.
- **Weighting differences (6%):** Agencies applied different importance to the same attributes.

"This was actually good news for us," Alex explained to the investment committee. "The rating disagreement means ESG analysis requires sophisticated judgement and industry expertise—exactly the capabilities that create competitive advantages. If ESG assessment was as standardized as credit ratings, there'd be no edge to gain."

The implication was clear: successful ESG integration required primary research capabilities rather than reliance on third-party ratings. Private equity firms with superior analytical frameworks and industry expertise could identify material ESG factors that rating agencies and competitors missed.

2.2 The Riviera Specialty Crisis: A Case Study in ESG Materiality

2.2.1 Traditional Due Diligence Limitations

Alex's weekend at Riviera Specialty provided painful first-hand education in traditional due diligence limitations. Kerring Capital Partners had conducted exhaustive financial, commercial, and operational analysis during the 18-month acquisition process, but had systematically overlooked environmental, social, and governance factors that ultimately determined investment success.

The financial analysis had been sophisticated: detailed cash flow modelling, competitive benchmarking, market share analysis, and management assessment. Commercial due diligence examined customer relationships, supplier agreements, and competitive positioning. Operational review identified efficiency improvements and growth opportunities.

However, the analysis had fundamental blind spots that proved catastrophic:

Environmental Assessment: Limited to basic compliance verification without deeper investigation of operational practices, stakeholder relationships, or cultural factors affecting environmental performance.
Social Factor Analysis: No systematic assessment of employee relations, community relationships, or stakeholder management capabilities.
Governance Evaluation: Focused primarily on formal board structures and reporting systems without examining decision-making culture, operational accountability, or ethical conduct.

"We'd spent €340,000 on due diligence," Alex recounted bitterly to Jim Kerring the following week. "Every number in the financial model was validated to three decimal places. But we never actually talked to employees about operational culture. We never asked community leaders about relationships, never dug into why environmental compliance costs were consistently below industry averages; which should have been a red flag, not a competitive advantage."

2.2.2 Discovery Process

The investigation that followed Riviera Specialty' shutdown revealed how systematically traditional due diligence had failed:

Employee Interviews: Anonymous conversations with workers revealed that environmental compliance was routinely compromised during busy periods. Equipment maintenance was delayed, safety protocols were abbreviated, and environmental monitoring was manipulated to avoid regulatory scrutiny. "Everyone knew," one long-time operator admitted. "Management just didn't want to hear it."

Community Relations: Local residents had complained for years about odours and suspected contamination, but management had dismissed these concerns as uninformed opposition to industrial development. The community relations failure turned what might have been a technical compliance issue into a criminal investigation.

Supplier Relationships: Chemical suppliers had raised questions about usage volumes and disposal practices, but these concerns were also not documented or escalated to senior management. The suppliers' risk management systems had identified problems that Riviera Specialty own processes missed.

Customer Feedback: Some customers had quietly expressed preferences for suppliers with stronger environmental credentials, but sales teams had dismissed this as peripheral concern. These early signals of market evolution went unheeded.

"The investigation revealed that traditional due diligence was fundamentally inadequate," Alex reflected. "We had analysed financial statements, market dynamics, and competitive positioning in exhaustive detail. But we'd completely ignored the stakeholder relationships and operational culture that actually determined business sustainability."

2.2.3 Financial and Personal Impact

The Riviera Specialty crisis ultimately cost Kerring Capital Partners €15.3 million in direct remediation expenses, €8.7 million in lost revenue from operational shutdowns, and €12 million in legal settlements with affected communities. Beyond financial losses, the crisis damaged relationships with limited partners and required 18 months to rebuild the company's customer base.

For Alex personally, the crisis triggered profound re-evaluation of fundamental assumptions about value creation and risk assessment.

"That weekend changed how I think about everything," Alex admitted during a retrospective with the investment team. "I realized that ESG factors weren't peripheral considerations—they were core business fundamentals that traditional analysis systematically overlooked. Our 'thorough' due diligence had been fundamentally incomplete."

2.2.4 The Learning Process

Following the crisis, Alex embarked on intensive study of sustainability research and ESG integration methodologies. This wasn't ideological conversion but analytical response to the recognition that traditional frameworks were inadequate for identifying and managing real business risks.

"I approached ESG like any other analytical challenge," Alex explains. "I read the academic research, studied successful implementations, and developed frameworks for systematic assessment. The goal wasn't to become a sustainability advocate—it was to become a better investor."

The research revealed that Riviera Specialty represented a common pattern: companies often failed on ESG dimensions not because of resource constraints or regulatory complexity, but because management systems did not systematically account for stakeholder relationships and long-term operational sustainability.

2.3 Seven Mechanisms of ESG Value Creation

Alex's portfolio research identified seven systematic mechanisms through which ESG factors create measurable business value. Understanding these mechanisms was crucial for distinguishing value-creating sustainability initiatives from expensive virtue signalling.

2.3.1 Revenue Enhancement through Stakeholder Relationships

The first mechanism involved revenue enhancement through improved stakeholder relationships, particularly with customers increasingly concerned about supplier sustainability practices.

"We saw this pattern repeatedly," Alex explained during a presentation on ESG value drivers. "Companies with strong sustainability credentials gained market access, commanded pricing premiums, and won competitive bids that their peers couldn't even participate in."**Customer Preference Evolution:** Research by NYU Stern's Center for Sustainable Business (2019) found that 73% of global consumers would change consumption habits to reduce environmental impact, with younger demographics showing even stronger preferences. For B2B companies, procurement policies increasingly required supplier sustainability credentials as table stakes for consideration.

Brand Value Premium: Companies with strong ESG reputations commanded pricing premiums across multiple sectors. Unilever announced in 2019 that its sustainable brands grew 69% faster than traditional brands in 2018, demonstrating that sustainability positioning could drive top-line growth. Similarly, Tesla achieved luxury pricing (average $54,660 in 2020) based partly on environmental positioning and technological innovation.
Market Access: ESG credentials increasingly determined access to customers, particularly in regulated industries and international markets. European companies often required supplier ESG certification, while government procurement policies favoured sustainable suppliers. "For our manufacturing portfolio companies," Alex noted, "strong ESG credentials opened doors that financial engineering alone never could."

2.3.2 Operational Efficiency and Cost Reduction

The second value creation mechanism involved systematic operational improvements driven by environmental and social initiatives. Contrary to popular perception, sustainability improvements often reduced costs while enhancing performance:

Energy Efficiency: Portfolio companies implementing systematic energy management achieved cost reductions while improving operational reliability. The The Solid Hej Components case study would later showcase 34% energy cost reduction over three years while expanding production capacity—demonstrating that environmental performance and operational growth were complementary rather than conflicting.
Waste Reduction: Circular economy principles drove both cost savings and operational efficiency. Through Alpine Foods' transformation, 18% raw material cost reduction through waste stream optimization would improve both environmental performance and product quality consistency—waste often signalled process inefficiency rather than inevitable operational reality.
Productivity Gains: Employee engagement initiatives consistently improved productivity metrics. Summit Peak Facility Services would achieve productivity improvements following comprehensive workplace culture transformation, while simultaneously reducing turnover costs by 35 percentage points—engaged employees generated superior performance.

2.3.3 Risk Mitigation and Operational Resilience

ESG factors significantly affected business risk profiles across environmental, regulatory, operational, and reputational dimensions. Systematic ESG management provided superior risk intelligence compared to traditional assessment approaches.

"The Riviera Specialty crisis taught me that ESG risks can destroy value faster than operational improvements can create it," Alex emphasized. "Companies with strong environmental management systems experience fewer operational disruptions, regulatory violations, and community conflicts. That operational resilience translates directly into financial performance advantages."

Environmental Risk Management: Companies with robust environmental systems experienced fewer operational disruptions and avoided enforcement actions. The operational resilience translated into sustained cash flow generation and preserved stakeholder relationships.
Supply Chain Resilience: ESG assessment identified supply chain vulnerabilities that traditional analysis missed. Companies with diverse, well-managed supplier relationships showed greater resilience during disruptions like COVID-19 or climate events—sustainability assessment provided early warning of operational fragility.
Regulatory Risk Mitigation: ESG-integrated companies anticipated regulatory changes more effectively, achieving compliance ahead of competitors while avoiding enforcement actions that disrupted operations. Early movers established competitive advantages that later entrants struggled to replicate.

2.3.4 Capital Access and Cost Advantages

ESG performance increasingly affected capital market access and pricing across debt and equity markets. Companies with superior ESG credentials achieved lower borrowing costs, better insurance pricing, and improved investor valuations.

"We started seeing this concretely in our portfolio by 2018," Alex recalled. "Companies with strong ESG performance received better loan pricing—25–50 basis points was common. Insurance carriers offered better terms. And strategic buyers paid higher multiples at exit, explicitly citing ESG capabilities as value drivers."

Research by Pedersen, Fitzgibbons, and Pomorski (2021) demonstrated that responsible investing strategies could achieve competitive returns while reducing risk. Their analysis suggested that ESG factors provided valuable information about business quality and management effectiveness that traditional financial metrics missed.

2.3.5 Talent Attraction and Retention

The fifth mechanism involved competitive advantages in talent markets, particularly for knowledge-intensive businesses where human capital determined value creation.

Companies with strong ESG credentials and authentic commitment to stakeholder value demonstrated systematic advantages in recruiting and retaining top talent. Summit Peak Facility Services would showcase this mechanism through dramatic turnover reduction from 47% to 12%—below industry averages—following comprehensive workplace culture transformation.

"Millennial and Gen Z workers consistently prefer employers with genuine sustainability commitments," Alex noted. "For professional services and technology companies, this talent advantage creates competitive moats that pure financial incentives can't replicate."

2.3.6 Innovation and Long-term Thinking

Focus on sustainability fosters innovation mindsets and long-term thinking that generates competitive advantages beyond immediate financial returns. Companies systematically considering environmental and social impacts developed products, services, and business models that anticipated rather than reacted to market evolution.

Ridgeline Solutions would later develop a patent portfolio around sustainable packaging solutions—intellectual property that created licensing revenue and competitive differentiation. The innovation emerged from systematic consideration of customer sustainability needs rather than traditional product development processes.

2.3.7 Licence to Operate and Stakeholder Support

The final mechanism involved maintaining and enhancing social licence to operate—the informal permission granted by communities, regulators, and broader stakeholders for business operations. Companies with strong stakeholder relationships navigated regulatory processes more effectively, avoided community opposition, and secured necessary permits and approvals.

"This one's hard to quantify but easy to see in action," Alex explained. "Companies with strong community relationships get expansion permits approved in months. Companies with hostile stakeholder relationships spend years in regulatory battles—if they succeed at all. The value impact is massive but traditional analysis completely misses it."

2.4 Challenges and Critical Perspectives

2.4.1 Data Quality and Measurement Issues

Despite accumulating evidence for ESG value creation, significant challenges remained in implementation and measurement. Alex learned that acknowledging these challenges honestly was crucial for developing effective approaches.

"One of the biggest mistakes I see is treating ESG as fully mature and standardized," Alex told new analysts. "The data is still messy, methodologies vary widely, and measurement remains challenging. Ignoring these issues doesn't make them go away—it just means we're not prepared to address them."

The data quality challenges were substantial:

Inconsistent Reporting Standards: Companies reported ESG performance using different frameworks (GRI, SASB, TCFD, CDP, etc.), making comparisons difficult and requiring sophisticated normalization.

Limited Historical Data: Many ESG metrics lacked the multi-year track records necessary for robust trend analysis, particularly for privately held companies.
Verification Gaps: While financial data underwent rigorous audit, many ESG metrics relied on self-reporting without independent verification—creating greenwashing risks.

2.4.2 *Greenwashing and Authenticity Concerns*

The risk of greenwashing—superficial ESG marketing without genuine substance—created both reputational and analytical challenges for investors.

Dempere, Alamash, and Mattos (2024) highlighted the prevalence of greenwashing in sustainable finance, finding that many companies made ambitious sustainability claims without corresponding operational changes or performance improvements. Their critique emphasized the importance of authentic commitment to stakeholder value creation rather than superficial compliance with reporting requirements.

"We've seen this first-hand," Alex acknowledged. "Companies that treat ESG as marketing exercise rather than operational transformation achieve no value creation—and sometimes destroy value through wasted resources and stakeholder cynicism. The key is distinguishing authentic integration from expensive virtue signalling."

For private equity firms, greenwashing risks created both competitive opportunities and implementation challenges. Firms developing genuine ESG capabilities could differentiate themselves from those pursuing superficial approaches, but they needed sophisticated measurement and verification systems to demonstrate authentic performance.

2.4.3 *Cost–Benefit Analysis*

Critics questioned whether ESG integration costs justified financial benefits, particularly for smaller companies with limited resources. Raghunandan and Rajgopal (2022) found that ESG funds did not consistently make more stakeholder-friendly investments than traditional funds, suggesting that ESG marketing might exceed actual practice differences.

"The cost question is legitimate," Alex engaged with this criticism directly during limited partner presentations. "ESG implementation requires investment—in systems, capabilities, and sometimes operational changes that have near-term costs. The question is whether the long-term benefits justify these investments."

Alex's portfolio experience suggested that ESG implementation costs varied significantly based on approach and industry context. Companies pursuing material ESG factors typically achieved positive returns, while those implementing generic programmes often struggled to justify costs. The key was rigorous materiality assessment and focused resource allocation.

Common Questions Alex Fields

Q: How do we respond to the greenwashing criticism? Isn't all ESG just marketing?

A: "Show them the operational changes and financial results. At Solid Hej Components, we documented €456,000 in annual value creation from €596,000 in ESG investments over four years. That's not marketing—that's genuine value creation that competitors couldn't replicate.

Q: What about the cost? Can smaller companies afford ESG integration?

A: Materiality is your answer. Small companies can't afford comprehensive ESG programmes—but they can focus on the 3–5 factors that actually drive their business. Alpine Foods' first 100 days generated €546,000 in annual benefits from €114,000 in investment. That's accessible even for mid-market companies.

Q: How do we distinguish authentic ESG from superficial approaches?

A: Three tests: (1) Are initiatives tied to material business factors? (2) Do they generate measurable operational improvements? (3) Can you demonstrate financial ROI? If you can't answer these clearly, you're probably doing ESG theatre rather than value creation.

2.5 The Future of ESG Integration

2.5.1 Technology and Data Revolution

Looking forward, Alex anticipated that technology would fundamentally transform ESG measurement and management capabilities. Artificial intelligence, satellite monitoring, blockchain verification, and Internet of Things (IoT) sensors would enable real-time sustainability monitoring and automated reporting.

"The twin transition is already happening," Alex explained, referencing recent research by Shajari and David (2025) on the convergence of digitalization and sustainability. "Digital transformation accelerates sustainability actions while sustainability goals drive digital innovation. Companies that master this convergence create synergies that competitors struggle to match."

These technological advances would address many current ESG implementation challenges:

Data Quality: Automated monitoring would improve data accuracy and reduce reporting burdens.
Verification: Blockchain and IoT would enable transparent, verifiable sustainability performance tracking.
Analysis: AI would identify patterns and opportunities that manual analysis might miss.
Efficiency: Technology would reduce ESG management costs while improving performance.

2.5.2 Regulatory Standardization

Global regulatory convergence towards mandatory sustainability disclosure would transform ESG integration from voluntary best practice to required business capability. The EU's Corporate Sustainability Reporting Directive (CSRD), US SEC climate disclosure rules, and similar initiatives across Asia-Pacific markets would create standardized frameworks and accountability requirements.

"For private equity firms, regulatory standardization creates both opportunities and challenges," Alex noted during a strategy session. "Standardized disclosure will improve due diligence data availability and quality but will also increase compliance requirements and transparency obligations that may affect competitive dynamics."

The strategic imperative was clear: build advanced ESG capabilities ahead of regulatory requirements, creating competitive advantages that late movers would struggle to replicate. A late-2025 policy signal reinforces this strategic logic. In November 2025, the European Commission published proposed reforms to SFDR explicitly aimed at simplifying disclosures and improving decision-usefulness for investors, while reducing unnecessary reporting burden (European Commission, 2025). This matters for private markets because it indicates the regulatory direction of travel is towards clearer product information and more enforceable governance expectations, rather than a steady expansion of disclosure volume.

2.5.3 Stakeholder Capitalism Evolution

The broader evolution towards stakeholder capitalism—where companies systematically consider impacts on employees, customers, suppliers, communities, and the environment alongside shareholder returns—would reshape business strategy and operations across all sectors.

"This evolution aligns naturally with private equity's operational approach," Alex reflected. "Unlike public market investors who rely primarily on financial analysis and market timing, we've always needed deep understanding of stakeholder relationships to drive value creation. ESG integration is simply the logical extension—applying systematic analysis to factors that materially affect business performance."

As Morgan Stanley's (2025) research demonstrated, 88% of companies now see sustainability as a long-term value creation opportunity. ESG integration was no longer optional or experimental—it had become essential for competitive success in modern private equity.

As Alex wrapped up the post-mortem presentation on Riviera Specialty to the Kerring Capital Partners partnership, the transformation from that painful weekend to systematic framework was complete. The crisis had cost them dearly—but it had also revealed opportunities that traditional analysis systematically missed.

Jim Kerring leaned forward. "Alright, Alex. You've convinced me that ESG matters and that there's solid research behind it. But Riviera Specialty was a defensive case—avoiding disaster. You mentioned earlier that our best-performing deals also had strong ESG characteristics. Show me the offensive case—how ESG creates value, not just prevents destruction."

Alex smiled. The question opened the door to the next phase of Kerring Capital Partners' evolution, moving from ESG as risk management to ESG as systematic value creation. Over the following quarters, Alex would develop the frameworks and case studies that demonstrated ESG's power as a competitive advantage. It all started with understanding how sustainability could drive superior financial performance through concrete, measurable mechanisms.

That journey from theory to practice, from avoiding disasters to creating competitive advantages, is where we turn next. In Chapter 3, we'll see how systematic ESG integration generates returns that exceed traditional private equity approaches, using real portfolio examples that demonstrate sustainability and profitability as complementary rather than conflicting objectives.

Chapter Summary

Core Insight

ESG evolved from 1970s compliance to 2020s stakeholder capitalism, with material ESG factors demonstrating clear financial impact. Riviera Specialty' €36 million crisis revealed that environmental, social, and governance factors aren't peripheral—they're core business fundamentals that traditional analysis systematically overlooks.

Critical Success Factors

- **Build on research foundation**: Friede et al.'s meta-analysis of 2,000+ studies shows 90% non-negative ESG-financial relationships—overwhelming evidence base.
- **Focus on materiality**: Khan et al. demonstrated that material ESG factors drive 4.2% outperformance while immaterial initiatives waste resources—sophisticated analysis required.
- **Understand seven value mechanisms**: Revenue enhancement, operational efficiency, risk mitigation, capital access, talent advantage, innovation, and licence to operate—ESG creates value through multiple channels.
- **Don't rely on ratings alone**: Berg et al. showed ESG rating correlations of only 0.54 vs 0.99 for credit ratings—primary research capabilities essential.
- **Embrace technology evolution**: The twin transition (digitalization + sustainability) creates synergies that amplify value creation when managed strategically.

Watch Out For

⚠ Greenwashing—superficial ESG marketing without genuine operational change destroys value through wasted resources and stakeholder cynicism.
⚠ Generic ESG programmes without materiality assessment show no financial benefit despite implementation costs.
⚠ Traditional due diligence blind spots—financial sophistication doesn't compensate for missing stakeholder and operational culture analysis.
⚠ Cost–benefit imbalance—ESG investments must focus on material factors that generate measurable returns.

Tools You Can Use Now

- **Seven value creation mechanisms framework**: Map which mechanisms matter most for your industry and business model.
- **Materiality filter**: Focus resources on 3–5 ESG factors with clear business relevance rather than comprehensive programmes.
- **Rating system scepticism**: Use ratings as starting point but conduct primary research on material factors.
- **Crisis autopsy methodology**: When deals fail, systematically analyse whether ESG blind spots contributed.

What's Next

Chapter 3 presents the offensive case for ESG—moving beyond risk mitigation to systematic value creation. Using Nordic Components, Alpine Foods, and Summit Peak Facility Services case studies, you'll see how material ESG factors generate 3.8 percentage point IRR improvements and 1.3× higher exit multiples. Alex demonstrates that sustainability and profitability aren't competing objectives—they're mutually reinforcing when approached with analytical rigour and operational discipline.

References

Berg, F., Kölbel, J., & Rigobon, R. (2022). Aggregate confusion: The divergence of ESG ratings. *Review of Finance*, 26 (6), 1315–1344. doi:10.1093/rof/rfac037.

Clark, G. L., Feiner, A., & Viehs, M. (2015). From the stockholder to the stakeholder: How sustainability can drive financial outperformance. University of Oxford & Arabesque Partners. doi:10.2139/ssrn.2508281.

Dempere, J., Alamash, E., & Mattos, P. (2024). Unveiling the truth: Greenwashing in sustainable finance. *Frontiers in Sustainability*, 5, Article 1362051. doi:10.3389/frsus.2024.1362051.

Eccles, R. G., Ioannou, I., & Serafeim, G. (2014). The impact of corporate sustainability on organizational processes and performance. *Management Science*, 60 (11), 2835–2857. doi:10.1287/mnsc.2014.1984.

European Commission. (2025). Commission proposes improvements to SFDR (21 November).

European Commission. (2025). Commission simplifies transparency rules for sustainable financial products (20 November)

Friede, G., Busch, T., & Bassen, A. (2015). ESG and financial performance: Aggregated evidence from more than 2000 empirical studies. *Journal of Sustainable Finance & Investment*, 5 (4), 210–233. doi:10.1080/20430795.2015.1118917.

Khan, M., Serafeim, G., & Yoon, A. (2016). Corporate sustainability: First evidence on materiality. *The Accounting Review*, 91 (6), 1697–1724. doi:10.2308/accr-51383.

Morgan Stanley. (2025, June). Sustainable Signals: Corporates 2025. Morgan Stanley Institute for Sustainable Investing.

NYU Stern Center for Sustainable Business. (2019). Sustainable market share index. New York University Stern School of Business.

Orlitzky, M., Schmidt, F. L., & Rynes, S. L. (2003). Corporate social and financial performance: A meta-analysis. *Organization Studies*, 24 (3), 403–441. doi:10.1177/0170840603024003910.

Pedersen, L. H., Fitzgibbons, S., & Pomorski, L. (2021). Responsible investing: The ESG-efficient frontier. *Journal of Financial Economics*, 142 (2), 572–597. doi:10.1016/j.jfineco.2020.11.004.

Raghunandan, A., & Rajgopal, S. (2022). Do ESG funds make stakeholder-friendly investments? *Review of Accounting Studies*, 27 (3), 822–863. doi:10.1007/s11142-022-09693-1.

Shajari, S., & David, S. (2025, June). Bridging the silos of digitalization and sustainability by twin transition. arXiv preprint.

Unilever. (2019). Unilever's purpose-led brands outperform. https://www.unilever.com/news/press-and-media/press-releases/2019/unilevers-purpose-led-brands-outperform/.

World Commission on Environment and Development. (1987). *Our common future*. Oxford University Press.

3 Building ESG Advantage

From Compliance to Competitive Edge

The Money Case

Jim Kerring's voice boomed across the Kerring Capital Partners' boardroom as Alex finished presenting their Solid Hej Components investment—a Danish wind turbine manufacturer that had become their most successful ESG-integrated deal. "I need you to prove this sustainability stuff isn't just expensive virtue signalling."

Alex clicked to the results slide, knowing this moment would determine whether ESG integration remained a side project or became central to their investment strategy. The numbers were stark: Solid Hej Components had generated a 3.2× return and 22% IRR, outperforming portfolio averages by 3.8 percentage points. More importantly, €12–15 million of the exit value was directly attributable to the sustainability infrastructure they had built—turning environmental and social improvements into hard financial returns.

But the evidence went far beyond one successful deal. After two decades of tracking performance across dozens of investments, Alex had assembled compelling data showing that their most profitable deals shared an unexpected characteristic: they were also their most sustainable.

"Look at the pattern," Alex continued, advancing to the next slide. "This isn't cherry-picking one success story. It's systematic analysis of our entire portfolio over ten years."

Kerring Capital Partners' portfolio analysis: ESG integration vs financial performance:

- **High ESG Integration** (top quartile): 25.3% IRR, 3.2× average multiple.
- **Medium ESG Integration**: 19.7% IRR, 2.6× average multiple.
- **Low ESG Integration** (bottom quartile): 16.4% IRR, 2.1× average multiple.

"The correlation is undeniable," Alex emphasized. "Companies where we systematically addressed material ESG factors generated superior returns across all three value creation mechanisms. Better operational improvements. Higher exit multiples. More resilient through economic cycles."

DOI: 10.4324/9781003625636-4

This portfolio performance trend reflected broader market evolution. PwC (2022) projected that sustainable finance assets would increase from 14.4% of total assets under management in 2021 to 21.5% in 2026—driven not by ideology but by growing recognition of ESG factors' financial materiality. The question was no longer whether sustainability mattered, but whether private equity firms could afford not to integrate ESG into their value creation strategies.

3.1 The Financial Evidence for ESG Integration

3.1.1 Portfolio Performance Analysis

Alex's systematic analysis of Kerring Capital Partners' portfolio revealed compelling patterns that aligned with broader academic research. The data spanned 47 investments across manufacturing, services, consumer goods, and technology sectors from 2010 to 2024.

"We started this analysis sceptically," Alex admitted to the room. "I wanted to prove that our ESG efforts weren't hurting returns—I didn't expect to find they were driving them. But the statistical relationship between material ESG integration and financial performance was too strong to ignore."

The analysis controlled for multiple variables: deal size, industry sector, entry timing, market conditions, and leverage levels. Across all these controls, the ESG-performance relationship persisted. Companies with high ESG integration consistently outperformed, achieving 8.9 percentage points higher IRR than low-integration peers—a difference that compounded to substantial value over typical hold periods.

More granularly, the analysis revealed specific mechanisms:

Operational Performance: High ESG companies achieved 34% better EBITDA growth on average, driven by energy efficiency, waste reduction, and productivity improvements.
Risk Profile: High ESG companies experienced 42% fewer material operational incidents, regulatory violations, or stakeholder conflicts requiring intervention.
Exit Performance: High ESG companies commanded 1.5× higher exit multiples on average, with buyers explicitly citing sustainability capabilities as valuation drivers.

3.1.2 Academic Research Foundation

"The portfolio evidence is compelling," Jim Kerring interjected, "but is this just our firm's experience, or is there broader research supporting this?"

Alex had anticipated the question. "The academic evidence is overwhelming. Let me walk you through the key studies that shaped our thinking."

Eccles, Ioannou, and Serafeim (2014) conducted an 18-year longitudinal study at Harvard Business School that provided perhaps the most rigorous evidence. They compared 180 US companies (90 high-sustainability firms adopting ESG policies by 1993, against 90 carefully matched controls). Their analysis found that high sustainability companies significantly outperformed on both stock market returns (4.8% higher annually) and accounting performance (16% higher return on assets (ROA), 13% higher return on equity (ROE)).

"What makes this research particularly compelling," Alex explained, "is the methodology. They didn't just look at companies claiming to be sustainable—they identified firms that had systematically integrated sustainability into operations and governance structures early. Then they tracked them for nearly two decades."

The performance gap was not immediate. During the first few years, high sustainability companies showed similar or slightly lower returns as they invested in building capabilities. But over time, the investments compounded. Improved stakeholder relationships reduced friction. Better risk management avoided crises. Enhanced reputation attracted talent and customers. The cumulative effect was substantial and persistent.

Clark, Feiner, and Viehs (2015) took a different approach through meta-analysis at the University of Oxford, synthesizing 200+ primary sources and finding that 80% showed positive effects of sustainability practices on stock price performance and 88% demonstrated operational improvements. The evidence suggested that ESG integration created value through multiple channels rather than a single mechanism.

Perhaps most comprehensive is the Friede, Busch, and Bassen (2015) earlier mentioned which aggregated results from over 2,000 empirical studies with the clear majority demonstrating positive correlations.

"Think about what that means," Alex emphasized. "Over 2,000 studies, across different time periods, different markets, different methodologies—and 90% find that sustainability either helps or doesn't hurt performance. That's not ideological bias. That's empirical reality."

Table 3.1 Eccles et al.'s (2014) sustainability performance study. *18-year longitudinal analysis of 90 high sustainability companies vs 90 matched controls showing systematic outperformance across multiple financial metrics*

Performance Metric	*High Sustainability Companies*	*Matched Control Group*	*Outperformance*
Annual Stock Returns	14.3%	9.5%	+4.8%
Return on Assets (ROA)	+16% vs control	Baseline	+16%
Return on Equity (ROE)	+13% vs control	Baseline	+13%
Study Period	1993–2011 (18 years)	—	—
Sample Size	90 companies	90 matched pairs	—

Source: Eccles et al. (2014).

Note: High sustainability companies defined as those adopting sustainability policies by 1993. Control group carefully matched on industry, size, and other characteristics. Results demonstrate systematic financial outperformance attributable to early ESG adoption across multiple performance dimensions.

The most important research for Kerring Capital Partners' practical implementation came from Khan, Serafeim, and Yoon (2016). Their materiality framework revolutionized how Alex thought about ESG integration.

"This research changed everything for us," Alex explained, clicking to a slide showing the materiality matrix. "Khan and colleagues demonstrated that companies performing well on material ESG issues—factors that actually affect their specific business model—generated 4.2 percentage point annual outperformance. Meanwhile, companies pursuing generic ESG initiatives across immaterial factors showed no benefit whatsoever."

The materiality insight meant that effective ESG integration required sophisticated industry analysis and business judgement. Energy efficiency mattered enormously for manufacturers but barely registered for software companies. Labour practices were critical for retail and hospitality but less material for capital-intensive industries. Environmental compliance was existential for chemicals but peripheral for professional services.

"This explains why some companies see great ESG returns and others see nothing," Alex continued. "The difference isn't whether sustainability matters. It comes down to whether you're focused on the sustainability factors that actually matter for your specific business."

Common Questions Alex Fields

Q: Doesn't this correlation just mean successful companies can afford to do ESG, not that ESG drives success?

A: Eccles and colleagues controlled for this through matched-pair analysis. They compared companies that were initially similar on all dimensions except sustainability commitment, then tracked them for 18 years. The high sustainability firms pulled ahead over time—suggesting causation, not just correlation.

Q: What about the studies showing ESG hurts performance? Don't they balance out the positive ones?

A: Friede's meta-analysis found roughly 10% of studies show negative relationships. But most of those studied immaterial factors or short-term costs without long-term benefits. When you focus on material factors with proper time horizons, the relationship becomes consistently positive.

Q: How do we know which ESG factors are material for our portfolio companies?

A: Khan and colleagues provide industry-specific frameworks through SASB standards. But the real work is business analysis—understanding your company's value drivers, stakeholder relationships, and operational risks. Material factors are those that affect these business fundamentals.

3.1.3 Value Creation Mechanisms

Alex advanced to the next section of the presentation, where the abstract research became concrete business cases. "Here's how ESG actually creates value in our portfolio. Not theory—operational reality."

Operational Efficiency through Resource Optimization

Environmental improvements consistently drove cost reductions across portfolio companies. Energy efficiency, waste reduction, and resource optimization generated direct bottom-line savings while improving sustainability metrics.

"Take Solid Hej Components," Alex said, bringing up detailed financials. "Systematic efficiency improvements achieved €456,000 in annual operating cost savings—money that dropped straight to EBITDA. The company reduced energy consumption by 31% through LED lighting retrofits saving €67,000 annually, HVAC optimization adding €98,000, and process equipment upgrades contributing €187,000."

These were not one-time savings from deferred maintenance or corner-cutting. They represented genuine efficiency improvements that improved operational reliability while reducing costs. The lighting upgrade improved workplace conditions and reduced maintenance needs. The HVAC optimization enhanced manufacturing environment stability. The equipment upgrades increased throughput while consuming less energy.

This experience aligned with broader industry evidence. Research by the International Energy Agency (2021) found that energy efficiency improvements in industrial settings typically generated 15–30% cost reductions while enhancing operational reliability and competitiveness. The IEA analysis suggested that efficiency represented one of the most underutilized profit improvement opportunities in manufacturing.

Risk Mitigation and Insurance Cost Reduction

"But cost reduction is just the beginning," Alex continued. "ESG integration systematically reduces various risk categories—from regulatory compliance to operational disruptions."

Research by Swiss Re Institute (2021) found that companies with superior ESG performance achieved 10–15% lower insurance premiums on average, reflecting reduced risk profiles across environmental, social, and governance dimensions. The insurance industry's sophisticated risk modelling had independently validated what ESG proponents argued: sustainability management correlated with better risk outcomes.

At Solid Hej Components, improved safety performance—achieving an industry-leading total recordable incident rate of 0.8 per 100,000 work hours—reduced insurance costs by €73,000 annually while preventing the operational disruptions and human costs of workplace accidents. But the risk mitigation value extended far beyond insurance savings.

"The Riviera Specialty Foods crisis taught us that ESG risks can destroy value faster than operational improvements can create it," Alex noted soberly. "Companies with strong environmental management systems experience fewer operational disruptions, regulatory violations, and community conflicts. That operational resilience translates directly into sustained cash flow generation."

Revenue Enhancement through Market Positioning

Market research by McKinsey & Company (2023) found that 77% of business-to-business (B2B) buyers considered supplier sustainability credentials in procurement decisions, with 34% willing to pay premiums for verified sustainable suppliers. This trend created systematic revenue advantages for companies with authentic ESG capabilities.

"Sustainability capabilities increasingly open new market opportunities and support premium pricing," Alex explained. "At Solid Hej Components, sustainability credentials enabled two major contract wins worth €340,000 annually with customers prioritizing environmental performance from suppliers."

But the revenue enhancement went beyond specific contracts. Strong ESG performance created brand value and competitive positioning that influenced customer decisions across the entire business. Solid Hej's reputation for sustainability leadership opened doors with procurement managers, differentiated them in competitive bids, and provided negotiating leverage for premium pricing.

"One customer told us explicitly," Alex recounted, "'We're willing to pay more for your components because your sustainability performance helps us meet our own commitments. You make us look good to our stakeholders.'"

Talent Attraction and Retention Value

Companies with strong ESG practices consistently outperformed on employee metrics that directly impacted operational performance. Deloitte's 2023 Global Millennial and Gen Z Survey found that 83% of respondents considered a company's environmental and social impact when deciding where to work, with 44% making career decisions based on personal values. This demographic shift created systematic talent advantages for ESG-integrated companies.

"The talent impact shows up most dramatically in turnover reduction," Alex explained. "At Summit Peak Facility Services, our facilities management company, comprehensive well-being programmes reduced annual turnover from 47% to 12%—saving over €600,000 annually in recruitment and training costs."

But turnover savings understated the full value. Lower turnover meant more experienced workforce, stronger institutional knowledge, better customer relationships, and enhanced service quality. These operational advantages compounded over time, creating competitive edges that pure financial incentives could not replicate.

Access to Capital and Financing Benefits

Portfolio companies with strong ESG credentials increasingly accessed better financing terms and attracted more investor interest. Research by the Bank for International Settlements (2021) documented systematic financing advantages for ESG-performing companies, with green bonds trading at 20–30 basis points below conventional debt and sustainability-linked loans showing similar pricing benefits.

"We've seen this concretely in refinancing negotiations," Alex noted. "Companies with strong, verified ESG performance receive better loan pricing—25–50 basis points was common across our portfolio. That might sound small, but on €20 million of debt, it's €50,000–100,000 in annual interest savings."

Beyond pricing, ESG credentials opened access to capital pools that traditional companies could not tap. Green bonds, sustainability-linked loans, and ESG-mandated funds represented growing capital sources actively seeking investments in companies with verified sustainability performance. New empirical work focused on private equity and published in January 2026 provides additional evidence linking structured ESG integration to value-creation disciplines across the investment life cycle. Using data and case examples drawn from a large institutional investor's private-market activity, the authors show how ESG integration is operationalized through diligence, ownership governance, and portfolio execution—emphasizing mechanisms such as operational risk reduction, performance discipline, and exit readiness rather than disclosure alone (Greenfield, Monk, and Rook, 2026). While this research is presented as a working paper rather than a peer-reviewed journal article, it is useful here because it is specific to private equity implementation and connects sustainability actions to recognized value-creation levers.

Table 3.2 Seven value creation mechanisms framework

Mechanism	*Description*	*Typical Impact*
1. Operational Excellence	Energy efficiency, waste reduction, process optimization, quality improvements	2–5% EBITDA improvement €500K–2M annual savings
2. Risk Mitigation	Regulatory compliance, reputation protection, supply chain security, cyber resilience	1–3% EBITDA protection Avoided costs €200K–1M
3. Revenue Enhancement	Market access, customer preference, sustainability premiums, innovation	3–8% revenue growth €1M–5M additional revenue
4. Cost of Capital	Better lending terms, lower insurance premiums, improved credit ratings	50–100 basis points €100K–500K annual savings
5. Talent Management	Attraction and retention, productivity gains, reduced turnover costs	1–2% EBITDA improvement €300K–1M value creation
6. Innovation	Sustainability-driven R&D, new products/services, market differentiation	Long-term growth 5–15% revenue upside
7. Exit Premium	Valuation multiple expansion, broader buyer pool, faster exit process	0.5–2.0× multiple uplift 10–30% value increase

3.2 Case Study: Solid Hej Components Value Creation Success

3.2.1 The Challenge and Opportunity

"Let me show you how this works in practice," Alex said, transitioning to the detailed Solid Hej Components case study. "This is where theory becomes operational reality."

Solid Hej Components, a €52 million Danish wind turbine parts manufacturer, appeared successful but was underperforming its potential when Kerring Capital Partners acquired it in 2019. The company served major turbine manufacturers across Northern Europe with precision-engineered components, maintaining steady revenue growth and healthy 14% EBITDA margins.

Traditional due diligence had identified operational efficiency opportunities and potential market expansion possibilities. However, Alex's enhanced ESG assessment revealed additional value creation opportunities that traditional analysis had missed:

Environmental Inefficiencies: Energy costs €450,000+ annually above industry benchmarks due to outdated equipment and processes. Waste disposal costing €89,000 annually from inefficient material utilization.
Employee Engagement Challenges: Turnover at 31% (industry average 22%) indicating cultural issues. Safety incident rates at 2.3 per 100,000 hours (industry average 1.8) suggesting operational problems. Limited training and development constraining innovation.
Sustainability Market Opportunity: Major customers increasingly requiring supplier ESG certification. Competitive advantage potential from demonstrable environmental leadership. Premium pricing opportunities for verified sustainable products.

"Traditional analysis saw a decent business with normal operational improvement potential," Alex explained. "Our ESG lens revealed a company leaving millions on the table through inefficiency, employee issues, and missed market positioning opportunities."

3.2.2 Systematic Implementation Approach

Kerring Capital Partners implemented a comprehensive ESG integration program focused on material factors that would drive measurable business improvements.

Year 1: Foundation Building (2019–2020):

Energy Efficiency Programme: LED lighting retrofit across all facilities (€178,000 investment, €67,000 annual savings). HVAC system optimization and controls upgrade (€156,000 investment, €98,000 annual savings). Process equipment energy audits identifying future improvement opportunities.

Employee Engagement Initiative: Anonymous engagement survey identifying key concerns and improvement opportunities. Management training on leadership and communication. Recognition programmes for safety excellence and innovation. Cross-functional improvement teams empowering employee problem-solving.
Sustainability Baseline: Comprehensive measurement of environmental and social performance. Industry benchmarking against peer companies and best practices. Goal-setting process establishing ambitious but achievable targets. External communication building reputation and customer awareness.

"The first-year investments totalled €334,000," Alex noted, "and generated €165,000 in annual savings—essentially a two-year payback just on the energy efficiency alone. But we were just getting started."

Year 2: System Integration (2020–2021):

Advanced Manufacturing Systems: Process equipment upgrades improving efficiency and reducing energy consumption (€312,000 investment, €187,000 annual savings). Waste stream optimization reducing material costs (€67,000 investment, €89,000 annual savings). Quality management system enhancement reducing defects and rework.
Safety Culture Transformation: Comprehensive safety training and certification for all employees. Near-miss reporting system and proactive hazard identification. Safety leadership training for supervisors and managers. Equipment and process improvements addressing identified risks.
Customer Sustainability Partnerships: Collaborative initiatives with major customers on supply chain sustainability. Joint goal-setting and progress tracking. Sustainability reporting and transparency programs. Innovation partnerships on next-generation sustainable products.

Year 3–4: Market Leadership (2021–2023):

Innovation and R&D: Sustainable product development creating differentiation opportunities. Process innovation reducing environmental impact while improving performance. Industry collaboration and thought leadership building reputation. Patent development protecting competitive advantages.
Advanced Performance Management: Real-time monitoring of energy, waste, and safety metrics. Predictive analytics identifying improvement opportunities. Continuous improvement culture and employee empowerment. Performance-based incentives aligning objectives.
Exit Preparation: Comprehensive documentation of ESG capabilities and competitive advantages. Financial impact quantification and third-party verification. Buyer education on sustainability value creation. Strategic positioning for premium exit opportunities.

3.2.3 Results and Value Creation

The systematic approach generated substantial financial returns that directly attributed to ESG initiatives:

Operational Performance Improvements:

- Energy costs reduced by 31% (€456,000 annual savings).
- Waste disposal costs eliminated through material optimization (€89,000 savings).
- Safety incidents reduced 65% (€43,000 insurance savings, avoided disruption costs).
- Employee turnover reduced to 14% (€167,000 recruitment/training savings).
- Customer contracts won based on sustainability credentials (€340,000 annual revenue).

Total Annual Value Creation: €1,095,000
Total ESG Investment Over Four Years: €596,000
ROI on ESG Investments: 4:1 within two years, continuing throughout ownership

But the financial impact extended beyond direct cost savings and revenue enhancement. The sustainability infrastructure created competitive advantages that buyers recognized and valued.

3.2.4 Exit Success and Buyer Rationale

Solid Hej Components sold in 2023 for €89 million—a 1.71× revenue multiple that exceeded industry benchmarks by 23%. The acquiring company, a major European industrial group, explicitly cited Solid Hej's ESG capabilities as justification for premium valuation.

"This is where ESG created exit value," Alex emphasized. "During the auction process, all six final bidders specifically mentioned sustainability infrastructure in their proposals. The winning bid included detailed plans for expanding Solid Hej's ESG approach across their global operations."

The buyer's due diligence report highlighted three factors that drove premium pricing:

Operational Excellence: Proven efficiency improvements and cost reduction capabilities that could be replicated across the buyer's portfolio. The systematic approach demonstrated scalability and transferability.
Market Positioning: Sustainability credentials enabling access to high-value customer segments and premium pricing opportunities. The competitive advantages were defensible and growing.
Risk Management: Comprehensive ESG systems reducing operational, regulatory, and reputational risks. The buyer's insurance and risk management teams specifically valued these capabilities.

"The buyer told us explicitly," Alex recounted, "'We're paying €12–15 million premium specifically for the ESG infrastructure you built. Rather than spending 3–4 years building these capabilities ourselves, we're acquiring a ready-made platform we can scale across our business.'"

This exit experience demonstrated that ESG capabilities create genuine asset value that sophisticated buyers recognize and pay for—contradicting persistent myths about sustainability's financial impact.

Common Questions Alex Fields

Q: How do you separate ESG value creation from normal operational improvements in the exit price?

A: The buyer's due diligence reports and bid rationale letters explicitly quantified it. They compared Solid Hej to peer transactions and identified the premium specifically attributable to sustainability capabilities. We also had independent valuation analysis supporting the attribution.

Q: Wasn't Solid Hej just a good company that happened to do ESG well?

A: The before-after comparison is clear. At entry, Solid Hej was average on most metrics—margins, growth, customer satisfaction. The ESG programme drove specific, measurable improvements that traditional operational playbooks don't address. Energy efficiency alone generated €456K annually—that's not generic operational improvement.

Q: How do we know these results are replicable across other companies and sectors?

A: We've seen similar patterns across manufacturing (Solid Hej), services (Summit Peak Facility), food production (Alpine), and packaging (Ridgeline). The specific initiatives vary by sector, but the material factors framework works consistently. That's why materiality is so important—it ensures you're focused on factors that actually drive your business.

3.3 Addressing Common Objections to ESG Integration

3.3.1 The Data Quality Concern

"Before we continue," Jim Kerring interjected, "I need to address the elephant in the room. Critics say ESG data is unreliable, ratings are inconsistent, and measurement is too subjective for serious investment analysis. How do you respond?"

Alex had anticipated this challenge. Berg, Kölbel, and Rigobon's (2022) analysis of ESG rating agencies had documented significant divergence in assessments, with rating correlations averaging only 0.54 compared to 0.99 for credit ratings. This "aggregate confusion" stemmed from measurement differences (56% of rating disparity), scope variations (38%), and weighting differences (6%).

"The rating agency critique is actually helpful," Alex responded. "It reveals that ESG integration's value doesn't depend on third-party ratings. It comes from systematic assessment and improvement of material business factors. Those rating divergences show that ESG requires sophisticated judgement and industry expertise, exactly the kind of analysis that creates competitive advantages."

Private equity firms' operational approach enabled primary research and direct performance measurement that avoided rating agency limitations. Unlike public market investors who might rely on third-party ratings, PE firms could conduct deep due diligence, implement systematic improvements, and measure actual performance.

"The materiality framework from Khan and colleagues provides crucial guidance," Alex continued. "Companies implementing material ESG improvements showed consistent outperformance regardless of rating agency scores. This suggests that authentic sustainability integration creates value independent of external recognition."

The key was building proprietary ESG assessment capabilities rather than outsourcing analysis to rating agencies. Kerring Capital Partners had invested in developing internal expertise, industry-specific frameworks, and systematic measurement approaches that generated insights competitors couldn't replicate.

3.3.2 The Implementation Cost Challenge

Another common objection involved ESG implementation costs, particularly for smaller companies with limited resources. Critics argued that sustainability initiatives required significant investment that might not generate adequate returns.

"The cost question is legitimate," Alex acknowledged. "ESG implementation requires investment—in systems, capabilities, and sometimes operational changes that have near-term costs. But our portfolio experience shows that when properly implemented, the returns justify the investment."

The key insight was resource prioritization based on materiality assessment. Companies pursuing material ESG factors typically achieved positive returns within 12–18 months, while those implementing generic programmes often struggled to justify costs.

"Look at Solid Hej Components' numbers," Alex pointed to the detailed financial analysis. "€596,000 total ESG investment over four years generated €1.095 million in annual value creation—achieving 4:1 return within two years. That's not a cost burden—that's a high-return investment opportunity."

The analysis also revealed that not all ESG spending generated returns. Companies implementing comprehensive sustainability programmes without materiality focus often wasted resources on immaterial initiatives that generated no business value. The difference between success and failure was which ESG factors to prioritize and how to implement effectively.

3.3.3 The Short-Term Focus Critique

Some critics argued that private equity's 3–7-year investment horizons were too short for sustainability benefits to materialize. ESG value creation, they suggested, required decade-long timeframes incompatible with PE ownership models.

"This critique misunderstands both ESG implementation and PE value creation," Alex countered. "Material ESG factors generate benefits across multiple timeframes—quick wins within months, strategic initiatives within 1–2 years, and transformational positioning over 3–5 years. These timeframes align perfectly with typical PE hold periods."

Solid Hej Components demonstrated this multi-timeframe value creation:

Quick Wins (Months 1–6): LED lighting retrofits, safety programme enhancements, employee engagement surveys—generating €165,000 annual value with minimal investment.
Strategic Initiatives (Years 1–2): Energy management systems, waste reduction programmes, customer sustainability partnerships—generating €450,000+ annual value with targeted investment.
Transformational Goals (Years 2–4): Industry leadership positioning, innovation platform development, competitive moat creation—generating premium exit valuation and strategic buyer interest.

"The full value may continue accruing beyond our ownership," Alex noted, "but that's true of any operational improvement. PE firms don't need to capture the entire long-term value—we need to create capabilities that buyers recognize and pay for at exit. ESG does exactly that."

3.3.4 The Greenwashing Risk

Perhaps the most serious critique involved greenwashing—superficial ESG marketing without genuine substance. Dempere, Alamash, and Mattos (2024) highlighted the prevalence of greenwashing in sustainable finance, finding that many companies made ambitious sustainability claims without corresponding operational changes or performance improvements.

"Greenwashing is a real risk," Alex acknowledged candidly. "We've seen companies that treat ESG as marketing exercise rather than operational transformation. They achieve no value creation and sometimes destroy value through wasted resources and stakeholder cynicism."

The key to avoiding greenwashing was rigorous materiality assessment, measurable performance targets, independent verification, and transparent communication. Kerring Capital Partners required portfolio companies to:

Focus on Material Factors: Only pursue ESG initiatives that demonstrably affected business performance through the mechanisms outlined earlier.
Measure and Report: Track specific, quantifiable metrics rather than vague aspirational statements.
Verify Claims: Obtain third-party certification and audits for significant sustainability claims.
Be Transparent: Acknowledge challenges and setbacks alongside successes, building credibility through honesty.

"Authentic ESG integration is distinguishable from greenwashing through three questions," Alex summarized. "First, are initiatives tied to material business factors? Second, can you demonstrate measurable operational improvements? Third, can you show financial ROI? If you can't answer these clearly, you're probably doing ESG theatre rather than value creation."

3.4 Broader Portfolio Evidence

3.4.1 Summit Peak Facility Services: Service Sector Value Creation

While Solid Hej Components demonstrated ESG value creation in manufacturing, Summit Peak Facility Services showed how the same principles worked in labour-intensive service businesses.

Summit Peak Facility Services, a €31 million facilities management company, faced chronic employee turnover (47% annually) that undermined service quality and customer relationships. Traditional approaches focused on compensation benchmarking and benefits packages had failed to address underlying cultural issues.

"We approached Summit Peak Facility differently," Alex explained. "Rather than treating employee issues as HR problems, we recognized them as core business challenges affecting service delivery, customer satisfaction, and competitive positioning."

The ESG-integrated approach included:

Workplace Culture Transformation: Comprehensive engagement surveys identifying improvement priorities. Management training on leadership and communication. Career development programmes and advancement pathways. Recognition systems celebrating excellence and innovation.
Well-being Programmes: Health and wellness initiatives addressing employee needs. Flexible scheduling accommodating work–life balance. Mental health resources and support systems. Inclusive workplace policies and practices.
Performance Management Integration: Employee engagement metrics tracked alongside operational KPIs. Customer satisfaction surveys including service quality feedback. Career advancement tied to skill development and performance. Compensation linked to individual and company success.
The results demonstrated that social factors could drive financial performance as powerfully as operational improvements:

- Employee turnover reduced from 47% to 12%.
- Customer retention improved from 78% to 96%.
- Revenue growth accelerated to 22% annually.
- EBITDA margins expanded from 9% to 14%.
- Exit multiple achieved 2.8× vs 2.1× industry average.

"Summit Peak Facility shows that ESG isn't just for manufacturers or environmental issues," Alex emphasized. "Social factors—employee engagement, workplace culture, stakeholder relationships—create massive value in service businesses where human capital drives performance."

3.4.2 Alpine Foods: Small Company Success

Critics often argued that ESG integration was only feasible for large companies with substantial resources. Alpine Foods, a €24 million family-owned Mediterranean speciality food producer, demonstrated otherwise.

With limited capital and modest margins, Alpine could not afford comprehensive sustainability programs. Instead, Kerring Capital Partners applied rigorous materiality assessment to identify the 3–5 factors that would drive the most business value:

Waste Stream Optimization: Reducing raw material waste by 18%, saving €124,000 annually while improving product consistency.
Supplier Relationship Enhancement: Strengthening local supplier partnerships, improving quality and reliability while reducing costs.
Customer Sustainability Positioning: Leveraging existing organic certification and local sourcing to command premium pricing.
The targeted approach generated substantial returns despite limited resources:

- Total ESG investment: €114,000 over first 100 days
- Annual value creation: €546,000
- First-year ROI: 379%
- Three-year revenue growth: 18% annually
- Exit multiple premium: 15% vs comparable transactions

"Alpine proves that ESG isn't about spending more—it's about focusing on what matters," Alex noted. "Small companies can achieve outstanding results by concentrating on material factors rather than pursuing comprehensive programs they can't afford."

3.5 The Competitive Advantage Dimension

3.5.1 First-Mover Advantages and Network Effects

Beyond direct financial returns, ESG integration created competitive advantages that compounded over time through first-mover benefits and network effects.

"Companies that built ESG capabilities early established relationships and reputation that later entrants struggled to match," Alex explained. "These advantages created self-reinforcing cycles where ESG excellence attracted better stakeholders, which enabled superior performance, which further enhanced reputation."

Customer Preference: Companies with established sustainability credentials became preferred suppliers, receiving early notification of opportunities,

favourable contract terms, and customer loyalty that insulated them from pure price competition.
Talent Attraction: ESG leaders attracted higher-quality candidates and experienced lower turnover, creating workforce advantages that competitors couldn't quickly replicate.
Supplier Collaboration: Strong relationships with sustainable suppliers provided preferential access, better terms, and collaborative innovation opportunities.
Regulatory Relationships: Companies with demonstrated ESG commitment gained more favourable regulatory treatment, faster permit approvals, and advance notice of regulatory changes.

"These network effects mean that ESG advantages compound over time," Alex emphasized. "The gap between leaders and laggards widens rather than narrows—creating sustainable competitive moats."

3.5.2 Technology and Innovation Platform

ESG integration increasingly required technology investments that created broader competitive advantages beyond sustainability metrics.

Solid Hej Components' sustainability journey drove technology adoption that enhanced operational performance:

- IoT sensors enabling real-time monitoring and optimization.
- Data analytics identifying efficiency improvement opportunities.
- Predictive maintenance reducing downtime and costs.
- Digital integration streamlining operations and communication.

"The technology we implemented for ESG monitoring became an innovation platform," explained Solid Hej's operations director. "We use the same systems for quality management, predictive maintenance, and process optimization. Sustainability drove digital transformation that transformed our entire operation."

This pattern repeated across the portfolio. Companies justified technology investments based on ESG requirements, then discovered broader applications that enhanced competitiveness beyond sustainability metrics.

3.6 Industry Evolution and Future Trends

3.6.1 LP Requirements and Fundraising Impact

The transformation of limited partner expectations created powerful incentives for ESG integration that extended beyond portfolio company performance.

By 2024, the Institutional Limited Partners Association reported that 67% of LPs required specific ESG reporting from their general partners, and 84% considered ESG factors when making allocation decisions. This wasn't ideological pressure—it reflected recognition that ESG factors materially affected investment performance.

"Our 2023 fundraising was completely different from previous rounds," Alex recounted. "Where we used to spend 80% of LP meetings discussing track record and investment strategy, we now spend 40% on ESG integration methodology, stakeholder engagement frameworks, and sustainability performance measurement."

LPs were asking increasingly sophisticated questions:

- How do you identify material ESG factors for different industries?
- What's your approach to portfolio company capability building?
- How do you measure ESG impact and attribute it to financial performance?
- What systems ensure ESG integration throughout the investment life cycle?
- How do ESG capabilities affect exit valuations and buyer interest?

"LPs aren't asking about ESG because they're trying to save the world," Alex emphasized. "They're asking because they recognize it affects returns, risk management, and competitive positioning. ESG has become table stakes for attracting capital from sophisticated institutional investors."

3.6.2 Regulatory Evolution and Standardization

Global regulatory convergence towards mandatory sustainability disclosure was transforming ESG from voluntary best practice to required business capability.

The EU's Corporate Sustainability Reporting Directive (CSRD), US SEC climate disclosure rules, and similar initiatives across Asia-Pacific markets were creating standardized frameworks and accountability requirements. Companies with advanced ESG capabilities found themselves 2–3 years ahead of competitors in regulatory compliance—creating competitive advantages that buyers increasingly valued.

"Regulatory evolution is accelerating the ESG advantage," Alex noted. "Companies that built capabilities early are prepared for requirements that will burden competitors for years to come. That preparation has real value that buyers recognize at exit."

3.6.3 Technology and Measurement Advances

Looking forward, technological advances would make ESG measurement more accurate, efficient, and verifiable—reducing implementation costs while improving performance transparency.

Artificial intelligence enabling real-time sustainability monitoring and optimization. Satellite imagery providing independent verification of environmental performance. Blockchain creating transparent and verifiable supply chain tracking. IoT sensors generating continuous operational data for analysis and improvement.

"The technology revolution in ESG is just beginning," Alex explained. "Companies mastering these tools will have systematic advantages in efficiency, verification, and stakeholder communication that competitors can't match."

This technological evolution would further reduce the distinction between ESG management and operational excellence, making sustainability integration increasingly synonymous with business excellence.

As Alex concluded the presentation to Kerring Capital Partners' investment committee, the transformation in the room's energy was palpable. What had started as a sceptical challenge "show me the money"—had evolved into strategic discussion about competitive positioning and capability building.

Jim Kerring, who had opened the session demanding proof, leaned forward with a different question entirely. "Alright, Alex. You've convinced me on the returns. But here's what I need to understand: if ESG is such a powerful value driver, why isn't everyone already doing this? What's our competitive advantage, and how do we scale this approach across our entire portfolio?"

Alex smiled, recognizing the shift from whether ESG mattered to how to operationalize it systematically. "That's exactly the right question. And the answer reveals why we're still in the early stages of a fundamental industry transformation. The competitive advantage comes from systematic implementation—embedding ESG throughout the entire investment life cycle rather than treating it as a separate initiative."

Over the following months, Alex would work with the team to develop comprehensive frameworks for ESG integration across deal sourcing, due diligence, value creation, and exit preparation. But the conversation had fundamentally shifted. ESG was no longer a defensive consideration or compliance requirement—it had become a central pillar of Kerring Capital Partners' value creation strategy.

The financial case was clear. The research foundation was solid. The portfolio evidence was compelling. The question was not whether to integrate ESG, it was how to do it systematically, efficiently, and at scale. That operational challenge of transforming theoretical frameworks into practical methodologies that could be deployed across diverse portfolio companies would require the systematic approach detailed in the next chapter.

In Chapter 4, we will follow Alpine Foods through Kerring Capital Partners' comprehensive ESG integration framework, seeing how materiality assessment, stakeholder engagement, and systematic implementation create value throughout the investment life cycle. The journey from acquisition through exit will reveal not just what to do, but how to do it in ways that generate measurable financial returns while building sustainable competitive advantages.

Chapter Summary

Core Insight

ESG integration generates superior financial returns through five systematic mechanisms: operational efficiency, risk mitigation, revenue enhancement, talent advantages, and capital access benefits. Kerring Capital Partners' portfolio analysis showed high-ESG companies achieved 25.3% IRR vs 16.4% for low-ESG peers—an 8.9 percentage point advantage that compounds to substantial value over typical hold periods.

Critical Success Factors

- **Focus on material factors**: Khan et al.'s research shows material ESG factors drive 4.2% outperformance while immaterial initiatives waste resources—rigorous materiality assessment essential.
- **Build on research foundation**: Friede et al.'s meta-analysis of 2,000+ studies shows 90% positive/neutral relationships; Eccles' 18-year study shows High Sustainability firms outperform by 4.8% annually.
- **Demonstrate financial ROI**: Solid Hej Components achieved 4:1 return on €596K ESG investment, generating €1.095M annual value and €12–15M exit premium.
- **Scale across company sizes**: Alpine Foods shows small companies can achieve 379% first-year ROI by focusing on 3–5 material factors rather than comprehensive programmes.
- **Create competitive moats**: First-mover advantages and network effects mean ESG leaders establish self-reinforcing advantages in customer preference, talent attraction, and stakeholder relationships.

Watch Out For

⚠ Generic ESG programmes without materiality assessment waste resources and show no financial benefit.

⚠ Greenwashing—superficial marketing without operational substance—destroys value through stakeholder cynicism.

⚠ Implementation cost concerns are valid but solvable through focused materiality-based approaches.

⚠ Rating agency inconsistency (0.54 correlation vs 0.99 for credit) means proprietary research capabilities essential.

Tools You Can Use Now

- **Seven value creation mechanisms framework**: Map which mechanisms (operational efficiency, risk mitigation, revenue enhancement, talent advantage, capital access) matter most for your business.
- **Solid Hej Components ROI model**: Template showing investment, annual returns, and exit value attribution for systematic ESG implementation.
- **Materiality assessment methodology**: Khan et al.'s framework adapted for private equity due diligence and value creation planning.
- **Three-question greenwashing test**: (1) Tied to material factors? (2) Measurable improvements? (3) Financial ROI?

What's Next

Chapter 4 demonstrates systematic ESG integration throughout the investment life cycle using Alpine Foods as the primary case study. You'll see how to conduct enhanced due diligence, develop stakeholder-centric value creation plans, implement the critical first 100 days, build sustainable competitive advantages, and position for premium exits. The chapter transforms theoretical frameworks into operational playbooks that can be deployed across portfolio companies regardless of industry or size.

References

Bank for International Settlements. (2021). Green bonds and carbon emissions: Exploring the case for a rating system at the firm level. BIS Quarterly Review, December.

Berg, F., Kölbel, J., & Rigobon, R. (2022). Aggregate confusion: The divergence of ESG ratings. *Review of Finance*, 26 (6), 1315–1344. doi:10.1093/rof/rfac037.

Clark, G. L., Feiner, A., & Viehs, M. (2015). From the stockholder to the stakeholder: How sustainability can drive financial outperformance. University of Oxford & Arabesque Partners. doi:10.2139/ssrn.2508281.

Deloitte. (2023). 2023 Gen Z and Millennial Survey. Deloitte Insights.

Dempere, J., Alamash, E., & Mattos, P. (2024). Unveiling the truth: Greenwashing in sustainable finance. *Frontiers in Sustainability*, 5, Article 1362051. doi:10.3389/frsus.2024.1362051.

Eccles, R. G., Ioannou, I., & Serafeim, G. (2014). The impact of corporate sustainability on organizational processes and performance. *Management Science*, 60 (11), 2835–2857. doi:10.1287/mnsc.2014.1984.

Friede, G., Busch, T., & Bassen, A. (2015). ESG and financial performance: Aggregated evidence from more than 2000 empirical studies. *Journal of Sustainable Finance & Investment*, 5 (4), 210–233. doi:10.1080/20430795.2015.1118917.

Greenfield, E., Monk, A. and Rook, D. (2026). ESG Value Creation in Private Equity: From Rhetoric to Returns. SSRN Working Paper (posted 6 January).

Institutional Limited Partners Association. (2024). ESG considerations for limited partners: A best practice guide. ILPA.

International Energy Agency. (2021). Energy efficiency 2021. IEA Publications.

Khan, M., Serafeim, G., & Yoon, A. (2016). Corporate sustainability: First evidence on materiality. *The Accounting Review*, 91 (6), 1697–1724. doi:10.2308/accr-51383.

McKinsey & Company. (2023). Does ESG really matter—and why? McKinsey Quarterly.

PwC. (2022). ESG-focused institutional investment seen soaring 84% to $33.9 trillion in 2026. PricewaterhouseCoopers.

Swiss Re Institute. (2021). The economics of climate change: No action not an option. Swiss Re Ltd.

Part II

Implementation Excellence

4 ESG Integration in Practice

The Systematic Approach

Alpine Foods: October 2018

"We need to talk about your integration approach." Imade Zala's blunt statement hung in the air as Alex walked into the company's Valencia headquarters three months after Kerring Capital Partners' acquisition closed. The speciality food manufacturer had seemed straightforward during due diligence—steady growth, strong margins, defensible market position in organic and locally sourced Mediterranean products.

But Imade's tone suggested complications. "Our employees are confused about priorities, customers are asking questions we cannot answer, and I am spending more time on stakeholder meetings than business management. Either this ESG thing becomes systematic, or it becomes a distraction."

Alex had heard similar concerns across portfolio companies as Kerring Capital Partners expanded ESG integration beyond Solid Hej Components' early success. The challenge was not whether ESG created value—the evidence was overwhelming. The challenge was developing systematic approaches that could be implemented efficiently across different companies, industries, and market contexts.

Over the next three years, Alpine Foods would become Alex's laboratory for developing and refining a comprehensive ESG integration methodology. The systematic approach they developed would generate superior financial performance while creating competitive advantages that persisted beyond Kerring Capital Partners' ownership period.

4.1 From Extraction to Creation: The Philosophical Shift

4.1.1 The Traditional Private Equity Model

Alex's early career had been built on the traditional private equity value creation model: acquire underperforming companies, implement operational improvements, optimize capital structures, and sell at higher valuations. This approach relied primarily on value extraction by reducing costs, increasing efficiency, and maximizing returns for shareholders.

DOI: 10.4324/9781003625636-6

The model worked effectively when targets were genuinely undervalued or inefficiently managed. Financial engineering, operational improvements, and multiple expansion could generate substantial returns when markets and credit conditions were favourable.

However, Alex's experience with Riviera Specialty, Solid Hej Components, and other portfolio companies revealed systematic limitations in this approach. Companies focused exclusively on shareholder value creation often ignored stakeholder relationships that actually determined long-term business sustainability.

4.1.2 The Stakeholder Value Creation Alternative

The ESG integration approach represented a fundamental shift from value extraction to value creation—building sustainable competitive advantages through systematic stakeholder relationship management. Instead of maximizing short-term returns through cost reduction, the approach focused on creating value for all stakeholders while driving superior financial performance.

Porter and Kramer's (2011) research on "Creating Shared Value" provided theoretical foundation for this approach, demonstrating that companies addressing social and environmental challenges often achieved competitive advantages and sustainable growth. The private equity industry's operational focus made it particularly well-suited to implement shared value strategies that combined stakeholder engagement with rigorous performance measurement.

4.1.3 Case Study: Peninsula Services Transformation

Summit Peak Facility Services exemplified this evolution from extraction to creation. When Kerring Capital Partners acquired the €31 million facilities management company, initial value creation plans focused on cost reduction and operational efficiency—traditional private equity approaches.

Traditional Approach (Years 1–2):

- Cost Reduction: Staff optimization, vendor renegotiation, facility consolidation.
- Operational Efficiency: Process standardization, technology implementation, management systems.
- Financial Engineering: Capital structure optimization, working capital management.
- Results: 12% EBITDA improvement, modest customer satisfaction gains.

Stakeholder Value Creation Approach (Years 3–5):

- Employee Investment: Training programmes, career development, workplace improvement.
- Customer Partnership: Collaborative service innovation, sustainability consulting, strategic planning support.

- Community Engagement: Local hiring initiatives, skills development programmes, environmental stewardship.
- Supplier Development: Vendor training, capability building, sustainability standard implementation.
- Results: 47% EBITDA improvement, industry-leading customer retention, 89% employee satisfaction.

The stakeholder approach generated nearly four times the value creation of traditional methods while building sustainable competitive advantages that persisted beyond exit.

4.1.4 Innovation through Stakeholder Engagement

The most significant value creation opportunities emerged from deep stakeholder engagement that identified unmet needs and collaborative innovation possibilities. At Peninsula Services, customer partnerships led to development of sustainability consulting services that generated €1.2 million in annual revenue while strengthening client relationships.

Employee engagement initiatives identified operational improvements that management had overlooked. Worker-suggested efficiency improvements generated €340,000 in annual cost savings while improving job satisfaction and retention.

Community partnerships created talent pipeline development that reduced recruitment costs while enhancing local relationships. The company's apprenticeship programme with local technical colleges generated qualified candidates while building community support for expansion projects.

Since 2025, investor expectations have broadened beyond climate risk towards nature-related dependencies and impacts. A concrete signal is Nature Action 100's first status report (October 2025), which sets out early investor engagement priorities and highlights that biodiversity and ecosystem risks are increasingly treated as financially relevant (Nature Action 100, 2025). For private equity owners, this reinforces the importance of systematically identifying material nature dependencies, particularly where supply chains, land use, water stress, or biodiversity-sensitive operations can affect resilience, permitting, or stakeholder legitimacy.

Table 4.1 Value creation evolution

Traditional PE Model	*Stakeholder Value Creation Model*
Financial Engineering	**Employee Engagement**
Cost Reduction	**Customer Partnership**
Multiple Expansion	**Community Investment**
	Supplier Development

4.2 The Systematic Integration Framework

4.2.1 Phase 1: Enhanced Due Diligence (Months 1–4)

The systematic ESG integration framework began during due diligence with comprehensive assessment of sustainability risks and opportunities. This assessment built on traditional commercial, operational, and financial analysis while adding systematic evaluation of environmental, social, and governance factors.

Environmental Assessment Protocol:

- Current performance analysis using relevant industry benchmarks.
- Regulatory compliance verification and future requirement anticipation.
- Resource efficiency opportunity identification (energy, water, waste).
- Climate risk assessment including physical and transition risks.
- Circular economy potential evaluation for waste stream optimization.

Social Factor Analysis Framework:

- Employee engagement assessment through anonymous surveys and interviews.
- Customer satisfaction evaluation including sustainability preferences.
- Community relationship analysis through stakeholder interviews.
- Supply chain labour practices verification and improvement opportunities.
- Health and safety performance benchmarking and improvement planning.

Governance Evaluation Methodology:

- Board effectiveness assessment including sustainability oversight capabilities.
- Management quality evaluation including ESG experience and commitment.
- Risk management system adequacy review with ESG integration assessment.
- Stakeholder engagement capability analysis and relationship quality evaluation.
- Ethics and compliance programme evaluation including implementation effectiveness.

4.2.2 Phase 2: Investment Committee Integration (months 4–5)

ESG findings were integrated into investment committee analysis rather than treated as separate considerations. This integration ensured that sustainability factors received appropriate weight in investment decisions and value creation planning.

Investment Memorandum ESG Section:

- Executive summary of material ESG risks and opportunities.
- Financial impact quantification for identified sustainability factors.
- Value creation potential assessment including implementation timelines.

- Risk mitigation requirements and associated costs.
- Stakeholder management plan and resource requirements.

Financial Model Integration:

- ESG-related cost savings incorporated into EBITDA projections.
- Revenue enhancement opportunities from sustainability initiatives.
- Risk adjustments reflecting ESG performance and management quality.
- Capital expenditure requirements for environmental and social improvements.
- Exit multiple assumptions adjusted for ESG competitive positioning.

4.2.3 Phase 3: First 100 Days Implementation (Months 5–8)

The critical post-acquisition period required intensive stakeholder engagement to build the foundation for systematic ESG integration. This phase emphasized trust building, quick wins identification, and cultural alignment around sustainability objectives.

Stakeholder Engagement Launch:

- Employee listening sessions to understand concerns and identify improvement opportunities.
- Customer interviews to assess satisfaction and sustainability expectations.
- Supplier meetings to communicate standards and identify collaboration opportunities.
- Community leader engagement to understand local priorities and partnership possibilities.
- Investor communication regarding ESG objectives and performance measurement.

Quick Wins Implementation:

- High-impact, low-cost initiatives that demonstrated commitment to stakeholder value creation.
- Employee-suggested improvements that showed responsiveness to internal feedback.
- Customer-requested sustainability enhancements that strengthened commercial relationships.
- Community partnership opportunities that built local support and goodwill.
- Supplier engagement initiatives that improved performance and reduced risks.

Cultural Foundation Building:

- ESG training programmes for management and employees.

- Communication campaigns explaining sustainability importance and individual contribution opportunities.
- Recognition programmes celebrating ESG achievements and innovation.
- Goal setting processes that included sustainability metrics alongside financial targets.
- Performance management system updates to include ESG accountability.

4.2.4 Phase 4: Operational Excellence Development (Months 6–24)

Long-term value creation required systematic capability building and process improvement across all business functions. This phase emphasized material factor focus, systematic measurement, and continuous improvement methodologies.

Operational Performance Optimization:

- Energy efficiency programmes targeting material consumption reduction.
- Waste reduction initiatives focusing on material cost savings.
- Quality improvement systems reducing defects and rework.
- Productivity enhancement through employee engagement and training.
- Supply chain optimization improving reliability and sustainability.

Market Positioning Enhancement:

- Sustainability credential development and third-party verification.
- Customer partnership programmes creating shared value and competitive differentiation.
- Brand positioning leveraging environmental and social leadership.
- Market expansion into sustainability-focused customer segments.
- Premium pricing justification through verified performance excellence.

Risk Management System Development:

- Environmental compliance monitoring and proactive risk mitigation.
- Social risk assessment including labour practices and community relationships.
- Governance system enhancement including board oversight and accountability.
- Scenario planning incorporating ESG factors and stakeholder expectations.
- Incident response protocols addressing environmental and social events.

4.2.5 Phase 5: Exit Preparation and Value Capture (Months 18–36)

As companies approached exit, the framework shifted to documenting ESG capabilities and educating potential buyers about sustainability-driven competitive advantages. This phase emphasized market positioning, buyer education, and value documentation.

Competitive Advantage Development:

- Industry leadership positioning through sustainability performance and innovation.
- Customer relationship strengthening through shared sustainability initiatives.
- Employee attraction and retention advantages through workplace excellence.
- Supplier partnership development creating mutual value and operational resilience.
- Community leadership recognition enhancing brand value and stakeholder support.

Exit Value Enhancement:

- ESG capability documentation demonstrating competitive advantages and growth potential.
- Financial impact quantification showing ROI for sustainability investments.
- Buyer education programmes highlighting ESG value creation and market positioning benefits.
- Third-party verification of sustainability performance and management system effectiveness.
- Strategic narrative development connecting ESG capabilities to long-term value creation.

4.3 Alpine Foods: Systematic Implementation in Action

4.3.1 Baseline Assessment and Opportunity Identification

Alpine Foods' ESG assessment during due diligence revealed a company with strong environmental credentials but significant social and governance improvement opportunities. The family-owned business had achieved organic certification and local sourcing leadership but lacked systematic employee engagement and stakeholder management capabilities.

Environmental Performance Baseline:

- 78% local sourcing within 200km radius (industry-leading).
- Organic certification for 67% of product portfolio.
- Energy efficiency 15% below industry benchmarks.
- Waste disposal costs 23% above peer companies.
- Water consumption tracking limited to regulatory requirements.

Social Performance Assessment:

- Employee turnover at 28% (industry average 22%).
- Customer satisfaction scores at 73% (good but not exceptional).

- Limited formal training and development programmes.
- Health and safety performance meeting but not exceeding standards.
- Community engagement limited to regulatory compliance.

Governance Evaluation:

- Family ownership providing stability but limiting professional management development.
- Board composition lacking independent oversight and sustainability expertise.
- Management systems focused on operational efficiency rather than stakeholder value creation.
- Limited stakeholder feedback mechanisms and engagement strategies.
- Financial management strong but sustainability performance measurement minimal.

"We saw a company doing many things right instinctively," Alex explained to the Kerring Capital Partners investment committee. "But the practices were informal, unmeasured, and unscalable. Our job was to systematize what worked while filling obvious gaps."

4.3.2 Value Creation Planning and Resource Allocation

The comprehensive assessment enabled development of a three-year ESG value creation plan focused on material factors that could drive measurable business improvements. Resource allocation prioritized initiatives with highest potential for financial return and stakeholder impact.

Year 1: Priorities (€234,000 investment):

- Employee engagement programme development and implementation.
- Energy efficiency improvements targeting 25% consumption reduction.
- Customer partnership initiatives for product development and market expansion.
- Community outreach programme establishing local stakeholder relationships.
- Management system development for ESG performance tracking and improvement.

Year 2: Expansion (€187,000 additional investment):

- Organic certification expansion to 85% of product portfolio.
- Supply chain sustainability programme development and implementation.
- Employee training and development programme launch.
- Customer satisfaction enhancement through service quality improvement.
- Environmental management system certification (ISO 14001).

Year 3: Optimization (€146,000 additional investment):

- Technology integration for real-time performance monitoring and optimization.
- Market expansion into sustainability-focused customer segments.
- Employee leadership development and career advancement programme implementation.
- Community partnership expansion including local supplier development.
- Third-party sustainability performance verification and reporting.

4.3.3 Implementation Results and Performance Measurement

Alpine Foods' systematic ESG implementation generated measurable improvements across all stakeholder dimensions while driving superior financial performance. The results validated the systematic approach and provided evidence for scaling across other portfolio companies.

Research by Morningstar (2021) found that sustainable equity funds incorporating ESG criteria consistently outperformed traditional counterparts, with 71% delivering better risk-adjusted returns over five-year periods. Alpine's experience demonstrated how these advantages manifested in private equity contexts through systematic implementation and measurement.

Year One Implementation Results:

- ESG integration methodology application: €114,000 investment.
- Systematized value creation: €546,000 annual benefits.
- Methodology validation: 379% first-year ROI.

The measurement framework enabled quarterly tracking of ESG performance alongside financial metrics. Monthly management reviews integrated sustainability analysis with operational and financial reporting. Department heads presented metrics relevant to their functions, discussed variances from targets, and developed improvement plans for underperforming areas.

Whelan, Atz, Van Holt, and Clark (2021) found that approximately 58% of corporate studies showed positive ESG-financial performance links, supporting the integration of sustainability metrics into core business management rather than treating them as peripheral reporting requirements.

"When sustainability metrics received equal management attention with financial results, behaviour changed immediately," observed Imade Zala. "Managers prioritized employee satisfaction and energy efficiency because performance reviews held them accountable."

Common Questions Alex Fields

Q: How do you ensure ESG implementation does not become just another compliance burden?
A: The key is material factor focus. We only pursue ESG initiatives that demonstrably affect business performance—cost reduction, revenue enhancement, risk mitigation, talent attraction. When sustainability drives financial results, it becomes value creation rather than compliance.
Q: What's the biggest implementation mistake companies make?
A: Imposing external frameworks without understanding existing culture and capabilities. Peninsula Services taught us that lesson painfully. You need to build on what the company already does well while filling obvious gaps, not replace everything with a predetermined playbook.
Q: How long does it take to see ROI from ESG investments?
A: For material factors, typically 12–18 months. The key is focusing on initiatives with clear business cases rather than pursuing comprehensive programmes without prioritization.

4.4 Technology Integration for ESG Excellence

4.4.1 Digital Infrastructure Development

Systematic ESG integration required technology infrastructure that could collect, analyse, and report sustainability data efficiently. Alpine Foods invested in integrated management systems that connected environmental monitoring, employee engagement tracking, and customer feedback collection.

Environmental Monitoring Technology:

- IoT sensors for real-time energy, water, and waste monitoring.
- Automated reporting systems reducing administrative burden while improving data accuracy.
- Predictive analytics identifying optimization opportunities before problems developed.
- Integration with financial systems enabling cost tracking and ROI analysis.
- Mobile dashboards providing managers with real-time performance visibility.

Social Performance Tracking:

- Employee engagement platforms enabling anonymous feedback and sentiment tracking.

- Customer relationship management systems enhanced with sustainability preference tracking.
- Training management systems monitoring programme completion and effectiveness.
- Health and safety incident reporting and analysis systems.
- Community engagement tracking including partnership development and local impact measurement.

Governance and Reporting Systems:

- Board reporting dashboards providing ESG performance visibility and trend analysis.
- Stakeholder communication platforms enabling transparent information sharing.
- Risk management systems incorporating environmental and social factors.
- Third-party verification systems supporting credible sustainability reporting.
- Integration with financial reporting enabling comprehensive performance analysis.

4.4.2 Data Analytics and Performance Optimization

Advanced analytics capabilities enabled identification of patterns and opportunities that manual analysis could not detect. Machine learning algorithms analysed environmental performance data to predict equipment maintenance needs, reducing downtime while improving efficiency.

Customer analytics identified sustainability preferences that informed product development and marketing strategies. Employee engagement analytics predicted turnover risk enabling proactive retention interventions.

The technology investment generated measurable returns: €45,000 in energy savings through automated optimization, €67,000 in employee retention through predictive analytics, and €23,000 in customer acquisition through preference analysis—total annual value of €135,000 from technology investments that enhanced ESG performance while reducing implementation costs.

"The technology was not about replacing human judgement," Alex emphasized. "It was about providing better information for decision-making and freeing up time from data collection for actual relationship building and problem solving."

4.5 Stakeholder Governance and Engagement

4.5.1 Board-Level Sustainability Oversight

Alpine Foods established board-level sustainability oversight to ensure ESG integration received appropriate strategic attention and resource allocation. The enhanced board included independent directors with sustainability expertise alongside traditional financial and operational capabilities.

Board Sustainability Committee Responsibilities:

- Quarterly ESG performance review including progress against targets and industry benchmarking.
- Annual sustainability strategy approval including resource allocation and priority setting.
- Risk assessment oversight incorporating environmental and social factors.
- Stakeholder feedback review and response planning.
- Executive compensation decisions including ESG performance metrics.

Management Accountability Framework:

- CEO performance evaluation including sustainability leadership and stakeholder relationship management.
- Department head objectives including ESG metrics relevant to functional responsibilities.
- Employee recognition programmes celebrating sustainability achievements and innovation.
- Annual sustainability reporting including third-party verification and stakeholder communication.
- Continuous improvement planning based on performance analysis and stakeholder feedback.

4.5.2 Stakeholder Advisory Mechanisms

Systematic stakeholder engagement required formal mechanisms for collecting feedback, addressing concerns, and identifying collaboration opportunities. Alpine Foods established advisory groups representing key stakeholder categories.

Employee Advisory Council:

- Quarterly meetings with representative employees from all departments and levels.
- Anonymous feedback collection and response systems.
- Workplace improvement suggestion and implementation processes.
- Training and development programme input and evaluation.
- Recognition programme development and administration.

Customer Partnership Forum:

- Semi-annual meetings with key customers to discuss sustainability preferences and collaboration opportunities.
- Product development input and market trend insights.
- Service quality feedback and improvement planning.
- Joint sustainability initiatives development and implementation.
- Market expansion strategy input and support.

Community Stakeholder Group:

- Regular meetings with local government representatives, community leaders, and environmental organizations.
- Community impact assessment and mitigation planning.
- Local hiring and supplier development programme input.
- Environmental stewardship project development and implementation.
- Social investment priority setting and impact measurement.

4.5.3 Continuous Improvement and Learning

The stakeholder engagement process enabled continuous learning and improvement rather than static compliance with predetermined standards. Regular feedback collection identified emerging requirements and optimization opportunities.

Quarterly stakeholder satisfaction surveys tracked relationship quality and identified areas requiring attention. Annual stakeholder forums brought all groups together for collaborative planning and shared learning.

The engagement process generated competitive intelligence about market trends, regulatory developments, and innovation opportunities that traditional analysis methods could not provide. This stakeholder insight became a source of strategic advantage that differentiated Alpine from competitors focused solely on financial metrics.

"Our stakeholder advisory mechanisms were not about compliance or public relations," Imade Zala explained. "They were genuine sources of business intelligence that informed strategic decisions and identified opportunities competitors missed."

4.6 Exit Strategy and Value Realization

4.6.1 ESG Value Documentation

As Alpine Foods approached exit, Alex worked with management to document the ESG capabilities and competitive advantages created during ownership. This documentation became crucial for buyer education and premium value realization.

Capability Documentation Framework:

- Environmental management system effectiveness including cost savings and risk reduction.
- Employee engagement excellence including retention advantages and productivity improvements.
- Customer relationship strength including loyalty metrics and referral generation.
- Community partnership value including local support and development opportunities.
- Governance system maturity including risk management and stakeholder oversight capabilities.

Financial Impact Quantification:

- Direct cost savings from environmental efficiency improvements: €124,000 annually.
- Revenue enhancement from customer retention and premium positioning: €340,000 annually.
- Risk reduction value from improved stakeholder relationships and governance systems.
- Market positioning advantages enabling continued growth and expansion.
- Operational excellence capabilities transferable to other business contexts.

4.6.2 Buyer Education and Premium Capture

The exit process included systematic buyer education regarding ESG value creation and competitive advantages. Strategic buyers recognized the sustainability capabilities as valuable intellectual property that could accelerate their own transformation efforts.

Three strategic buyers competed for Alpine Foods, with the winning bidder specifically citing ESG capabilities as justification for premium pricing. The acquirer's due diligence report highlighted environmental management systems, employee engagement excellence, and customer partnership development as factors driving competitive advantage.

The exit multiple reflected recognition that ESG capabilities represented genuine asset value rather than compliance costs. Post-acquisition performance validated this assessment as the buyer continued investing in sustainability capabilities while expanding the business model to other markets.

"The buyer told us explicitly they were paying a premium for the ESG infrastructure we built," Alex recounted. "They could have spent three years developing these capabilities internally, or they could acquire a ready-made platform. The premium reflected that value."

4.7 The Full Cycle Success

4.7.1 Portfolio-Wide Methodology Validation

By 2024, Alpine Foods had become Kerring Capital Partners' methodology showcase for systematic ESG integration throughout the private equity deal cycle. The systematic approach produced the results detailed in Chapter 3: 18% annual revenue growth, three new market expansions, and sustainability credentials that commanded premium acquisition interest.

The exit validated the systematic methodology rather than just the individual company success. Multiple strategic buyers competed for Alpine's systematically developed ESG capabilities, viewing the integrated approach as transferable intellectual property that would accelerate their transformation across other acquisitions.

For Alex, Alpine Foods represented methodological proof that systematic ESG integration throughout the investment cycle created replicable competitive advantages that buyers recognized and valued at exit.

4.7.2 Systematic Approach Components

Due Diligence Phase: The enhanced assessment framework enabled identification of material ESG risks and opportunities that traditional analysis missed, revealing €280,000 in annual cost savings opportunities and €340,000 in premium pricing potential through stakeholder-focused assessment.

Value Creation Phase: The stakeholder-centric approach generated superior performance through authentic relationship building and operational excellence, transforming informal family practices into systematic competitive advantages.

Measurement Phase: The material metrics framework provided the management systems necessary to track performance and optimize results, integrating ESG factors into monthly reviews and quarterly board assessments.

Exit Preparation: The systematic ESG capabilities developed during ownership became valuable assets that attracted strategic buyer interest and commanded premium pricing, demonstrating that sustainability creates genuine asset value.

This integrated approach across all deal cycle phases enabled value creation that exceeded traditional private equity returns while building stakeholder relationships that supported long-term success.

4.7.3 Methodology Transferability and Scaling

The Alpine Foods methodology proved transferable across different industries, company sizes, and market contexts. Peninsula Services, Solid Hej Components, and other portfolio companies achieved similar results using adapted versions of the systematic approach.

The key insight was methodological consistency combined with content flexibility. The assessment frameworks, stakeholder engagement processes, and measurement systems could be standardized while specific initiatives and priorities varied based on materiality analysis and company context.

This combination of systematic methodology with contextual adaptation enabled Kerring Capital Partners to scale ESG integration across their entire portfolio while maintaining the quality and effectiveness that generated superior returns.

As Imade Zala reflected three years after acquisition: "What Alex and the team built was not just a set of sustainability programmes. They created a systematic approach to stakeholder value creation that fundamentally transformed how we think about business success. That capability persisted long after Kerring Capital Partners' exit; it became part of our competitive DNA."

The success of Alpine Foods' transformation demonstrated that systematic ESG integration was not just possible but profitable—when approached with the right methodology, measurement discipline, and stakeholder focus. The question was no longer whether to integrate ESG throughout the investment life cycle, but how to do it efficiently and effectively across diverse portfolio contexts.

Chapter 5 addresses the critical foundation for this systematic approach: enhanced due diligence that could identify hidden ESG risks and opportunities before they affected investment performance.

Chapter Summary

Core Insight

Systematic ESG integration throughout the investment life cycle generates superior returns by transforming sustainability from compliance burden to competitive advantage. Alpine Foods achieved 379% first-year ROI on €114,000 ESG investment, generating €546,000 annual value creation, demonstrating that methodological consistency combined with contextual flexibility enables scaling across portfolio companies.

Critical Success Factors

- **Stakeholder value creation:** Peninsula Services' transformation from traditional PE approach (12% EBITDA improvement) to stakeholder focus (47% improvement) shows value creation over extraction.
- **Five-phase framework:** Enhanced Due Diligence, Investment Committee Integration, First 100 Days, Operational Excellence, Exit Preparation provide systematic methodology.
- **Material factor focus:** Porter & Kramer's (2011) shared value principles plus Morningstar's (2021) evidence of 71% sustainable fund outperformance validate approach.

- **Technology enablement:** Alpine's €135,000 annual technology ROI through automation, predictive analytics, and performance optimization demonstrates digital enhancement value.
- **Board-level governance:** Stakeholder advisory mechanisms generate competitive intelligence and relationship advantages beyond traditional shareholder governance.

Watch Out For

⚠ Value extraction mindsets that prioritize short-term cost cutting over stakeholder relationship building.
⚠ Implementation without cultural assessment—Peninsula's initial approach failed before stakeholder focus succeeded.
⚠ Generic ESG programmes without materiality-driven prioritization waste resources on immaterial initiatives.
⚠ Treating sustainability as separate workstream rather than integrated business strategy.

Tools You Can Use Now

- **Five-Phase Integration Framework:** Systematic methodology from due diligence through exit preparation with specific activities and deliverables.
- **Technology Platform Architecture:** Integrated systems for environmental monitoring, social performance tracking, and governance reporting.
- **Stakeholder Advisory Structure:** Employee councils, customer forums, and community groups providing competitive intelligence.
- **Exit Value Documentation Framework:** Capability assessment and financial impact quantification for buyer education.

What's Next

Chapter 5 demonstrates how enhanced ESG due diligence transforms from defensive risk assessment to offensive value discovery tool. Through the Alpine Foods case study, you will see how systematic assessment uncovers risks and opportunities that traditional analysis misses. The chapter provides detailed frameworks for climate scenario analysis, stakeholder mapping, and materiality assessment that enable superior investment decisions.

References

CFGI. (2021). Navigating those critical first 100 days of private equity ownership. Retrieved from https://www.cfgi.com/resources/articles/navigating-those-critical-first-100-days-of-private-equity-ownership/.

Morningstar. (2021). Sustainable funds U.S. landscape report. Morningstar Research.

Nature Action 100 (2025). Nature Action 100 releases its first status report showcasing initiative progress and investor insights (28 October).

Porter, M. E., & Kramer, M. R. (2011). Creating shared value. *Harvard Business Review*, 89(1/2), 62–77.

Whelan, T., Atz, U., Van Holt, T., & Clark, C. (2021). ESG and financial performance: Uncovering the relationship by aggregating evidence from 1,000 plus studies published between 2015–2020. NYU Stern Center for Sustainable Business.

5 Due Diligence that Delivers

Finding Gold and Avoiding Landmines

The €15 Million Discovery

The mass balance analysis did not lie. As Alex stared at the spreadsheet showing 1,820 tons of toxic chemicals that had seemingly vanished from Helix Chemicals, a €78 million speciality chemical manufacturer's books, a cold dread settled over the team as the significance of the numbers dawned on them. The fluorescent-lit conference room felt smaller. Someone's coffee had gone cold hours ago. Ivie Chen's carefully-prepared presentation lay forgotten—these numbers rewrote everything. Their target company reported purchasing 2,000 tons of methylene chloride annually but only declared 180 tons in emissions—a discrepancy that would either kill the deal or transform it.

"Chemistry does not lie," Alex announced to the stunned investment committee. "Those missing chemicals are going somewhere—either into unreported emissions or undisclosed waste. We need to find out which."

What followed was a forensic investigation involving former employees, satellite imagery, and soil testing that uncovered €15 million in hidden environmental liabilities while revealing operational inefficiencies that created even greater value creation opportunities.

This discovery crystallized Alex's philosophy: effective ESG due diligence is not about checking compliance boxes—it is about using sustainability factors as a lens to see business realities that traditional financial analysis might miss. This chapter presents the tools, frameworks, and methodologies Alex developed through dozens of deals to transform due diligence from a defensive exercise into a value creation goldmine.

The tension in that Kerring Capital Partners conference room was thick enough to cut with a knife. What should have been a straightforward investment committee discussion about a speciality chemicals deal had turned into something resembling a crime scene investigation. Alex watched the environmental consultant shuffle through his papers for the third time, looking as though he was wishing he had called in sick that morning.

DOI: 10.4324/9781003625636-7

5.1 Enhanced ESG Due Diligence Framework

5.1.1 The Integration Imperative

Traditional due diligence focused on financial, commercial, and operational analysis while treating environmental, social, and governance factors as peripheral considerations. This approach worked adequately when ESG factors had minimal impact on business performance, but increasing stakeholder awareness, regulatory requirements, and market dynamics made systematic ESG assessment essential for comprehensive risk evaluation and opportunity identification.

Alex's enhanced framework integrated ESG analysis with conventional due diligence rather than treating sustainability as a separate workstream. This integration reflected Khan, Serafeim, and Yoon's (2016) research demonstrating that companies performing well on financially material ESG issues substantially outperformed those with poor material ESG performance—a finding that transformed how Alex approached investment analysis.

The framework balanced comprehensive assessment with practical resource constraints through materiality-driven prioritization. High-impact ESG factors received intensive analysis, while lower-priority issues were assessed at summary level. This approach enabled thorough evaluation within typical deal timelines and budgets.

5.1.2 Four-Dimensional Assessment Matrix

Environmental Risk and Opportunity Analysis:

- Regulatory compliance verification including historical violations and pending litigation.
- Resource efficiency assessment identifying cost reduction opportunities through energy, water, and waste optimization.
- Climate risk evaluation using scenario analysis to understand physical and transition risks.
- Circular economy potential assessment identifying revenue opportunities from waste stream monetization.
- Environmental liability quantification including remediation costs and ongoing compliance obligations.

Social Factor Evaluation:

- Employee engagement measurement through anonymous surveys and third-party assessment platforms.
- Customer satisfaction analysis incorporating sustainability preferences and loyalty drivers.
- Community relationship evaluation assessing local stakeholder support and potential conflicts.

- Supply chain assessment identifying labour practices risks and collaborative improvement opportunities.
- Health and safety performance benchmarking against industry standards and regulatory requirements.

Governance Quality Assessment:

- Board effectiveness evaluation including diversity, expertise, and oversight capabilities.
- Management quality assessment including ESG experience and stakeholder engagement capabilities.
- Risk management system evaluation incorporating ESG factors and scenario planning.
- Ethics and compliance programme assessment including implementation effectiveness and cultural integration.
- Stakeholder engagement capability analysis evaluating systematic relationship management and feedback mechanisms.

Materiality-Driven Prioritization:

- Industry-specific factor identification using SASB frameworks and peer benchmarking.
- Stakeholder impact assessment ranking factors by business impact and stakeholder importance.
- Financial materiality evaluation quantifying potential effects on revenue, costs, and capital requirements.
- Time horizon analysis distinguishing short-term operational factors from long-term strategic considerations.
- Implementation feasibility assessment evaluating improvement potential and resource requirements.

Assessment Methodology:

- Score each dimension on a 1–5 scale (1 = Critical Risk, 5 = Leading Practice).
- Conduct stakeholder interviews to validate findings.
- Use data triangulation: company disclosures, third-party assessments, and primary research.
- Prioritize material issues based on financial impact and stakeholder importance.

Reporting readiness is also becoming more dynamic as European sustainability reporting standards evolve in response to implementation feedback. In December 2025, EFRAG submitted technical advice and published draft simplified ESRS materials designed to reduce reporting burden while maintaining materiality discipline (EFRAG, 2025). For private equity due diligence, this reinforces the need to

Table 5.1 Four-dimensional assessment matrix. *Due diligence framework for ESG risk and opportunity assessment*

Dimension	*Key Assessment Criteria*
ENVIRONMENTAL	**Compliance & Regulatory** • Environmental permits and violations history • Remediation liabilities and ongoing environmental issues • Regulatory compliance track record
	Resource Efficiency • Energy consumption per unit of production • Water usage and wastewater management • Waste generation and recycling rates
	Climate Impact • GHG emissions (Scope 1, 2, 3) • Climate transition risks and physical risks • Renewable energy adoption and carbon reduction targets
SOCIAL	**Employee Relations** • Workforce demographics and turnover rates • Labour relations history and union engagement • Employee satisfaction and engagement scores
	Health & Safety • Incident rates (TRIR, LTIR) and safety record • Safety management systems and culture • Worker health and wellbeing programmes
	Community & Supply Chain • Community relations and social license to operate • Supply chain labour practices and human rights • Product safety and customer satisfaction
GOVERNANCE	**Corporate Structure** • Board composition, independence, and diversity • Management quality and succession planning • Ownership structure and related-party transactions
	Ethics & Compliance • Business ethics policies and code of conduct • Anti-corruption and anti-bribery controls • Regulatory compliance history and legal disputes

Dimension	*Key Assessment Criteria*
	Risk Management • Enterprise risk management framework • Cybersecurity and data privacy controls • Internal controls and financial reporting quality
MATERIALITY	**Industry-Specific Factors** • Sector-specific ESG risks and opportunities • Industry benchmarking and peer comparison • Regulatory and market trends affecting the sector **Stakeholder Priorities** • Customer and investor ESG expectations • Employee and community concerns • Lender requirements and covenant considerations **Value Creation Potential** • Quick wins and low-hanging fruit • Medium-term value creation opportunities • Long-term strategic positioning advantages

evaluate not only current disclosure gaps, but management's ability to maintain decision-useful reporting systems as standards are refined and assurance expectations increase.

5.1.3 Technology-Enhanced Assessment

Modern ESG due diligence leverages technological capabilities that enable more comprehensive and efficient analysis than traditional approaches. Alex's team integrated multiple technology platforms to enhance assessment accuracy while reducing time and cost requirements:

AI-Powered Document Review: Natural language processing tools analysed thousands of regulatory filings, court documents, and media reports to identify potential ESG risks that manual review might miss. Machine learning algorithms identified patterns indicating compliance issues or operational problems.
Alternative Data Sources: Social media sentiment analysis provided insights into employee satisfaction and community relationships. Online review platforms revealed customer satisfaction trends and brand reputation issues. Supply chain databases enabled verification of supplier practices and relationship quality.
Satellite Imagery and Remote Sensing: Environmental monitoring capabilities enabled independent verification of operational claims. Satellite imagery could

detect unreported emissions, waste disposal practices, and facility expansion without relying exclusively on company-provided information.
Digital Materiality Assessment Platforms: Automated tools conducted preliminary materiality assessments based on industry classifications, business model analysis, and stakeholder mapping. These platforms provided systematic starting points that human analysts could refine based on company-specific factors.

5.2 The Chemical Company Investigation: Forensic ESG Analysis

5.2.1 Initial Red Flags and Investigation Process

Helix Chemicals appeared to be a textbook acquisition candidate during initial screening. Revenue growth averaged 12% annually, EBITDA margins exceeded industry benchmarks, and the management team had strong operational credentials. However, Alex's enhanced due diligence protocols identified several red flags that warranted deeper investigation:

Environmental Data Inconsistencies: Company environmental reports showed dramatically lower emissions than expected based on production volumes and chemical input quantities. Industry benchmarking suggested emissions should be 8–10 times higher than reported levels.
Employee Interview Insights: Anonymous conversations with current and former employees revealed systematic pressure to minimize environmental reporting and expedite processes during peak production periods. Several workers mentioned concerns about waste disposal practices and equipment maintenance deferrals.
Regulatory Pattern Analysis: Analysis of regulatory inspection records revealed an unusual pattern of violations clustered around specific time periods, suggesting systematic rather than random compliance failures.

Table 5.2 Technology-enhanced assessment tools

Technology	*Application*	*Benefits*
AI Document Review	Automated analysis of permits, contracts, compliance documents, historical records	80% time reduction 95% accuracy Identifies hidden risks
Alternative Data Sources	Social media sentiment, news monitoring, supplier databases, employee reviews	Real-time insights Stakeholder perspectives Early warning signals
Satellite Imagery	Land use monitoring, deforestation tracking, facility verification, environmental compliance	Independent verification Historical trends Remote assessment
Digital Materiality Platforms	Industry-specific ESG risk identification, peer benchmarking, stakeholder mapping	Data-driven prioritization Industry expertise Automated scoring

Community Relations Assessment: Local environmental groups had raised concerns about air quality and groundwater contamination near company facilities, though these concerns had not resulted in formal enforcement actions.

"The pattern was too consistent to ignore," Alex explained to the investment committee. "When you see environmental data that defies chemistry, combined with employee concerns and regulatory patterns, you have a systematic problem that needs forensic investigation."

5.2.2 Mass Balance Analysis and Discovery

Alex's team brought in specialized environmental consultants to conduct mass balance analysis—a technique that tracks material flows through production processes to identify discrepancies between inputs, outputs, and reported emissions or waste.

The analysis revealed the stark reality: 1,820 tons of methylene chloride annually could not be accounted for through reported emissions, product output, or declared waste disposal. The missing chemicals represented either massive unreported environmental releases or undisclosed hazardous waste that would require expensive remediation.

Further investigation using former employee interviews, satellite imagery analysis, and soil testing revealed the truth: decades of improper waste disposal had contaminated soil and groundwater across multiple sites. The company had systematically underreported emissions and waste to avoid regulatory scrutiny and compliance costs.

Liability Quantification:

- Immediate soil remediation: €8 million
- Groundwater treatment systems: €4 million
- Regulatory fines and penalties: €2 million
- Ongoing monitoring and compliance: €1 million (present value)
- Total environmental liability: €15 million

5.2.3 Value Creation Opportunity Identification

While the environmental investigation revealed substantial liabilities, it also uncovered significant value creation opportunities that traditional analysis had missed. The forensic approach identified operational inefficiencies and competitive positioning advantages that could offset remediation costs.

Operational Improvement Identification: The investigation revealed that environmental compliance failures coincided with production quality issues, energy inefficiency, and raw material waste. Addressing environmental problems would likely improve overall operational performance.

Technology Upgrade Opportunities: Compliance requirements necessitated process technology upgrades that would reduce costs while improving environmental performance. Modern equipment could achieve both compliance and efficiency objectives simultaneously.
Management System Enhancement: Environmental management system improvements would create operational transparency and control systems that enhanced general business performance beyond compliance requirements.
Competitive Positioning: Achieving industry-leading environmental performance would create competitive advantages in customer relationships and regulatory interactions while reducing operational risks.

5.2.4 Deal Structure and Value Creation Planning

The investigation results enabled informed deal structuring that allocated environmental risks appropriately while capturing value creation opportunities. Rather than simply adjusting the purchase price downward to reflect environmental liabilities, Alex's team developed a comprehensive approach that addressed both risks and opportunities.

Environmental Liability Management: Purchase price adjustment of €12 million reflected immediate remediation requirements, with additional €3 million held in escrow pending regulatory resolution and long-term monitoring requirements.
Value Creation Investment: €4.5 million investment in process technology upgrades and environmental management systems expected to generate €2.8 million annual cost savings while achieving full regulatory compliance.
Performance Monitoring: Comprehensive environmental performance monitoring system enabling real-time optimization and continuous improvement beyond compliance requirements.
Stakeholder Engagement: Proactive communication with regulators, community groups, and employees demonstrating commitment to environmental excellence and operational transparency.

Helix Chemicals ultimately generated 2.8× returns over four years, with environmental improvements contributing €11.2 million to enterprise value through cost savings, risk reduction, and competitive positioning advantages.

"This case demonstrated that ESG due diligence is not just about avoiding disasters," Alex reflected. "It is about understanding business reality more completely than competitors—seeing risks they miss and opportunities they overlook."

Common Questions Alex Fields

Q: How do you balance thorough ESG assessment with typical deal timelines?
A: Materiality-driven prioritization is essential. We focus intensive resources on high-impact factors while using efficient screening for lower-priority issues. Technology tools handle routine data collection and analysis, freeing

human expertise for complex evaluation. The Helix investigation took extra time, but the €15 million discovery justified the investment.

Q: What if target companies lack ESG data or have poor disclosure quality?

A: Berg and colleagues' (2022) research shows ESG rating agencies only correlate 0.54 versus 0.99 for credit ratings, so we never rely solely on third-party assessments. We use primary data collection through site visits, employee interviews, and specialized testing. The missing data itself often signals management quality issues worth investigating.

Q: How do you avoid false positives where ESG concerns turn out to be immaterial?

A: Materiality assessment distinguishes real risks from noise. We ask: Does this factor affect revenue, costs, or capital requirements? Will stakeholders penalize poor performance? Can improvements create competitive advantage? If the answers are no, we acknowledge the issue but do not let it drive decisions.

5.3 Stakeholder Analysis Framework

5.3.1 Comprehensive Stakeholder Assessment

Effective ESG due diligence required systematic stakeholder analysis that went beyond traditional customer and supplier evaluation. Alex's framework assessed all stakeholder relationships that could materially affect business performance, using structured interviews, surveys, and third-party research to understand stakeholder perspectives and expectations:

Employee Engagement Evaluation: Anonymous employee surveys measured engagement levels, satisfaction with management, workplace culture quality, and retention intentions. Exit interview analysis identified systematic issues affecting turnover and productivity. Management assessment included leadership quality, communication effectiveness, and change management capabilities.

Customer Relationship Analysis: Customer interviews explored satisfaction with current services, sustainability preferences, future requirements, and competitive evaluations. Analysis of customer concentration, retention rates, and feedback patterns identified relationship quality and potential risks.

Community Stakeholder Mapping: Systematic identification and assessment of local government officials, environmental groups, community leaders, and other stakeholders who could influence operational licence and expansion opportunities. Relationship quality assessment and potential conflict identification.

Supply Chain Relationship Evaluation: Supplier interviews assessed relationship quality, capacity constraints, sustainability practices, and collaboration opportunities. Analysis of supplier concentration, performance metrics, and contract terms identified risks and improvement potential.

Regulatory Relationship Assessment: Analysis of interactions with key regulators, compliance history, and regulatory positioning relative to competitors. Assessment of regulatory change preparedness and stakeholder relationship quality with enforcement authorities.

5.3.2 *Alpine Foods Stakeholder Discovery*

The Alpine Foods due diligence process, building on the financial performance documented in Chapter 3, revealed how family-owned sustainable practices could be scaled through institutional partnership. The ESG analysis identified €280,000 in annual cost savings opportunities and €340,000 in premium pricing potential that traditional due diligence would have missed—hidden value visible only through stakeholder-focused assessment frameworks:

Employee Interview Insights: Staff interviews revealed unusually high engagement levels (87% satisfaction versus 64% industry average) and extremely low turnover (8% versus 23% industry average). Employees cited company values, local community connection, and management accessibility as key retention factors. However, interviews also identified training and career development gaps that limited productivity and innovation potential.

Customer Relationship Analysis: Customer interviews uncovered deep loyalty based on product quality, reliability, and shared sustainability values. Several customers expressed willingness to pay 10–15% premiums for enhanced sustainability credentials and supply chain transparency. However, customers also identified product innovation and service enhancement opportunities that could strengthen competitive positioning.

Supplier Partnership Potential: Local supplier relationships created cost advantages and quality benefits, but systematic supplier development could enhance capabilities while strengthening community relationships. Organic certification support for additional suppliers could expand certified product portfolio while reducing costs.

Community Integration Advantages: Strong community relationships provided operational advantages including streamlined permitting, local talent access, and community support for expansion projects. However, systematic community investment could enhance these advantages while creating shared value opportunities.

5.3.3 *Materiality Assessment Integration*

Stakeholder analysis informed materiality assessment by identifying which ESG factors actually mattered to key stakeholders and affected business performance. This stakeholder-informed materiality approach provided more accurate prioritization than generic industry frameworks alone:

Stakeholder Priority Mapping: Different stakeholder groups prioritized different ESG factors based on their interests and concerns. Employees emphasized workplace culture and development opportunities. Customers focused on product quality and sustainability credentials. Communities prioritized environmental stewardship and local economic contributions.

Business Impact Quantification: Stakeholder priorities were evaluated for potential business impact through revenue effects, cost implications, and risk considerations. Factors that multiple stakeholders considered important typically had higher business materiality.

Dynamic Materiality Updates: Regular stakeholder feedback collection enabled materiality assessment updates as stakeholder priorities evolved, and business circumstances changed. This dynamic approach ensured continued relevance and accuracy of materiality frameworks.

5.4 Climate Risk Assessment and Scenario Analysis

5.4.1 Physical and Transition Risk Evaluation

Climate change represented both physical risks (extreme weather, sea-level rise, temperature changes) and transition risks (policy changes, technology disruption, market shifts) that could materially affect business performance. Alex's framework incorporated climate scenario analysis based on frameworks developed by the Task Force on Climate-related Financial Disclosures (TCFD) and the Network for Greening the Financial System (NGFS).

Physical Risk Assessment:

- Facility location vulnerability to extreme weather events and sea-level rise.
- Supply chain exposure to climate-related disruptions.
- Operational impacts from temperature changes and water availability.
- Infrastructure resilience and adaptation requirements.
- Insurance availability and cost implications.

Transition Risk Evaluation:

- Carbon pricing exposure and regulatory compliance costs.
- Technology disruption affecting product competitiveness.
- Market demand changes from customer sustainability preferences.
- Stranded asset risks from policy or market shifts.
- Reputation risks from perceived climate performance.

5.4.2 Sector-Specific Climate Analysis

Different industries faced distinctive climate risks that required specialized assessment approaches. Alex's team developed sector-specific climate analysis frameworks that addressed industry-particular vulnerabilities and opportunities:

Manufacturing Sector Analysis: Focus on energy costs, supply chain disruption, extreme weather operational impacts, and regulatory compliance requirements. Assessment of energy efficiency opportunities and renewable energy potential. Evaluation of product demand changes related to climate policies.
Consumer Goods Climate Assessment: Analysis of changing consumer preferences, sustainable product opportunities, packaging requirements, and supply chain sustainability. Assessment of brand reputation risks related to climate positioning and competitive advantages from sustainability leadership.
Healthcare Sector Evaluation: Climate-related health impacts affecting demand patterns, facility resilience requirements for continuity of care, and regulatory requirements for environmental health protection. Energy cost management and sustainability positioning for institutional customers.
Technology Sector Analysis: Energy consumption assessment for data centres and operations, supply chain minerals and rare earth element availability, customer sustainability requirements, and competitive positioning through climate technology innovation.

5.4.3 Scenario Modelling and Financial Impact Quantification

Alex's team used NGFS climate scenarios to model potential financial impacts under different future states, incorporating both physical and transition risks into investment analysis and valuation adjustments.

Scenario Framework:

- Orderly transition (early policy action, gradual change).
- Disorderly transition (late policy action, rapid disruption).
- Hot house world (limited policy action, severe physical impacts).

For each scenario, the team quantified potential impacts on revenue, costs, capital requirements, and asset values over different time horizons. This analysis informed risk adjustments in financial models and identified adaptation strategies that could reduce vulnerability.

"The goal was not to predict the future," Alex explained. "It was to understand how different climate futures could affect business performance and ensure we were not surprised by plausible scenarios that would materially impact returns."

5.5 Data Quality Management and Verification

5.5.1 Addressing ESG Data Challenges

ESG due diligence faced systematic data quality challenges that required sophisticated verification and triangulation approaches. Berg, Kölbel, and Rigobon's (2022) comprehensive analysis of ESG rating agencies revealed that

Table 5.3 Climate scenario analysis framework. Network for Greening the Financial System (NGFS) scenarios

Scenario	*Description*	*Key Risks*
Orderly Transition	Early policy action, gradual transition to net zero by 2050 Global warming: 1.5–2°C	Transition risks: Carbon pricing, technology shifts, stranded assets Physical risks: Moderate
Disorderly Transition	Late policy action, abrupt changes after 2030 Global warming: 1.5–2°C	Transition risks: Sudden policy shifts, market disruptions, write-downs Physical risks: Moderate–High
Hot House World	Limited policy action, minimal transition Global warming: 3°C+	Transition risks: Minimal Physical risks: Severe—extreme weather, sea-level rise, ecosystem collapse

measurement differences account for 56% of rating disparity, while scope variations contribute another 38%. This fundamental disagreement among professional rating agencies illustrated why due diligence teams could not rely solely on third-party assessments.

"In an ideal world, we would have complete, verified ESG data for every company we evaluate," Alex acknowledged. "In reality, we often encounter gaps, especially in emerging markets or family-owned businesses."

Rather than accepting these limitations, Alex's team developed several practical approaches informed by both research best practices and implementation experience:

Primary Data Collection Protocols: When existing information was insufficient, they implemented structured data gathering during due diligence through on-site assessments, targeted interviews, and specialized questionnaires based on GRI and SASB frameworks.

Multiple Source Triangulation: Instead of relying on single data sources, they cross-referenced company disclosures with industry benchmarks, regulatory filings, employee accounts, and third-party assessments to identify inconsistencies and verify accuracy.

Independent Verification Methods: Satellite imagery, environmental testing, customer surveys, and employee sentiment analysis provided objective data that did not depend on company cooperation or disclosure quality.

Data Quality Scoring: A systematic framework assessed information reliability based on source independence, verification methodology, and consistency across multiple sources—enabling appropriate confidence levels in assessment conclusions.

5.5.2 *Site Visits and Operational Assessment*

Technology tools provided valuable insights, but on-site assessment remained essential for verifying claims and understanding operational reality. Alex's team conducted systematic facility tours, employee interviews, and community engagement during due diligence.

Table 5.4 Data quality scoring framework

Criterion	*High (5)*	*Medium (3)*	*Low (1)*	*Score Weight*
Collection Method	Automated metering	Semi-automated systems	Manual recording	25%
Verification Level	Third-party assured	Internal audit	Self-reported	30%
Timeliness	Real time/monthly	Quarterly	Annual/ad hoc	20%
Completeness	>95% data points	80–95% coverage	<80% coverage	25%

Overall Score Interpretation: 4.0–5.0 = Investment Ready | 3.0–3.9 = Improvement Needed | <3.0 = High Risk

Facility Assessment Protocols:

- Environmental management system inspection and documentation review.
- Equipment condition assessment and maintenance practice evaluation.
- Workplace safety observation and employee feedback collection.
- Waste management and disposal practice verification.
- Community relationship assessment through local stakeholder interviews.

On-site assessment enabled verification of claims and identification of issues that document review might miss. The physical inspection often revealed cultural factors and operational practices that determined ESG performance more accurately than formal systems or policies.

5.5.3 Managing Resource Constraints

Conducting thorough ESG due diligence within typical deal timelines and budgets required careful prioritization and efficient deployment of resources. This challenge became more acute as ESG expectations grew while deal execution timelines compressed.

"We are always balancing thoroughness with practicality," Alex explained. "The key is focusing intensive assessment on material factors while using efficient screening approaches for lower-priority issues."

Risk-Based Assessment Prioritization: High-risk industries, companies, and ESG factors received intensive analysis, while lower-risk situations used standardized screening approaches. Risk assessment considered industry factors, company characteristics, and stakeholder concerns.

Technology-Enabled Efficiency: Automated tools handled routine data collection and analysis, enabling human resources to focus on complex evaluation and verification activities. AI-powered document review, automated benchmarking, and digital survey platforms improved efficiency.

Collaborative Assessment Approaches: Coordination with other due diligence workstreams to share information and avoid duplicated effort. Integration of ESG assessment with commercial, operational, and financial analysis to maximize information value while minimizing resource requirements.

Scalable Assessment Frameworks: Standardized assessment approaches that could be adapted to different company sizes, industries, and complexity levels. Framework consistency enabled efficient deployment while maintaining assessment quality and comparability.

5.6 Sector-Specific ESG Assessment

5.6.1 Industry Materiality Frameworks

Different sectors faced distinctive ESG risks and opportunities that required specialized assessment approaches. Alex's team developed sector-specific frameworks based on materiality research, regulatory analysis, and portfolio experience across various industries:

Manufacturing Sector Assessment: Focus on environmental efficiency, workplace safety, supply chain management, and regulatory compliance. Key metrics included energy consumption, waste generation, worker safety performance, and environmental compliance history. Assessment emphasized operational efficiency opportunities and regulatory risk management.

Consumer Goods Evaluation: Emphasis on brand reputation, product safety, supply chain labour practices, and customer sustainability preferences. Assessment included social media sentiment analysis, product recall history, supplier audit results, and customer satisfaction research. Focus on brand value protection and enhancement opportunities.

Healthcare Sector Analysis: Priority on patient safety, regulatory compliance, data privacy, and community health impacts. Key factors included clinical quality metrics, regulatory violation history, cybersecurity capabilities, and stakeholder trust measures. Assessment emphasized risk mitigation and stakeholder confidence building.

Technology Industry Framework: Focus on data privacy, cybersecurity, employee retention, and innovation capabilities. Assessment included data breach history, employee satisfaction scores, intellectual property protection, and customer trust metrics. Emphasis on talent management and competitive positioning.

5.6.2 Regulatory Environment Analysis

ESG assessment required comprehensive understanding of current and anticipated regulatory requirements affecting target companies. Regulatory analysis informed risk assessment and value creation planning while identifying compliance costs and competitive positioning opportunities:

Current Compliance Status: Analysis of existing regulatory requirements and company compliance performance. Review of violation history, enforcement actions, and ongoing regulatory proceedings. Assessment of management commitment to compliance and system effectiveness.

Emerging Regulatory Requirements: Analysis of pending and anticipated regulatory changes that could affect business operations and competitive positioning. Assessment of preparation status and compliance costs for emerging requirements.

Cross-Jurisdictional Analysis: For companies operating across multiple jurisdictions, assessment of varying regulatory requirements and compliance complexity. Identification of regulatory arbitrage opportunities and harmonization challenges.

Regulatory Relationship Quality: Assessment of company relationships with key regulators and enforcement authorities. Analysis of compliance culture and proactive engagement with regulatory authorities.

5.6.3 Competitive Positioning Assessment

ESG factors increasingly affected competitive positioning as customers, employees, and other stakeholders incorporated sustainability considerations into their decision-making. Assessment of ESG competitive positioning informed both risk evaluation and value creation planning:

Peer Benchmarking: Systematic comparison of ESG performance against industry peers using publicly available data and third-party assessments. Identification of competitive advantages and disadvantages in sustainability performance.

Customer Preference Analysis: Assessment of customer sustainability preferences and procurement requirements. Analysis of competitive positioning based on ESG credentials and identification of market opportunities from sustainability leadership.

Employee Attraction and Retention: Evaluation of competitive positioning for talent acquisition and retention based on workplace culture, values alignment, and career development opportunities. Assessment of employee value proposition relative to industry competitors.

Stakeholder Perception Analysis: Assessment of brand reputation and stakeholder perception relative to competitors. Analysis of media coverage, social media sentiment, and stakeholder feedback to understand competitive positioning.

5.7 Integration with Traditional Due Diligence

5.7.1 Cross-Functional Assessment Integration

The most successful ESG due diligence implementations integrated sustainability assessment with traditional due diligence workstreams rather than treating them as separate activities. This integration reflected research showing that ESG factors often correlated with operational and financial performance indicators:

Commercial Due Diligence Integration: ESG factors affecting market positioning, customer relationships, and competitive advantages were assessed alongside traditional commercial analysis. Customer interviews included sustainability preferences and procurement requirements. Brand reputation analysis incorporated ESG factors affecting market positioning.

Operational Due Diligence Integration: Environmental efficiency, workplace safety, and operational resilience were evaluated as part of operational assessment. Energy and resource efficiency analysis identified cost reduction opportunities. Workplace culture evaluation informed operational effectiveness assessment.

Financial Due Diligence Integration: ESG-related costs, liabilities, and value creation opportunities were incorporated into financial models and projections. Environmental liability assessment informed balance sheet analysis. Efficiency improvement opportunities were included in operational improvement planning.

Management Assessment Integration: ESG experience and commitment were evaluated as part of management team assessment. Leadership capabilities included stakeholder engagement and sustainability implementation experience. Management incentive systems were reviewed for ESG performance inclusion.

5.7.2 *Investment Committee Presentation Integration*

ESG findings were integrated into investment committee presentations rather than reported separately. This integration ensured that sustainability factors received appropriate consideration in investment decisions and value creation planning:

Executive Summary Integration: Key ESG risks and opportunities were highlighted in executive summaries alongside traditional commercial and financial highlights. Material ESG factors were presented with quantified business impact assessment.

Financial Impact Integration: ESG-related costs, savings, and revenue opportunities were incorporated into financial projections and valuation analysis. Risk adjustments reflected ESG performance quality and improvement potential.

Value Creation Planning: Sustainability initiatives were included in value creation plans with specific targets, timelines, and resource requirements. ESG improvements were integrated with operational enhancement and growth strategies.

Risk Assessment Integration: ESG risks were evaluated alongside traditional operational and financial risks. Risk mitigation planning included ESG factors and stakeholder management requirements.

5.8 Building Competitive Advantage through Superior Due Diligence

5.8.1 *Due Diligence as Strategic Intelligence*

As Alex concluded the investment committee presentation on the Helix Chemicals discovery, the room's energy had shifted from tension to excitement. What could have been a catastrophic investment had become an opportunity to demonstrate the value of systematic ESG due diligence.

"The future belongs to firms that can systematically identify sustainability factors that others overlook," Alex told the team. "This is not about compliance or social responsibility—though those matter. It is about seeing the complete picture of risks and opportunities that determine investment success."

The committee voted to proceed with the acquisition, adjusting the purchase price to reflect environmental remediation costs while incorporating specific sustainability initiatives expected to generate substantial operational improvements and EBITDA enhancement.

For Alex, this represented the culmination of years refining due diligence approaches across dozens of transactions. The methodology developed through experience and continuous improvement now helped the firm consistently find value where others saw only problems—or missed issues entirely.

5.8.2 Competitive Differentiation through ESG Excellence

Kerring Capital Partners' enhanced ESG due diligence capabilities created competitive advantages in deal origination, execution, and value creation. Superior assessment capabilities enabled the firm to:

Identify Hidden Value: ESG analysis often revealed value creation opportunities that traditional due diligence missed. Environmental efficiency improvements, employee engagement enhancements, and customer relationship strengthening created measurable financial benefits.

Avoid Catastrophic Risks: Systematic ESG assessment identified potential disasters that could destroy investment returns. Environmental liabilities, social conflicts, and governance failures often escaped traditional analysis but created material business risks.

Enhance Deal Sourcing: Investment bankers and business owners increasingly preferred buyers with sophisticated ESG capabilities who could recognize and capture sustainability value. ESG expertise became a competitive advantage in deal origination.

Improve Value Creation: Comprehensive ESG assessment informed value creation planning and identified improvement opportunities that competitors might overlook. Sustainability integration often created competitive advantages that persisted beyond ownership periods.

5.8.3 Continuous Improvement and Learning

The ESG due diligence methodology continued evolving based on experience, academic research, and industry best practice development. Alex's team systematically captured lessons learned and refined approaches to improve effectiveness and efficiency:

Portfolio Feedback Integration: Post-investment performance analysis identified which ESG factors actually affected business results and which assessment techniques predicted outcomes most accurately. This feedback informed methodology refinements and resource allocation optimization.

Academic Research Integration: New research findings were systematically evaluated and incorporated into assessment frameworks when relevant. Collaboration with academic institutions provided access to emerging methodologies and validation of assessment approaches.

Industry Best Practice Adoption: Participation in industry associations and working groups enabled learning from peer experiences and adoption of proven best practices. Collaboration with other private equity firms advanced industry-wide ESG capabilities.

Technology Enhancement: Continuous evaluation and adoption of new technology tools that improved assessment efficiency and accuracy. Investment in technology platforms that enabled scalable deployment across portfolio companies.

Common Questions Alex Fields

Q: How do you handle situations where ESG assessment reveals deal-breaking issues late in the process?

A: The chemical company case is instructive. We discovered €15 million in liabilities but also identified value creation opportunities that offset them. The key is early assessment—ideally in LOI stage—and maintaining deal flexibility. Sometimes we walk away, sometimes we restructure pricing and indemnities, sometimes we see opportunities others miss.

Q: Do sellers resist providing ESG data during due diligence?

A: Sophisticated sellers recognize that buyers will eventually uncover issues, so transparency serves their interests. We frame ESG assessment as value discovery rather than fault-finding. The Alpine Foods family was initially nervous but came to see our assessment as validation of their practices and identification of improvement opportunities.

Q: How do you compare ESG performance across industries with different material factors?

A: We do not try to create universal ESG scores. Instead, we assess performance on industry-specific material factors. A manufacturer's energy efficiency matters more than a software company's. We benchmark within industries and focus on whether ESG performance creates competitive advantages in that specific context.

5.9 Future Evolution of ESG Due Diligence

5.9.1 Regulatory Standardization and Data Improvement

Looking forward, Alex anticipated several trends that would continue reshaping ESG due diligence capabilities and requirements. Regulatory development would improve data availability while creating new compliance requirements:

Expanding Disclosure Requirements: Initiatives like the EU Corporate Sustainability Reporting Directive (CSRD) would improve ESG data availability and quality for assessment purposes. Standardized disclosure requirements would enable more efficient and accurate ESG analysis.
Mandatory Climate Reporting: Climate disclosure requirements would provide comprehensive data for climate risk assessment and scenario analysis. Carbon accounting and emissions reporting would become routine business practices.
Supply Chain Transparency: Regulatory requirements for supply chain due diligence would improve visibility into supplier practices and enable more comprehensive risk assessment. Supply chain sustainability reporting would become standard practice.

5.9.2 Technology Integration and Automation

AI and Machine Learning: Advanced analytics would enable pattern recognition and risk identification that manual analysis cannot achieve. Machine learning algorithms would improve assessment accuracy while reducing time and cost requirements.
Satellite Monitoring and Remote Sensing: Environmental monitoring capabilities would enable independent verification of operational claims and identification of undisclosed environmental issues. Real-time monitoring would supplement periodic assessment with continuous surveillance.
Blockchain Verification: Distributed ledger technology would enable transparent and verifiable ESG data sharing. Supply chain tracking and verification would become more efficient and reliable through blockchain implementation.

5.9.3 Stakeholder Engagement Evolution

Digital Stakeholder Platforms: Technology would enable more efficient and systematic stakeholder engagement during due diligence. Digital platforms would facilitate stakeholder feedback collection and analysis at scale.
Collaborative Value Creation: Due diligence processes would increasingly involve stakeholder co-creation of value creation plans. Employee input, customer collaboration, and supplier partnership discussions would occur during assessment phases rather than post-acquisition.
Transparent Reporting: Public ESG reporting would provide additional data sources while creating accountability for performance improvement. Third-party verification would become standard practice for material ESG disclosures.

The evolution of ESG due diligence from compliance exercise to competitive intelligence tool represented one of private equity's most significant methodological advances. Firms that mastered comprehensive ESG assessment would consistently outperform competitors who treated sustainability as peripheral consideration.

As Kerring Capital Partners demonstrated through the chemical company discovery, Alpine Foods' opportunity identification, and systematic methodology development, enhanced ESG due diligence was not just about avoiding disasters. It was about understanding business reality more completely seeing risks others missed and opportunities others overlooked.

Due diligence identified opportunities and risks, but successful ESG integration depended on those critical first 100 days post-acquisition. Chapter 6 reveals how to build momentum that lasts throughout the entire ownership period, transforming assessment insights into operational reality.

Chapter Summary

Core Insight

Enhanced ESG due diligence transforms from defensive compliance to offensive competitive intelligence by systematically uncovering risks and opportunities traditional analysis misses. The €15 million chemical company discovery and Alpine Foods' €620,000 hidden value identification demonstrate how materiality-driven assessment enables superior investment decisions.

Critical Success Factors

- **Materiality-driven prioritization:** Khan et al.'s (2016) research showing material factors drive 4.2% outperformance validates focusing intensive resources on high-impact ESG factors.
- **Technology-enabled efficiency:** AI document review, satellite imagery, and alternative data sources enhance assessment accuracy while managing resource constraints.
- **Stakeholder analysis integration:** Alpine Foods case shows employee interviews, customer feedback, and community assessment reveal hidden value (€620K opportunities) traditional due diligence misses.
- **Climate scenario analysis:** TCFD/NGFS frameworks enable quantification of physical and transition risks across different future states.
- **Data quality management:** Berg et al.'s (2022) finding of 0.54 ESG rating correlation (vs 0.99 credit) requires primary data collection and multiple-source triangulation.

Watch Out For

⚠ Treating ESG as separate workstream rather than integrating with commercial, operational, and financial due diligence.

⚠ Relying solely on third-party ratings when measurement differences account for 56% of rating disparity.

⚠ Generic industry frameworks without company-specific materiality assessment miss context-dependent risks.
⚠ Insufficient resource allocation for forensic investigation when red flags appear—chemical company required intensive analysis.

Tools You Can Use Now

- **Four-Dimensional Assessment Matrix:** Environmental, social, governance, and materiality evaluation framework with technology enhancement overlay.
- **Chemical Company Investigation Playbook:** Mass balance analysis, forensic techniques, and value creation identification from liability discovery.
- **Alpine Foods Stakeholder Framework:** Employee, customer, supplier, community assessment protocols revealing hidden opportunities.
- **Climate Scenario Modelling:** NGFS orderly/disorderly/hot house scenarios with financial impact quantification methodology.
- **Data Triangulation Approach:** Primary collection, multiple sources, independent verification, and quality scoring framework.

What's Next

Chapter 6 demonstrates how the critical first 100 days post-acquisition determine long-term ESG success. Through the case studies of Precision Peak Manufacturing and Solid Hej Components' breakthrough, you will discover battle-tested strategies for securing executive buy-in, overcoming stakeholder resistance, and creating cultural change.

References

Berg, F., Kölbel, J. F., & Rigobon, R. (2022). Aggregate confusion: The divergence of ESG ratings . *Review of Finance*, 26 (6), 1315–1344. doi:10.1093/rof/rfac037.

Cohen, L., Gurun, U. G., & Nguyen, Q. (2024, July 10). It's time to change how ESG is measured. *Harvard Business Review*. https://hbr.org/2024/07/its-time-to-change-how-esg-is-measured.

Eccles, R. G., Ioannou, I., & Serafeim, G. (2014). The impact of corporate sustainability on organizational processes and performance. *Management Science, 60*(11), 2835–2857. doi:10.1287/mnsc.2014.1984.

EFRAG (2025). EFRAG provides its technical advice on draft simplified ESRS to the European Commission (News release, 3 December).

EFRAG (2025). Draft Simplified ESRS (Resource hub, November/December 2025 materials).

Khan, M., Serafeim, G., & Yoon, A. (2016). Corporate sustainability: First evidence on materiality. *The Accounting Review, 91*(6), 1697–1724. doi:10.2308/accr-51383.

Network for Greening the Financial System. (2022). Progress report on bridging data gaps. NGFS Secretariat.

Task Force on Climate-related Financial Disclosures. (2017). Recommendations of the Task Force on Climate-related Financial Disclosures. TCFD.

6 Value Creation Playbook

The First 100 Days and Beyond

The First 100 Days

The Precision Peak Manufacturing boardroom felt like a courtroom. Three months after Kerring Capital Partners' acquisition, what should have been a routine quarterly review had devolved into something resembling a hostage negotiation. Employee satisfaction scores glowed an ominous red on the projection screen: down from 72% to 48% in just 90 days.

"Let me be clear about what we are looking at," Alex said, clicking to the next slide that showed turnover climbing toward 34%. "We acquired a profitable company with a decent workplace culture and somehow managed to make it worse. We are now facing our first-ever strike vote, productivity has dropped 12%, and three key customers have expressed concerns about service quality."

The silence stretched uncomfortably. Alex had learned the hard way at Precision Peak Manufacturing that the first 100 days make or break ESG integration. Get it wrong, as they had here, and the result was potential strikes and 34% employee turnover. Get it right, as they later did at Solid Hej Components with €67,000 in immediate LED upgrade savings, and unstoppable momentum builds.

Kenyon Iken, Precision Peak's CEO, shifted uncomfortably. "Alex, we implemented everything you suggested. The new reporting systems, the sustainability committees, the environmental audits—"

"That is exactly the problem," Alex interrupted. "We imposed our playbook without understanding the company culture. Transformation is not about systems—it is about people. Here we treated symptoms instead of building relationships."

Research by the Principles for Responsible Investment (2023) found that successful ESG integration during the first 100 days required systematic stakeholder engagement and cultural assessment before implementing new processes. The Precision Peak experience became Alex's master class in what not to do during the critical first 100 days. It also sparked development of a systematic framework that would later generate superior results across Kerring Capital Partners' portfolio.

DOI: 10.4324/9781003625636-8

6.1 The Foundation Framework: Four Critical Elements

6.1.1 Cultural Assessment Before Action

Rather than imposing external ESG frameworks, effective integration started with understanding existing organizational culture and building on authentic strengths. Alex's revised approach, developed after Precision Peak's failure, emphasized assessment before action.

Based on lessons learned from Precision Peak and refined through subsequent acquisitions, Alex's framework rested on four foundation elements that must be established during the first 100 days. These aligned with established change management principles while incorporating ESG-specific considerations identified in recent private equity research. CFGI (2021) emphasized that "the first 100 days following an acquisition are a critical period for private equity sponsors and their newly acquired portfolio companies," requiring systematic approaches that address people, processes, and technology within compressed timeframes.

The Four Foundation Elements

Rather than imposing predetermined sustainability programmes, successful integration starts with understanding what the company already does well and where employees see opportunities for improvement. This approach reflected both Schein's (2010) work on organizational culture, which demonstrated that successful change required understanding and respecting existing cultural norms before introducing new practices, and Cooperrider and Srivastva's (1987) foundational research on appreciative inquiry, which showed that organizations perform better when change efforts focus on strengths rather than deficits.

At Precision Peak's recovery, Alex's team spent the first month conducting systematic interviews with employees at all levels to understand existing

Table 6.1 Four foundation elements

Element	*Purpose*	*Key Components*
🔍 Cultural Assessment	Understand current state, readiness, and barriers to change	• Employee surveys • Leadership interviews • Culture diagnostic • Readiness assessment
⚡ Quick Wins	Build credibility and momentum with visible early successes	• Energy efficiency • Waste reduction • Safety improvements • Cost savings
💬 Communication Rhythm	Keep stakeholders informed, engaged, and aligned throughout journey	• Monthly updates • Quarterly reviews • Success stories • Feedback channels
🤝 Trust Building	Establish credibility through transparency, consistency, and follow-through	• Open dialogue • Consistent messaging • Deliver promises • Celebrate progress

strengths and improvement aspirations. They discovered that Precision Peak workers took immense pride in their precision manufacturing capabilities and safety record but felt frustrated by wasteful processes and lack of recognition for efficiency improvements.

"Instead of telling them what was wrong, we asked what they were proud of and what they wanted to improve," Alex explained. "That shift in framing changed everything."

At Alpine Foods, this same approach revealed different strengths. Alpine Foods had strong sustainability practices but lacked systematic measurement and improvement processes that could support institutional scalability. Rather than replacing family practices with corporate systems, Alex's team built on the existing local sourcing relationships (78% within 200km), long-term supplier partnerships (12-year average), and low employee turnover (8%) to develop measurement and governance systems that could capture and expand their value.

6.1.2 Trust Building through Transparency

Every action during the first 100 days either builds or erodes trust with the management team and workforce. Small gestures matter enormously during this period, when everyone watches to understand what the new ownership really values.

Alex learned this lesson painfully at Precision Peak, where initial meetings focused on cost reduction and efficiency metrics without acknowledging employee expertise or company heritage. The recovery process included regular "coffee conversations" where Alex and team members shared meals with different employee groups, discussing challenges and opportunities in informal settings.

"Trust is not built through presentations," Alex reflected. "It is built through presence, consistency, and genuine curiosity about people's experiences and insights."

6.1.3 Quick Wins That Demonstrate Partnership

The most effective early initiatives address problems the company already recognizes and has wanted to solve but lacked resources or focus to tackle. These create credibility for larger changes later while demonstrating that new ownership adds value rather than just imposing requirements.

At Alpine foods, the first quick win came from employee suggestions during listening sessions. Workers had identified energy efficiency opportunities in building systems that could be addressed with modest investment. The €52,000 LED retrofit generated €74,000 in annual savings while involving maintenance staff in the planning and implementation.

"The financial return was nice, but the real value was showing employees that we listened to their ideas and acted on them," noted Hans Mueller, who became one of the transformation's strongest champions.

6.1.4 Communication Rhythms that Build Confidence

Regular, transparent communication about intentions, progress, and challenges prevents the rumour mill from filling information gaps with worst-case scenarios. This reflected established change management principles while addressing the specific transparency expectations that ESG initiatives typically generate among stakeholders.

Alex established weekly email updates to all employees, monthly all-hands meetings with Q&A sessions, and quarterly stakeholder forums that included suppliers and community representatives. The content focused less on achievements and more on learnings, challenges, and next steps—building credibility through honest assessment rather than promotional messaging.

This credibility standard is reinforced by the direction of EU sustainable finance reform. The European Commission's 2025 SFDR reform proposal places emphasis on simplifying disclosures and improving the usability of sustainability information for investors (European Commission, 2025). For ownership teams, the practical implication is to prioritize internal governance, quality controls, and consistent reporting rhythms that withstand both LP scrutiny and regulatory review (European Commission, 2025).

6.2 The ESG Quick Start Programme

6.2.1 Structured 90-Day Implementation Process

One of the most effective tools Alex developed was the "ESG Quick Start Programme"—a structured 90-day process that identified and implemented high-impact, low-controversy sustainability initiatives while building the foundation for larger changes. This approach reflected research showing that early wins increased the probability of long-term change success.

Week 1–2: Discovery and Assessment

- Stakeholder interviews with employees, customers, suppliers, and community representatives.
- Operational assessment of existing environmental and social practices.
- Governance structure review and board effectiveness evaluation.
- ESG baseline measurement and benchmarking against industry standards.

Week 3–4: Opportunity Identification

- Quick win analysis focusing on high-impact, low-cost initiatives.
- Employee suggestion collection and evaluation for improvement opportunities.
- Customer feedback analysis to identify satisfaction and loyalty drivers.
- Supplier collaboration opportunities assessment.

Week 5–8: Implementation Planning

- Resource allocation for priority initiatives.
- Timeline development with clear milestones and accountability.
- Stakeholder communication plan and engagement strategy.
- Performance measurement system design and implementation.

Week 9–12: Execution and Monitoring

- Quick win implementation with employee involvement and recognition.
- Progress monitoring and course correction as needed.
- Stakeholder feedback collection and response planning.
- Results documentation and success story development.

6.2.2 Alpine Foods Implementation Case Study

Alpine Foods exemplified successful ESG Quick Start Programme implementation. The company had strong sustainability practices but lacked systematic measurement and improvement processes that could support institutional scalability.

Month 1 Activities:

- Stakeholder interviews with employees, customers, suppliers, and community representatives.
- Operational assessment of environmental and social practices.
- Governance structure review and board effectiveness evaluation.
- ESG baseline measurement and benchmarking against industry standards.

Table 6.2 ESG Quick Start Programme timeline (90 days)

Phase	*Key Activities*	*Deliverables*
Days 1–30 Assessment	• Conduct baseline ESG assessment • Review existing data and systems • Interview key stakeholders • Identify quick wins • Benchmark against peers	• ESG baseline report • Gap analysis • Quick win identification • Stakeholder map • 100-day roadmap
Days 31–60 Foundation	• Launch quick win projects • Set up data collection systems • Establish governance structure • Begin training programmes • Communicate vision and plan	• Quick wins implemented • Data collection protocols • ESG governance charter • Training curriculum • Communication plan
Days 61–90 Momentum	• Report early results • Scale successful pilots • Engage broader organization • Set annual targets • Celebrate wins and recognize team	• Progress dashboard • Scaled initiatives • Annual ESG targets • Performance metrics • Team recognition programme

Month 2–3 Initiatives:

- Quick-win implementation: LED lighting retrofit, employee recognition programme, supplier communication enhancement.
- Strategic planning sessions combining traditional business planning with ESG integration.
- Management development programme including sustainability leadership training.
- Customer engagement programme highlighting quality and sustainability practices.

6.2.3 *Results and Momentum Building*

The Alpine Foods Quick Start Programme generated €546,000 in annual benefits from €114,000 in initial investment, achieving 379% first-year ROI while building stakeholder confidence and engagement. More importantly, the early successes created momentum for larger transformational initiatives during years two and three of ownership.

Employee satisfaction scores improved from 78% to 91% during the first 100 days, while customer satisfaction increased from 73% to 89%. These engagement improvements provided foundation for sustained performance enhancement and competitive advantage development.

Common Questions Alex Fields

Q: What's the biggest mistake companies make in the first 100 days?
A: Imposing solutions before understanding problems. Precision Peak taught us that lesson brutally. We arrived with our playbook and started implementing systems without asking what employees were proud of or what they wanted to improve. The result was resistance, turnover, and strike threats. Cultural assessment must come before programme implementation.
Q: How do you balance speed with stakeholder engagement during the first 100 days?
A: Quick wins demonstrate momentum while listening sessions build trust. At Alpine, we implemented LED upgrades and recognition programmes within weeks while conducting comprehensive stakeholder interviews. The key is choosing initiatives that employees already wanted—then they feel heard rather than imposed upon.
Q: What if management resists ESG integration from the start?
A: Frame sustainability as solutions to their existing problems rather than new requirements. Energy efficiency reduces costs. Employee engagement improves retention. Customer partnerships strengthen relationships. When you connect ESG to business challenges they already care about, resistance transforms into interest.

Table 6.3 Stakeholder mapping matrix (influence/interest)

Quadrant	*Stakeholder Type*	*Engagement Strategy*
High Interest High Influence (Manage Closely)	• Board members • Key investors/LPs • Senior management • Major customers	• Regular one-on-one meetings • Strategic input solicitation • Early involvement in decisions • Detailed progress reporting
High Interest Low Influence (Keep Informed)	• Employees • Local community • Industry associations • NGOs	• Regular updates • Feedback channels • Transparency • Responsive communication
Low Interest High Influence (Keep Satisfied)	• Regulators • Financial institutions • Industry analysts • Rating agencies	• Meet requirements • Proactive compliance • Professional relationships • Periodic updates
Low Interest Low Influence (Monitor)	• General public • Distant suppliers • Peripheral competitors	• General communications • Monitor for changes • Minimal direct engagement

6.3 Value Creation Planning: Beyond Financial Engineering

6.3.1 Stakeholder-Centric Value Creation Framework

Traditional private equity value creation focused primarily on revenue growth, margin improvement, and multiple expansion through operational efficiency and strategic initiatives. Alex's ESG-integrated approach expanded this framework to include stakeholder value creation that drives superior financial performance.

Traditional Value Creation Levers:

- Revenue Growth: Market expansion, product development, pricing optimization.
- Margin Improvement: Cost reduction, operational efficiency, technology adoption.
- Multiple Expansion: Competitive positioning, market leadership, strategic buyer appeal.

ESG-Enhanced Value Creation Framework:

- Stakeholder Value Integration: Employee engagement, customer loyalty, supplier collaboration.
- Operational Excellence Through Sustainability: Resource efficiency, waste reduction, quality improvement.
- Market Positioning Through ESG Leadership: Brand enhancement, customer preference, regulatory advantage.
- Risk Mitigation Through Stakeholder Relationships: Operational resilience, regulatory compliance, community support.

Table 6.4 Stakeholder engagement protocol

Stakeholder	*First 30 Days*	*Days 31–60*	*Days 61–90*
Employees	• Town halls • Surveys • Skip-level meetings	• Training begins • Quick win updates • Feedback loops	• Results sharing • Recognition events • Next phase preview
Customers	• Key account meetings • Needs assessment • Expectations mapping	• Progress updates • Pilot collaborations • Feedback integration	• Results presentation • Future roadmap • Partnership opportunities
Suppliers	• Supplier summits • Requirements sharing • Capability assessment	• Development programmes • Performance tracking • Support provision	• Recognition program • Best practice sharing • Long-term planning
Community	• Community meetings • Impact assessment • Concern identification	• Quick response actions • Partnership building • Regular updates	• Progress celebration • Ongoing engagement • Future commitments

6.3.2 Employee Engagement as Value Driver

Research consistently demonstrates that employee engagement correlates strongly with operational performance, customer satisfaction, and financial results. Alex's framework systematically leveraged this relationship to drive value creation while building authentic workplace culture.

Employee Engagement Investment Approach:

- Training and development programmes aligned with business needs and career aspirations.
- Recognition and reward systems celebrating both performance and sustainability contributions.
- Workplace improvement initiatives addressing employee-identified priorities.
- Career advancement opportunities including sustainability leadership roles.
- Communication systems enabling employee feedback and idea contribution.

Summit Peak Facility Services Employee Engagement Success:

Summit Peak Facility Services, a facilities management company, exemplified employee engagement value creation. When Kerring Capital Partners acquired the company, employee satisfaction was 52% and annual turnover reached 47%—far above industry averages.

The ESG-integrated approach included comprehensive workplace culture transformation:

- Anonymous employee survey identified key satisfaction drivers and improvement opportunities.
- Training programme development addressing both technical skills and career development aspirations.
- Workplace improvement initiatives based on employee suggestions and priorities.
- Recognition programme celebrating both individual achievement and team collaboration.
- Management development focusing on employee engagement and sustainability leadership.

Results achieved over three years:

- Employee satisfaction improved from 52% to 89%.
- Annual turnover reduced from 47% to 12%.
- Productivity per employee increased by 34%.
- Customer satisfaction improved from 67% to 94%.
- EBITDA growth averaged 22% annually versus 8% industry average.

The employee engagement transformation generated €1.7 million in annual cost savings through reduced recruitment and training costs, while productivity improvements contributed €2.3 million in additional EBITDA annually.

6.3.3 Customer Partnership and Market Positioning

ESG factors increasingly influenced customer purchasing decisions across B2B and B2C markets. Alex's framework systematically leveraged sustainability capabilities to strengthen customer relationships while accessing premium market segments.

Customer Partnership Strategy:

- Sustainability preference assessment through customer interviews and surveys.
- Collaborative initiative development creating shared value for customers and company.
- Transparent communication about sustainability practices and performance improvement.
- Joint innovation projects addressing customer sustainability objectives.
- Premium positioning based on verified sustainability leadership.

Solid Hej Components Customer Partnership Success:

Solid Hej Components, the Danish wind turbine manufacturer featured in Chapter 3, demonstrated customer partnership value creation through systematic sustainability engagement. Sustainability credentials enabled two major contract wins worth €340,000 annually with customers prioritizing environmental performance from suppliers.

Beyond specific contracts, strong ESG performance created brand value and competitive positioning that influenced customer decisions across the entire business. Solid Hej's reputation for sustainability leadership opened doors with procurement managers, differentiated them in competitive bids, and provided negotiating leverage for premium pricing.

"One customer told us explicitly," the operations director recounted, "'We are willing to pay 8–12% more for your components because your sustainability performance helps us meet our own commitments. You make us look good to our stakeholders.'"

6.4 Overcoming Resistance and Building Champions

6.4.1 Understanding Five Types of Resistance

Stakeholder resistance to ESG initiatives typically stemmed from five distinct sources, each requiring different engagement approaches. Alex's framework systematically addressed these resistance patterns rather than dismissing them as obstruction:

Resource Resistance: "We do not have time or budget for sustainability initiatives on top of existing priorities." This reflected genuine resource constraints rather than values opposition. Response: Demonstrate ROI through quick wins and integrate ESG into existing workflows rather than creating separate programmes.

Competence Resistance: "We do not understand sustainability well enough to implement it effectively." This reflected knowledge gaps rather than unwillingness. Response: Provide training, external expertise, and peer learning opportunities that build capability systematically.

Values Resistance: "Sustainability conflicts with our business model or shareholder obligations." This reflected genuine philosophical disagreement. Response: Reframe ESG as stakeholder value creation that drives shareholder returns rather than constrains them.

Priority Resistance: "Other initiatives are more important right now—we will address sustainability later." This reflected competing demands rather than rejection. Response: Demonstrate material business impact and integrate with existing priorities rather than competing for attention.

Trust Resistance: "Previous owners made promises they did not keep—why should we believe new commitments?" This reflected historical experience rather than current relationship. Response: Build credibility through transparency, quick wins, and consistent follow-through over time.

Table 6.5 Stakeholder engagement methods by group

Stakeholder Group	*Primary Methods*	*Frequency & Format*
Board & Investors	• Board presentations • Quarterly ESG reports • Annual impact reviews • Strategic planning sessions	Quarterly formal updates Annual in-depth review Ad-hoc strategic discussions Written + in-person
Employees	• Town halls • Team meetings • Surveys • Intranet updates • Training programmes	Monthly town halls Weekly team updates Quarterly surveys Ongoing training Multiple channels
Customers	• Account reviews • Sustainability reports • Product updates • Industry events	Quarterly account meetings Annual sustainability report Ongoing product communications Digital + in-person
Community	• Public meetings • Community investment • Local partnerships • Facility tours	Bi-annual community meetings Ongoing partnership activities Annual open days Local presence

6.4.2 Converting Sceptics to Champions

The most powerful advocates for ESG integration often emerged from initial sceptics who developed understanding through direct involvement. Alex's framework included systematic champion development that converted resistance into advocacy.

Four-Step Champion Development Process:

Step 1: Identify Potential Champions: Look for employees with informal influence, technical expertise in relevant areas, and demonstrated problem-solving orientation regardless of initial ESG scepticism.
Step 2: Provide Expertise and Resources: Offer training, external expert access, industry best practice exposure, and resources that enable champions to develop genuine sustainability knowledge.
Step 3: Create Leadership Opportunities: Assign meaningful responsibilities for specific ESG initiatives, involve in planning and decision-making, provide visibility with senior management, and enable ownership of outcomes.
Step 4: Recognize and Reward Success: Celebrate achievements publicly, incorporate ESG performance into compensation and advancement, share success stories across organization, and use champions as mentors for others.

Hans Mueller Champion Development Case:

After the initial 100-day failure at Precision Peak, Alex's team identified several employees who had shown interest in efficiency improvements and environmental responsibility despite management resistance.

Hans Mueller, a senior maintenance technician, had repeatedly suggested energy efficiency improvements that management had ignored due to budget constraints and competing priorities. Alex's team recognized Hans's expertise and provided development opportunities that transformed him into a sustainability champion.

Development Process:

- Formal recognition for energy efficiency expertise and improvement suggestions.
- Leadership role in LED retrofit project enabling hands-on implementation experience.
- Training programme attendance building systematic sustainability knowledge.
- Presentation opportunities sharing results with management team and other employees.
- Mentoring responsibilities helping other employees identify and implement efficiency improvements.

Results and Impact:

- Hans became leading advocate for sustainability initiatives throughout the organization.
- Employee-suggested improvements generated €340,000 in annual savings over three years.
- Hans's enthusiasm and expertise convinced sceptical colleagues about ESG value.
- Sustainability became integrated with operational excellence rather than separate requirement.
- Hans's leadership continued after Kerring Capital Partners' exit, ensuring sustainable transformation.

6.4.3 Tailoring Messages to Different Stakeholder Groups

Different organizational functions responded to different value propositions and messaging approaches. Alex's framework customized communication to resonate with existing motivations rather than imposing uniform ESG narratives:

Operations Teams: "Sustainability reduces waste, improves efficiency, and enhances operational reliability. Energy optimization cuts costs while improving equipment performance. Workplace safety programmes reduce incidents and productivity losses."
Sales and Marketing: "ESG credentials open new customer opportunities and differentiate us competitively. Sustainability leadership enables premium pricing and strengthens customer relationships. Brand enhancement through ESG performance attracts high-value clients."
Finance and Accounting: "Sustainability initiatives generate measurable ROI through cost savings, revenue enhancement, and risk reduction. ESG integration

improves access to capital and reduces financing costs. Performance tracking demonstrates financial impact."

Human Resources: "Workplace culture investments reduce turnover and recruitment costs. Employee engagement programmes improve productivity and service quality. Sustainability positioning enhances employer brand for talent attraction."

Research and Development: "Sustainability drives innovation opportunities and product differentiation. Customer sustainability requirements create development priorities. ESG leadership positions company for emerging market opportunities."

6.5 Cultural Integration and Sustainability

6.5.1 Embedding ESG in Organizational DNA

Successful ESG integration required embedding sustainability into organizational culture and systems rather than treating it as a separate programme or initiative. Alex's framework focused on cultural integration that would survive ownership transitions and leadership changes.

Five Cultural Integration Mechanisms:

Systems Integration: ESG metrics and processes integrated into existing management systems rather than created as separate tracking and reporting requirements. Performance management systems included sustainability metrics alongside traditional financial and operational measures. Budget planning processes incorporated ESG investment and ROI analysis. Strategic planning sessions included sustainability considerations in all business decisions. Risk management systems incorporated environmental and social factors.

Skills Development: Sustainability expertise development throughout the organization rather than concentrated in specialized roles. Management training programmes included sustainability leadership and stakeholder engagement. Employee education covered both individual contribution opportunities and organizational objectives. Technical skills development for environmental and social performance improvement. Cross-functional collaboration capabilities enabling integrated ESG implementation.

Values Alignment: Organizational values and culture evolution incorporating stakeholder value creation alongside shareholder returns. Mission and vision statements incorporated sustainability objectives and stakeholder consideration. Communication systems emphasized shared values and purpose rather than compliance requirements. Recognition systems celebrated sustainability achievements and innovation. Leadership behaviour modelled stakeholder engagement and long-term thinking.

Stories and Communication: Organizational narratives and communication emphasizing sustainability success stories and learning experiences. Success

story documentation and sharing across organization and external stakeholders. Learning experience communication including failures and course corrections. Customer and stakeholder feedback sharing demonstrating sustainability impact and value. Industry leadership positioning and external recognition highlighting sustainability achievements.
Measurement and Accountability: Performance measurement and accountability systems ensuring sustainability integration rather than peripheral consideration. Board-level sustainability performance review and strategic oversight. Management compensation and advancement criteria including ESG performance metrics. Employee performance evaluation including sustainability contribution and development. Customer and stakeholder feedback integration into performance management and improvement planning.

6.5.2 Measurement Systems That Drive Behaviour

Alex learned that measurement systems powerfully influenced behaviour and cultural development. The framework distinguished between leading indicators (behavioural changes) and lagging indicators (outcome improvements).

Leading Indicators of Cultural Integration:

- Voluntary ESG initiative participation rather than mandated compliance.
- Employee-generated improvement suggestions and innovation.
- Cross-functional collaboration on sustainability projects.
- Proactive stakeholder communication and engagement.
- Management decision-making incorporating ESG considerations.

Lagging Indicators of Sustained Change:

- Performance improvement persistence through leadership changes.
- Stakeholder satisfaction maintenance during ownership transitions.
- Competitive advantage preservation after exit.
- Industry recognition and leadership positioning.
- Financial performance improvement attribution to ESG capabilities.

6.6 Technology and Digital Enablement

6.6.1 Digital Tools for Engagement and Performance

Technology platforms enhanced ESG integration effectiveness while reducing administrative burden. However, Alex's framework emphasized that digital tools supplemented rather than replaced human-centred engagement strategies.

Employee Engagement Platforms: Anonymous feedback collection and sentiment tracking. Pulse surveys measuring engagement trends. Recognition and rewards programme administration. Training and development tracking. Communication and collaboration tools.

Stakeholder Communication Systems: Customer relationship management enhanced with sustainability preferences. Supplier performance tracking and collaboration platforms. Community engagement documentation and impact measurement. Investor reporting and transparency tools. Board-level performance dashboards.

Performance Analytics: Real-time environmental performance monitoring. Predictive analytics for equipment maintenance and optimization. Employee retention risk identification. Customer satisfaction trend analysis. Financial impact quantification and ROI tracking.

6.6.2 Balancing Automation with Human Connection

While technology improved efficiency, Alex emphasized that authentic stakeholder relationships required personal engagement that automation could not replicate. The most successful implementations used technology to enable rather than replace human interaction.

"Digital tools provide data and streamline processes," Alex explained. "But trust comes from conversations, not dashboards. Use technology to identify where human attention is needed, then invest time in genuine relationship building."

6.7 Measuring Cultural Integration Success

6.7.1 Beyond Compliance to Genuine Transformation

The ultimate test of ESG integration was whether sustainability became genuine organizational capability rather than externally imposed requirement. Alex's framework distinguished between leading indicators (behavioural changes) and lagging indicators (outcome improvements).

Quality Over Quantity Metrics: The framework emphasized behavioural quality rather than just participation quantity. Voluntary actions indicated genuine buy-in. Proactive communication demonstrated internalization. Cross-functional collaboration showed systematic integration. Innovation and improvement suggestions reflected ownership.

Durability Assessment: True cultural integration showed resilience through challenges. Performance maintained through ownership transitions. Engagement persisted through leadership changes. Initiatives continued without external prompting. Competitive advantages survived market changes.

6.7.2 Summit Peak Facility Services Cultural Integration Assessment

Summit Peak Facility Services provided compelling evidence for successful cultural integration through sustained performance improvement that persisted beyond Kerring Capital Partners' ownership.

Cultural Integration Evidence:

- ESG initiatives continued after ownership transition without external prompting.
- Employee satisfaction maintained high levels (87%) through leadership changes.
- Customer retention continued improving (96%) after new ownership.
- Industry recognition as sustainability leader expanded after Kerring Capital Partners' exit
- Financial performance improvements (22% annual EBITDA growth) continued under new ownership.

Measurement Results:

- Employee engagement surveys showed consistent high satisfaction (85%+) across three years post-exit.
- Customer feedback maintained strong loyalty and satisfaction scores.
- Operational performance improvements (productivity, quality, efficiency) continued.
- Sustainability performance maintenance and continued improvement.
- Competitive positioning preserved and enhanced under new ownership.

These results validated that ESG integration had become genuine organizational capability rather than externally imposed requirement.

6.8 Long-Term Sustainability and Exit Preparation

6.8.1 Building Capabilities That Survive Ownership Transitions

The ultimate test of ESG integration success was performance continuation after ownership transitions. Alex's framework emphasized building genuine organizational capabilities rather than dependence on external support or specific leadership.

Capability Institutionalization:

- Documented processes and systems enabling consistency without key individuals.
- Distributed expertise rather than concentrated in single roles.
- Stakeholder relationships maintained by organization rather than dependent on specific people.
- Performance measurement systems providing accountability and feedback.
- Cultural values and behaviours reinforced through multiple mechanisms.

Transition Preparation:

- Systematic documentation of ESG capabilities and competitive advantages.
- Management team development ensuring continued leadership.
- Stakeholder communication about ownership transition and commitment continuity.

- Performance tracking through transition period.
- Post-exit support and knowledge transfer to new ownership.

6.8.2 Exit Value Realization

ESG capabilities developed during ownership created tangible value that buyers recognized and paid for at exit. Alex's framework included systematic documentation and buyer education that captured sustainability premiums.

Value Documentation Approach:

- Financial impact quantification of ESG initiatives and competitive advantages.
- Third-party verification of sustainability performance and system effectiveness.
- Stakeholder testimonials and relationship quality evidence.
- Competitive positioning analysis demonstrating market advantages.
- Growth potential assessment enabled by sustainability capabilities.

Buyer Education Strategy:

- Early communication about ESG value creation and competitive advantages.
- Detailed capability documentation for due diligence teams.
- Management presentations on sustainability as strategic asset.
- Stakeholder introduction and relationship transfer planning.
- Post-acquisition support offering to ensure continuity.

Summit Peak Facility Services, Solid Hej Components, and Alpine Foods all demonstrated that systematic ESG capabilities commanded premium exit valuations. Buyers recognized that sustainability infrastructure represented valuable intellectual property that would accelerate their own transformation efforts.

6.9 Lessons Learned and Best Practices

6.9.1 Critical Success Factors

Alex's experience across dozens of ESG integration projects identified several critical success factors that determined implementation effectiveness and long-term sustainability.

Essential Elements for Success:

- Cultural assessment and respect before implementing new programmes or requirements.
- Trust building through transparency, consistency, and genuine stakeholder engagement.

- Quick wins demonstration showing immediate value creation and capability.
- Communication systems providing regular updates and response to stakeholder feedback.
- Champion development creating internal expertise and advocacy.

Common Implementation Mistakes:

- Imposing external frameworks without understanding existing culture and capabilities.
- Focusing on compliance and reporting rather than performance improvement and value creation.
- Underestimating change management requirements and resistance sources.
- Treating ESG as separate programme rather than integrated business strategy.
- Relying exclusively on external expertise rather than building internal capabilities.

6.9.2 Scaling Across Portfolio Companies

Kerring Capital Partners' success with ESG integration enabled scaling of approaches across portfolio companies while maintaining effectiveness and relevance to specific contexts.

Scaling Strategy:

- Standardized assessment frameworks adapted for industry and company characteristics.
- Best practice sharing and cross-portfolio learning opportunities.
- Common measurement systems enabling benchmarking and improvement identification.
- Technology platform deployment reducing implementation costs and improving efficiency.
- Expert team development providing consistent support while building internal capabilities.

The scaling approach generated portfolio-wide performance improvements while maintaining company-specific relevance and cultural fit. By 2024, Kerring Capital Partners had integrated ESG systematically across their entire portfolio, generating average IRR improvements of 3.8 percentage points and exit multiples averaging 1.3× higher than portfolio benchmarks.

The first 100 days built momentum, but sustained success required measuring what matters. The frameworks and tools developed through Alpine Foods, Summit Peak Facility Services, Solid Hej Components, and even the Precision Peak failure provided replicable approaches for transforming ESG from compliance burden to competitive advantage.

As Alex reflected on the journey from Precision Peak's painful beginning to the systematic methodology that emerged: "The first 100 days determine whether ESG becomes genuine value creation or expensive distraction. Get the foundation right—cultural assessment, trust building, quick wins, communication—and everything else becomes possible. Skip these steps, and even the best technical programmes will fail."

Chapter 7 addresses the next critical challenge: developing metrics that drive real performance improvements rather than just satisfy reporting requirements, building on the measurement framework introduced in this chapter's engagement assessment tools and performance tracking systems.

Chapter Summary

Core Insight

The first 100 days post-acquisition determine long-term ESG success by establishing cultural foundation, trust, and momentum. Precision Peak Manufacturing's failure (employee satisfaction 72% to 48%, turnover to 34%) versus Solid Hej Components' breakthrough (€89,000 immediate savings) and Alpine Foods' success (379% first-year ROI) demonstrate that cultural assessment before programme implementation separates success from disaster.

Critical Success Factors

- **Four foundation elements:** Cultural assessment, trust building, quick wins, and communication rhythms create platform for sustainable transformation validated by PRI (2023) research.
- **Appreciative inquiry approach:** Schein (2010) and Cooperrider & Srivastva (1987) research shows focusing on strengths rather than deficits drives superior organizational change.
- **Systematic 90-day framework:** Alpine Foods Quick Start Programme generated €546K annual benefits from €114K investment through structured discovery, planning, and execution.
- **Champion development:** Hans Mueller case shows four-step process (identify, provide expertise, create opportunities, recognize success) converts sceptics to advocates.
- **Cultural integration mechanisms:** Five-element framework (systems, skills, values, stories, measurement) embeds ESG into organizational DNA surviving ownership transitions.

Watch Out For

⚠ Imposing solutions before understanding problems—Precision Peak's biggest mistake leading to strike threats and 34% turnover.

⚠ Focusing on systems and compliance rather than people and culture—sustainability requires behavioural change not just reporting.
⚠ Treating ESG as separate programme rather than integrated business strategy creates resistance and wastes resources.
⚠ Underestimating five types of resistance (resource, competence, values, priority, trust) requiring different engagement approaches.

Tools You Can Use Now

- **ESG Quick Start Programme:** Structured 90-day framework with week-by-week activities from discovery through execution.
- **Alpine Foods Implementation Model:** €114K investment generating €546K annual benefits (LED upgrades, recognition programmes, supplier partnerships, customer communication).
- **Five Resistance Types Framework:** Resource, competence, values, priority, and trust resistance patterns with specific response strategies.
- **Champion Development Process:** Four steps transforming sceptics (like Hans Mueller) into advocates through expertise, leadership, and recognition.
- **Cultural Integration Checklist:** Systems, skills, values, stories, and measurement mechanisms embedding ESG into organizational DNA.
- **Stakeholder-Specific Messaging:** Tailored value propositions for operations, sales, finance, HR, and R&D teams.

What's Next

Chapter 7 reveals how to develop metrics that drive real performance improvements rather than just satisfy reporting requirements. You will discover material metrics frameworks that integrate ESG into monthly management reviews and quarterly board assessments, moving beyond generic sustainability scorecards to financially material performance indicators that actually influence business decisions.

References

A Simple Model. (2024). Post acquisition work: The first 100 days. Retrieved from https://www.asimplemodel.com/insights/post-acquisition-work-the-first-100-days.

CFGI. (2021). Navigating those critical first 100 days of private equity ownership. Retrieved from https://www.cfgi.com/resources/articles/navigating-those-critical-first-100-days-of-private-equity-ownership/.

Cooperrider, D. L., & Srivastva, S. (1987). Appreciative inquiry in organizational life. *Research in Organizational Change and Development*, 1, 129–169.

European Commission (2025). Commission proposes improvements to SFDR (21 November)

Financier Worldwide. (2022). M&A challenges: Employee engagement and retention. *Financier Worldwide Magazine*, December.

7 Metrics that Matter

Measuring What Drives Value

Measuring What Matters

"We are drowning in data, and we get nothing back from it."

Penelope Day's frustrated voice cut through the Monday morning silence at Apex Industries, her laptop screen displaying a spreadsheet that seemed to stretch into infinity. As chief financial officer of the €67 million automotive supplier, she had just spent her weekend wading through their latest ESG report—127 different metrics tracked across 15 categories, consuming 40 hours of staff time monthly, yet somehow telling her nothing useful about their business.

"Look at this," Penelope continued, gesturing at the screen. "We track the number of LED lightbulbs installed, the percentage of recycled paper used in our offices, and the gender ratio of our third-tier suppliers. Meanwhile, our biggest customer just told us they are prioritizing suppliers with carbon reduction plans, our energy costs spiked 23% last quarter, and we lost three skilled technicians to competitors who offer better work–life balance. But none of that shows up in our 'comprehensive' ESG dashboard."

Alex Morgan had seen this scenario too many times—companies drowning in measurement while missing what actually mattered. The problem was not lack of data; it was the absence of intelligence. In the rush to demonstrate ESG progress, companies often fell into the trap of measuring everything instead of measuring what moved the needle.

When Alex walked into a portfolio company and saw 127 different ESG metrics on spreadsheets, the diagnosis was clear: they were drowning in data but starving for insights. At Apex Industries, the solution was to cut that to 12 material metrics and reduce reporting time from 40 to 32 hours monthly. That transformation was when measurement became management.

The challenge reflected broader tensions in ESG implementation. Berg, Kölbel, and Rigobon (2022) found that approximately 56% of rating disparity among ESG rating agencies stemmed from measurement differences, while Khan, Serafeim, and Yoon (2016) found that material ESG factors generated 4.2 percentage points of annual outperformance, while non-material factors did not.

DOI: 10.4324/9781003625636-9

"Show me the three numbers that keep you awake at night," Alex said, pushing the massive report aside.

Penelope did not hesitate. "Customer complaints about product quality, which spiked 23% last quarter. Energy costs, which jumped €180,000 above budget due to equipment inefficiencies. And employee turnover in our skilled positions, which hit 31% this year."

"Those are your material ESG metrics," Alex replied. "Quality complaints connect to governance and process management. Energy costs link directly to environmental performance. And skilled worker retention is your most important social factor. Everything else is just noise."

This conversation became the foundation for completely rebuilding Apex's measurement approach. Over the following months, they would develop what became Alex's template for practical sustainability metrics—systems that drove performance instead of just documenting it.

7.1 Building Effective Reporting Frameworks

7.1.1 The Materiality Foundation

Khan, Serafeim, and Yoon's (2016) materiality research provided the foundational framework showing that firms performing well on material ESG issues outperformed peers with poor material ESG performance by 4.2 percentage points annually, while performance on immaterial ESG issues showed no benefit. This materiality principle—focusing resources on sustainability factors that actually drove business value—formed the cornerstone for measurement approaches that created genuine competitive advantages.

The problem with most ESG reporting, Alex had learned, was not the quality of the data—it was the lack of connection between what got measured and what actually mattered for business success. Companies were tracking generic sustainability indicators while ignoring the specific factors that drove their performance.

Research supported this materiality-focused approach. Whelan, Atz, Van Holt, and Clark (2021) found that 58% of corporate studies showed positive ESG–financial performance links, with only 8% showing negative results. However, these benefits materialized primarily when companies focused on financially material sustainability factors. This evidence contradicted earlier sceptical perspectives, suggesting that focused ESG efforts could indeed create value.

A parallel policy signal supports this materiality-first approach. In late 2025, the European Commission proposed reforms to SFDR intended to simplify disclosures and improve the usability of sustainability information for investors (European Commission, 2025). For private equity reporting systems, the implication is clear: measurement should prioritize materiality, comparability, and governance controls over disclosure volume, particularly where data quality and assurance requirements are rising.

7.1.2 Material Metrics Identification: Sector-Specific Approaches

The breakthrough at Apex Industries came from applying materiality assessment not as a theoretical exercise, but as a practical business diagnostic. Instead of starting with standard ESG frameworks, Alex's team began by mapping the company's value drivers and risk factors, then identified which sustainability issues most directly affected those business fundamentals.

For Apex Industries—an automotive parts manufacturer serving major European car companies—this analysis revealed a clear hierarchy of material factors:

Tier 1: Direct Financial Impact

- Energy efficiency (affecting 12% of operating costs).
- Quality management (influencing 67% of customer relationships).
- Skilled worker retention (controlling 43% of production capacity).

Tier 2: Medium-Term Competitive Position

- Supply chain reliability (affecting delivery performance).
- Innovation capability (determining market share in new technologies).
- Community relations (influencing permit approvals for expansion).

Tier 3: Long-Term Risk Management

- Climate adaptation (protecting coastal facilities).
- Regulatory compliance (avoiding future penalties).
- Brand reputation (maintaining customer trust).

This tiered approach allowed Apex to focus their measurement efforts where they would have the greatest impact. Instead of tracking 127 metrics superficially, they monitored 12 metrics intensively—with the depth and frequency needed to drive actual improvements.

"The difference was immediate," recalled Penelope Day. "Instead of producing reports that nobody read, we were generating intelligence that shaped our weekly management meetings."

7.1.3 Alpine Foods Material Metrics Framework

Alpine Foods' material metrics framework, developed during the value creation phase documented in Chapter 4, exemplified sector-specific approaches to sustainability measurement in food manufacturing. Rather than tracking generic ESG indicators, the company focused on local sourcing percentage (>75%), customer satisfaction scores (>90%), and community economic impact (€2M+ annually)—factors directly connected to their premium positioning and 18% revenue growth strategy.

Table 7.1 Material ESG metrics by industry sector

Sector	*Priority Metrics*	*Measurement Approach*
Manufacturing	• Energy per unit • Waste generation • Safety incidents (TRIR) • Employee turnover • Quality defects	IoT sensors, ERP integration, automated tracking, monthly reporting
Services	• Employee satisfaction • Training hours per FTE • Diversity metrics • Carbon footprint (Scope 1–3) • Customer satisfaction	HR systems, surveys, carbon accounting platforms, quarterly assessments
Technology	• Data privacy incidents • Cybersecurity breaches • Product accessibility • R&D sustainability focus • Supplier code compliance	Security monitoring, accessibility audits, supplier assessments, continuous tracking

7.1.4 Technology Integration for Measurement Efficiency

Alpine Foods implemented digital dashboards that tracked ESG metrics alongside financial performance, creating integrated management systems that treated sustainability factors as business drivers rather than separate reporting requirements.

The technology platform provided real-time monitoring capabilities that enabled proactive management rather than reactive reporting. IoT sensors tracked energy consumption and waste generation automatically, while employee engagement platforms collected feedback continuously rather than through annual surveys.

This technological integration reduced measurement administrative burden by 67% while improving data accuracy and decision-making speed. Management could identify problems and opportunities as they emerged rather than discovering issues weeks later through traditional reporting cycles.

Common Questions Alex Fields

Q: How do you determine which metrics are truly material versus just interesting?

A: Khan and colleagues provide the framework: does this factor affect revenue, costs, or capital requirements? Will stakeholders penalize poor performance? Can improvements create competitive advantage? At Apex, energy costs affected 12% of operating expenses—material. Office paper recycling affected 0.02%—interesting but immaterial.

Q: What if we cannot measure a material factor precisely?

A: Use proxy measures. At Summit Peak Services, we could not directly measure workplace culture quality, so we tracked turnover rates, employee satisfaction surveys, and exit interview themes. These proxies provided sufficient intelligence for management decisions without perfect precision.

Q: How often should we update our materiality assessment?
A: Annually for strategic review, with continuous monitoring for emerging issues. Alpine Foods discovered a new material factor—supply chain transparency—when major customers changed procurement requirements. The annual cycle ensures systematic review, but you need to stay alert for game-changing developments.

7.2 Data Collection and Management Systems

7.2.1 Practical Data Collection Strategies

One of the biggest challenges in ESG measurement was collecting reliable data efficiently across companies with varying levels of technological sophistication. Alex's framework provided scalable approaches that could work for both technology-enabled companies and those with basic systems.

Automated Data Collection Where Possible:

- Energy management systems providing real-time consumption data.
- HR information systems tracking employee engagement and turnover automatically.
- Customer relationship management platforms monitoring satisfaction and retention.
- Financial systems capturing cost and efficiency metrics.
- Environmental monitoring equipment providing emissions and waste data.

Manual Collection for Critical Gaps:

- Stakeholder surveys collecting qualitative feedback and satisfaction data.
- Site visits and audits verifying compliance and performance claims.
- Manager interviews assessing culture and relationship quality.
- Customer conversations understanding preferences and requirements.
- Supplier assessments evaluating capabilities and partnership potential.

Proxy Measures for Resource Constraints:

- Employee turnover rates indicating workplace culture quality.
- Customer complaint patterns revealing service and product quality issues.
- Energy consumption trends suggesting operational efficiency and management quality.
- Payment terms reflecting supplier relationship health.
- Community engagement levels indicating social licence and stakeholder support.

7.2.2 Apex Industries Data Transformation

Apex Industries' transformation from 127 metrics to 12 material measures required systematic overhaul of data collection and management processes. The company had been collecting vast amounts of information but lacked systems to turn data into actionable intelligence.

Before Transformation:

- 127 different metrics tracked across 15 sustainability categories.
- 40 hours monthly staff time dedicated to data collection and reporting.
- Multiple spreadsheets and systems with no integration or analysis capabilities.
- Quarterly reporting cycles providing information too late for management action.
- Generic benchmarking against ESG standards rather than business-relevant comparisons.

After Material Metrics Implementation:

- 12 material metrics aligned with business value drivers and stakeholder priorities.
- 32 hours monthly for data collection, analysis, and management action planning.
- Integrated dashboard providing real-time visibility and trend analysis.
- Weekly performance review enabling proactive management and rapid course correction.
- Sector-specific benchmarking against automotive industry leaders and customer requirements.

Results and Impact:

- Management decision-making improved through relevant and timely information.
- Employee engagement increased as sustainability efforts connected to business priorities.
- Customer satisfaction improved through systematic quality and service measurement.
- Cost reduction achieved through energy efficiency monitoring and optimization.
- Regulatory compliance strengthened through systematic tracking and accountability.

7.2.3 Scalable Technology Solutions

Alex's experience across companies of different sizes and technological capabilities led to development of scalable technology approaches that could be adapted based on resources and requirements.

Table 7.2 Data collection hierarchy

Collection Method	*Best For*	*Cost & Effort*
Automated (Preferred)	Energy consumption, water usage, production metrics, safety incidents, employee data	High initial setup (€50–200K) Low ongoing effort Best data quality
Semi-Automated	Waste tracking, supply chain data, customer feedback, training records	Medium setup (€20–50K) Moderate effort Good data quality
Manual (Minimize)	Qualitative assessments, stakeholder interviews, ad-hoc surveys, site observations	Low set-up cost High ongoing effort Variable data quality

Small Company Solutions (<€50M revenue):

- Cloud-based platforms requiring minimal IT infrastructure investment.
- Mobile applications enabling data collection from operational personnel.
- Integrated spreadsheet tools with automated data aggregation and visualization.
- Third-party service providers offering measurement and reporting support.
- Peer network platforms enabling benchmarking and best practice sharing.

Medium Company Solutions (€50–250M revenue):

- Enterprise software platforms integrating ESG with financial and operational systems.
- IoT sensors and automation providing real-time environmental performance data.
- Advanced analytics capabilities enabling predictive insights and optimization recommendations.
- Custom dashboards providing role-specific views and decision support.
- Professional services support for system implementation and capability building.

Large Company Solutions (>€250M revenue):

- Comprehensive enterprise resource planning systems with embedded ESG functionality.
- AI-powered analytics providing pattern recognition and opportunity identification.
- Distributed data architecture supporting multi-site operations and global reporting.
- Stakeholder portals enabling transparent communication and collaboration.
- Dedicated ESG technology teams managing continuous system improvement.

The key insight was matching technology sophistication to organizational capabilities and resources. Companies that over-invested in complex systems before building basic measurement competencies often wasted resources and generated frustration. Conversely, companies that under-invested in appropriate technology struggled with administrative burden and data quality issues that undermined decision-making.

7.3 Integration with Business Management

7.3.1 Embedding ESG in Monthly Reviews

The most successful ESG measurement implementations integrated sustainability metrics into existing business management processes rather than creating separate reporting systems. This integration ensured that ESG factors received appropriate attention in decision-making while avoiding administrative overhead.

Monthly Management Review Integration:

- ESG performance metrics included in standard monthly operational reviews.
- Department heads presented sustainability metrics relevant to their functional responsibilities.
- Variance analysis and improvement planning for underperforming ESG indicators.
- Cross-functional collaboration on sustainability initiatives affecting multiple departments.
- Resource allocation decisions incorporating ESG investment and ROI analysis.

Quarterly Board Review Incorporation:

- Executive summary of material ESG performance included in board packages.
- Annual sustainability strategy review and approval process.
- ESG risk assessment integration with traditional risk management oversight.
- Stakeholder feedback summary and management response planning.
- Competitive positioning analysis including sustainability leadership and market advantages.

Annual Strategic Planning Integration:

- Sustainability objectives incorporated into long-term strategic planning.
- Market analysis including ESG trends and customer preference evolution.
- Competitive assessment incorporating sustainability capabilities and positioning.

- Resource allocation planning including ESG investment requirements and expected returns.
- Performance target setting aligning sustainability and financial objectives.

7.3.2 Summit Peak Services Management Integration Example

Summit Peak Services, the facilities management company featured in previous chapters, demonstrated effective integration of ESG metrics into business management processes. Rather than treating sustainability as separate reporting requirement, the company embedded ESG factors into operational excellence and customer service management.

Daily Operations Integration:

- Employee satisfaction metrics tracked alongside productivity and quality indicators.
- Customer feedback collection included sustainability preferences and satisfaction.
- Energy efficiency monitoring integrated with facility management optimization.
- Safety performance tracking incorporated into operational excellence programmes.
- Supplier performance evaluation included sustainability criteria alongside cost and quality.

Management Decision-Making Enhancement:

- Service pricing decisions incorporated sustainability value propositions and customer willingness to pay premiums.
- Employee retention strategies addressed workplace culture and engagement factors identified through ESG measurement.
- Customer relationship management included sustainability collaboration opportunities and shared value creation.
- Investment planning incorporated energy efficiency and operational improvement ROI analysis.
- Risk management processes included ESG factors affecting operational resilience and customer satisfaction.

Results and Business Impact:

- Customer retention improved from 78% to 96% through systematic satisfaction monitoring and improvement.
- Employee turnover reduced from 47% to 12% through workplace culture enhancement and engagement tracking.

- Operational efficiency improved by 34% through energy monitoring and optimization
- Revenue growth accelerated to 22% annually through sustainability-enabled customer partnership and premium positioning.
- Competitive differentiation achieved through verified sustainability performance and customer value creation.

7.3.3 Solid Hej Components Technical Integration

Solid Hej Components, the wind turbine manufacturer featured in Chapter 3, exemplified technical integration of ESG measurement with engineering and manufacturing operations. The company's sustainability metrics directly supported operational excellence and customer value creation.

Production Process Integration:

- Energy efficiency metrics tracked alongside manufacturing productivity and quality indicators.
- Waste reduction measurement integrated with lean manufacturing and continuous improvement processes.
- Employee engagement surveys incorporated with operational safety and teamwork assessment.
- Customer satisfaction tracking included sustainability performance and innovation collaboration.
- Supply chain assessment integrated ESG factors with cost, quality, and delivery performance evaluation.

Technology Platform Implementation:

- IoT sensors provided real-time energy consumption data enabling immediate optimization.
- Manufacturing execution systems incorporated sustainability targets alongside productivity and quality goals.
- Customer relationship management platforms tracked sustainability preferences and collaboration opportunities.
- Employee engagement platforms collected continuous feedback supporting culture development and retention.
- Supplier portals facilitated ESG performance tracking and collaborative improvement initiatives.

Operational Excellence Results:

- Energy consumption reduced by 31% over three years through systematic monitoring and optimization.

- Manufacturing waste reduced by 45% through lean principles and circular economy implementation.
- Employee engagement improved from 67% to 89% through systematic feedback and workplace improvement.
- Customer satisfaction increased from 78% to 94% through quality improvement and sustainability collaboration.
- Supplier performance improved through systematic ESG assessment and collaborative development programmes.

"The beauty of integrated measurement was that sustainability became invisible," explained Solid Hej's operations director. "We were not doing ESG reporting—we were managing our business better. The fact that it generated great sustainability metrics was a by-product of operational excellence."

Common Questions Alex Fields

Q: How do you prevent ESG metrics from becoming just another compliance exercise?
A: Tie them to existing business problems and management priorities. At Summit Peak, we did not talk about "employee engagement metrics"—we discussed "turnover costs" and "service quality drivers". Same data, different framing. When sustainability metrics answer questions managers already have, they become management tools rather than compliance burdens.
Q: What's the right frequency for different types of metrics?
A: Match frequency to decision cycles. Energy consumption at Solid Hej? Daily monitoring for operations, weekly trends for management, monthly analysis for board. Community relationships at Alpine? Quarterly surveys with annual deep dives. The key is providing information when decisions are being made.
Q: How do you balance simplicity with comprehensiveness in measurement?
A: Start simple, add complexity only when it drives decisions. Apex began with 12 metrics. Over two years, they added five more as new material factors emerged. But they also eliminated three that stopped being relevant. Dynamic simplicity beats static comprehensiveness.

7.4 Stakeholder Reporting and Communication

7.4.1 Multi-Stakeholder Reporting Requirements

Effective ESG measurement systems needed to satisfy multiple stakeholder requirements while maintaining decision usefulness for internal management. Different stakeholder groups required different information formats and frequency, creating complexity that needed systematic management.

Investor Reporting Requirements:

- Quarterly performance updates on material ESG factors affecting investment value.
- Annual comprehensive sustainability reports documenting strategy, performance, and future plans.
- Real-time incident reporting for material ESG events requiring immediate disclosure.
- Benchmarking analysis comparing performance against industry peers and best practices.
- Forward-looking information including targets, roadmaps, and strategic initiatives.

Customer Communication Needs:

- Product-specific sustainability data supporting customer procurement decisions.
- Supply chain transparency demonstrating compliance with customer ESG requirements.
- Innovation collaboration opportunities addressing shared sustainability challenges.
- Performance improvement evidence showing continuous advancement and commitment.
- Third-party verification providing credibility for sustainability claims.

Employee Engagement Requirements:

- Regular updates on sustainability initiatives and performance achievements.
- Opportunities for employee participation and contribution to ESG programmes.
- Recognition of individual and team sustainability contributions and innovations.
- Transparency about challenges, setbacks, and lessons learned.
- Connection between company sustainability performance and employee pride and purpose.

Regulatory Compliance Obligations:

- Mandatory disclosure requirements varying by jurisdiction and industry.
- Standardized reporting formats enabling regulatory review and enforcement.
- Third-party assurance for material sustainability information.
- Historical data enabling trend analysis and compliance verification.
- Forward-looking information demonstrating regulatory preparedness.

7.4.2 Efficient Multi-Stakeholder Reporting Architecture

The key to managing multiple stakeholder reporting requirements was building integrated systems that could generate tailored reports from single data sources rather than creating separate measurement approaches for each audience.

Core Data Repository:

- Single source of truth for all sustainability performance data.
- Standardized metrics enabling consistent reporting across stakeholders.
- Historical tracking supporting trend analysis and performance verification.
- Quality assurance processes ensuring accuracy and credibility.
- Flexible architecture enabling adaptation to evolving requirements.

Stakeholder-Specific Outputs:

- Automated report generation tailored to each stakeholder group's needs.
- Role-based dashboards providing relevant information and decision support.
- Customizable communication formats addressing different technical sophistication levels.
- Transparent methodology documentation enabling stakeholder confidence.
- Feedback mechanisms ensuring continuous improvement based on stakeholder needs.

Technology-Enabled Efficiency:

- Cloud-based platforms enabling secure stakeholder access to relevant information.
- Automated data aggregation reducing manual reporting effort.
- Real-time updates providing current performance visibility.
- Mobile access enabling stakeholder engagement from any location.
- Integration with communication platforms facilitating efficient information sharing.

Alpine Foods' integrated reporting architecture generated investor reports, customer updates, employee communications, and regulatory filings from the same underlying data system. This integration reduced reporting preparation time by 73% while improving consistency and stakeholder satisfaction.

7.5 Benchmarking and Performance Context

7.5.1 Meaningful Benchmarking Approaches

Benchmarking provided essential context for ESG performance, enabling companies to understand whether their results represented leadership, parity, or underperformance relative to relevant comparison groups. However, effective benchmarking required careful selection of comparison groups and metrics.

Peer Company Benchmarking:

- Industry-specific comparison groups reflecting similar business models and stakeholder relationships.
- Size-adjusted metrics enabling fair comparison across different scale operations.
- Geographic context addressing regional variations in regulatory and market conditions.
- Performance trend analysis identifying improvement trajectories rather than just current position.
- Best practice identification revealing opportunities for learning and improvement.

Industry Standard Comparison:

- Sector-specific sustainability standards and frameworks.
- Regulatory requirement benchmarks ensuring compliance adequacy.
- Customer expectation alignment demonstrating market positioning.
- Investor criteria comparison addressing capital access requirements.
- Technology capability benchmarks revealing innovation opportunities.

Best-in-Class Leadership Assessment:

- Cross-industry excellence identification revealing aspirational targets.
- Innovation practice discovery demonstrating cutting-edge approaches.
- Technology platform comparison highlighting digital transformation opportunities.
- Stakeholder engagement models showcasing relationship management excellence.
- Value creation demonstration connecting sustainability to financial performance.

7.5.2 *Apex Industries Benchmarking Evolution*

Apex Industries' benchmarking journey illustrated the importance of selecting relevant comparison groups and evolving approaches as company performance matured.

Initial Benchmarking (Year 1):

- Comparison against automotive industry averages establishing baseline positioning.
- Identification as mid-pack performer on most material ESG factors.

- Recognition of significant gaps on energy efficiency and employee engagement.
- Establishment of improvement targets based on industry top quartile performance.
- Development of action plans addressing priority gaps.

Intermediate Benchmarking (Years 2–3):

- Progression to top quartile positioning on energy efficiency and quality management.
- Expansion of benchmark scope to include leading manufacturers across industries.
- Identification of best practices from adjacent sectors applicable to automotive context.
- Refinement of metrics to reflect more sophisticated performance measurement.
- Recognition as emerging leader in automotive sustainability.

Advanced Benchmarking (Year 4+):

- Comparison against global sustainability leaders across all industries.
- Contributing benchmarking data to industry associations and standard-setting organizations.
- Receiving recognition as benchmarking reference point for peer companies.
- Focus shifted from catching up to staying ahead of emerging best practices.
- Integration of benchmarking insights into innovation and strategic planning.

"Benchmarking was not about rankings—it was about understanding what excellence looked like and how to achieve it," explained Penelope Day. "Early on, we learned from industry leaders. Later, we learned from cross-industry innovators. Eventually, others started learning from us."

7.6 Future Trends in ESG Measurement

7.6.1 Regulatory Standardization Impact

Looking forward, Alex anticipated that regulatory evolution would fundamentally reshape ESG measurement requirements and practices. Standardization would improve comparability while creating compliance requirements that advantaged companies with advanced capabilities.

Mandatory Disclosure Requirements:

- EU Corporate Sustainability Reporting Directive (CSRD) creating standardized reporting requirements for large companies.

- US Securities and Exchange Commission climate disclosure rules requiring public company reporting.
- Asia-Pacific regulatory developments creating regional reporting standards and requirements.
- International coordination through organizations like the International Sustainability Standards Board (ISSB).
- Industry-specific requirements addressing sector-particular risks and opportunities.

Technology Integration Requirements:

- Automated reporting systems reducing compliance costs while improving accuracy.
- Third-party verification requirements ensuring credibility and preventing greenwashing.
- Real-time monitoring capabilities enabling continuous compliance and performance optimization.
- Integration with financial reporting systems creating comprehensive performance assessment.
- Stakeholder communication requirements ensuring transparency and accountability.

7.6.2 *Predictive Analytics and AI*

Emerging technologies would enable evolution from retrospective reporting to predictive management, allowing companies to anticipate problems and opportunities before they materialized.

AI-Powered Pattern Recognition:

- Machine learning algorithms identifying correlations between ESG factors and business performance.
- Predictive models forecasting performance trajectories based on current trends.
- Anomaly detection flagging unusual patterns requiring investigation.
- Optimization recommendations suggesting high-impact improvement opportunities.
- Scenario modelling assessing potential impacts of different strategic choices.

Real-Time Optimization:

- Continuous monitoring enabling immediate response to performance deviations.
- Automated optimization of energy consumption, waste generation, and resource utilization.

- Dynamic stakeholder sentiment analysis informing relationship management strategies.
- Competitive intelligence gathering and analysis supporting strategic positioning.
- Innovation opportunity identification through trend analysis and pattern recognition.

7.6.3 Stakeholder Expectation Evolution

Stakeholder expectations would continue evolving, requiring measurement systems that could adapt to changing requirements while maintaining decision usefulness for management.

Investor Sophistication Growth:

- Increased focus on financially material ESG factors rather than generic sustainability metrics.
- Demand for forward-looking information and strategic roadmaps.
- Expectation of third-party verification and assurance for material claims.
- Interest in ESG integration with financial analysis and valuation.
- Requirement for transparent disclosure of both achievements and challenges.

Customer Requirement Expansion:

- Growing procurement criteria including comprehensive ESG performance.
- Demand for supply chain transparency and traceability.
- Expectation of collaboration on shared sustainability objectives.
- Requirement for continuous improvement demonstration.
- Interest in innovation partnerships addressing emerging challenges.

Employee Engagement Deepening:

- Increasing workplace culture and values alignment importance for talent attraction and retention.
- Expectation of authentic sustainability commitment rather than superficial programmes.
- Desire for meaningful participation opportunities in ESG initiatives.
- Requirement for transparent communication about challenges and progress.
- Interest in career development opportunities related to sustainability capabilities.

As measurement systems evolved to address these trends, the companies that would thrive were those that maintained focus on materiality, business value creation, and stakeholder needs rather than pursuing measurement for its own sake.

Alex smiled as Penelope Day reviewed Apex Industries' transformed measurement approach two years after their initial conversation. "You have come a long way from 127 metrics," Alex observed.

"The irony," Penelope laughed, "is that we now know more about our business than when we were measuring everything. Focusing on what matters gave us the clarity to drive real performance improvements."

"That is the entire point," Alex replied. "The next frontier is predictive sustainability—using AI and advanced analytics to anticipate problems before they happen and identify opportunities before competitors recognize them. But that is a topic for our next session."

Effective measurement drives operational performance, but the ultimate test is exit value creation. Chapter 8 reveals how systematic ESG implementation creates competitive advantages that buyers will pay premiums to acquire, building on the measurement foundations established in this chapter.

Chapter Summary

Core Insight

Material ESG metrics drive business value by focusing measurement on factors that actually affect financial performance rather than generic sustainability indicators. Apex Industries' transformation from 127 metrics to 12 material measures, reducing reporting time from 40 to 32 hours monthly while improving management decisions, demonstrates that effective measurement creates intelligence rather than administrative burden.

Critical Success Factors

- **Materiality-driven prioritization:** Khan et al.'s (2016) research showing material factors drive 4.2% outperformance while immaterial issues show no benefit validates focused measurement approaches.
- **Three-tier hierarchy:** Direct financial impact factors (energy, quality, retention) receive intensive monitoring; medium-term competitive factors (supply chain, innovation, community) get regular review; long-term risks (climate, regulation, reputation) merit annual assessment.
- **Technology appropriateness:** Scalable solutions from cloud platforms for small companies to AI-powered analytics for large operations—matching sophistication to organizational capabilities prevents waste.
- **Business process integration:** Summit Peak Services' embedding of ESG metrics in daily operations (96% customer retention, 12% turnover) shows sustainability measurement enhances rather than burdens management.
- **Multi-stakeholder efficiency:** Single data repository generating tailored reports for investors, customers, employees, and regulators reduces burden by 73% while improving consistency.

Watch Out For

⚠ Measuring everything instead of what matters—127 generic metrics provide less intelligence than 12 material indicators.
⚠ Creating separate ESG reporting systems rather than integrating with business management processes.
⚠ Over-investing in complex technology before building basic measurement competencies wastes resources.
⚠ Generic benchmarking against ESG standards rather than business-relevant comparisons misleads decision-making.

Tools You Can Use Now

- **Material Metrics Framework:** Three-tier hierarchy (financial impact, competitive position, risk management) with Alpine Foods sector-specific example.
- **Apex Industries Transformation Model:** Before/after comparison showing 127 to 12 metrics, 40 to 32 hours, improved decision quality.
- **Scalable Technology Matrix:** Company size (small/medium/large) matched to appropriate technology solutions (cloud/enterprise/AI-powered).
- **Integration Checklist:** Monthly management reviews, quarterly board reports, annual strategic planning touchpoints.
- **Stakeholder Reporting Architecture:** Core data repository generating customized outputs for different audiences from single source.

What's Next

Chapter 8 demonstrates how systematic ESG implementation—measured through frameworks established in this chapter—creates competitive advantages that buyers recognize and pay premiums to acquire. Through Solid Hej Components' €12–15 million exit premium, Ridgeline Solutions' circular economy innovation value, and Summit Peak Services' workforce advantage, you will discover how sustainability capabilities documented through rigorous measurement translate into tangible exit value.

References

Berg, F., Kölbel, J., & Rigobon, R. (2022). Aggregate confusion: The divergence of ESG ratings. *Review of Finance*, 26 (6), 1315–1344. doi:10.1093/rof/rfac037.
European Commission (2025). Commission simplifies transparency rules for sustainable financial products (20 November).
Global Reporting Initiative. (2021). GRI standards. GRI. doi:10.46234/gri2021.
Khan, M., Serafeim, G., & Yoon, A. (2016). Corporate sustainability: First evidence on materiality. *The Accounting Review*, 91 (6), 1697–1724. doi:10.2308/accr-51383.
Whelan, T., Atz, U., Van Holt, T., & Clark, C. (2021). ESG and financial performance: Uncovering the relationship by aggregating evidence from 1,000+ studies published between 2015–2020. NYU Stern Center for Sustainable Business.

8 The Exit Advantage

How Sustainability Boosts Your Multiple

The Exit Advantage

"I have never seen bidders get this excited about operational metrics before."

Ivie Chen, Director of ESG Integration at Kerring Capital Partners, was reviewing the preliminary bids for Solid Hej Components with a mixture of amazement and satisfaction. What should have been a straightforward auction for a profitable wind turbine manufacturer had evolved into something unprecedented: six qualified bidders actively competing not just on financial metrics, but on their ability to leverage and expand the company's sustainability capabilities.

The Solid Hej Components exit changed how Ivie thought about sustainability value. When all six bidders mentioned sustainability capabilities in their proposals, and the winner paid a 23% premium worth €12–15 million specifically for ESG infrastructure, Ivie and the Kerring team realized it was more than just avoiding risks—they were creating attractive assets that strategic buyers valued highly.

While critics like Pedersen, Fitzgibbons, and Pomorski (2021) had identified potential "greenium" costs where investors with strong sustainability preferences might sacrifice some return for ESG alignment, the Solid Hej Components exit was demonstrating the opposite phenomenon in private equity. The company's environmental, social, and governance leadership was driving a premium that exceeded traditional valuation multiples by 23%.

"Look at these buyer presentations," Ivie continued, spreading the proposals across the conference table. "Every single bidder is highlighting how Solid Hej's sustainability infrastructure fits their corporate strategies. This is not just about financial returns anymore—it is about strategic value creation."

The evidence before them reflected broader market trends documented in recent research. Kengelbach et al.'s (2024) survey of 115 mergers and acquisitions dealmakers found that 77% observed companies with higher ESG maturity commanding higher valuations, while Alvarez & Marsal's (2024) survey showed that 75% of private equity professionals were willing to pay a modest premium for assets with positive ESG track records.

DOI: 10.4324/9781003625636-10

8.1 The Exit Process through a Sustainability Lens

8.1.1 The Sustainability Story Development

Alex Morgan had learned through dozens of exits that sustainability integration was not just about operational improvements during the holding period—it fundamentally changed how buyers perceived value, risk, and future potential. This transformation required systematic preparation that began years before the actual sale process.

Unlike traditional exit preparation that focused primarily on financial optimization, ESG-enhanced exits required comprehensive documentation of sustainability value creation. This reflected Shandal and Entraygues's (2024) findings that private equity-backed companies often outperformed public companies on sustainability measures, creating differentiation opportunities that buyers increasingly valued.

At Solid Hej Components, exit preparation began 18 months before the sale process with systematic documentation of ESG achievements:

Performance Metrics: Third-party verification of 31% energy efficiency improvement, 43% waste reduction, and 38% carbon footprint reduction documented measurable operational excellence that buyers could validate.
Business Impact: €456,000 in annual value creation from €596,000 total ESG investment over four years demonstrated clear return on investment that justified premium pricing.
Capability Assessment: Advanced environmental management systems, employee engagement programmes, and supplier sustainability networks represented transferable intellectual property that buyers could leverage across their operations.

Table 8.1 ESG-driven exit value enhancement

Mechanism	*How It Works*	*Typical Value Impact*
Operational Excellence	ESG improvements translate to lower costs, higher margins, and efficiency gains visible in financials	2–5% EBITDA improvement €1M–3M additional value
Risk Mitigation	Clean ESG record reduces buyer due diligence concerns, eliminates contingencies, speeds closing	Faster process (2–4 weeks) Fewer holdbacks Higher certainty
Market Positioning	Sustainability credentials open doors to buyers with ESG mandates and strategic sustainability goals	30% broader buyer pool Competitive tension Premium pricing
Growth Narrative	ESG investments demonstrate management quality and create compelling future growth story	0.5–1.5× multiple uplift 10–25% value increase
Strategic Optionality	ESG leaders attract both PE buyers and strategics, including sustainability-focused acquirers	Multiple buyer types Bidding competition Best price/terms

Future Roadmap: Five-year sustainability plan showing continued value creation potential gave buyers confidence in ongoing performance improvements beyond the acquisition.

This comprehensive approach aligned with research from EY showing that funds with advanced ESG practices realize internal rate of return up to 5 percentage points greater than competitors, partly due to enhanced exit positioning (EY, 2024).

8.1.2 Market Positioning for ESG-Conscious Buyers

The universe of potential buyers increasingly included organizations with formal sustainability commitments. PwC's (2022) Global Investor Survey found that most investors wanted companies to report the relevance of sustainability factors to their business model, while ESG assets under management were projected to grow from 14.4% in 2021 to 21.5% in 2026.

Alex's team systematically analysed potential buyers across several dimensions:

Strategic Acquirers with ESG Commitments: Large corporations with public sustainability targets who needed proven capabilities to achieve their goals. These buyers often paid the highest premiums for companies that could immediately contribute to their ESG objectives.

ESG-Focused Financial Buyers: Private equity firms with dedicated sustainability strategies or funds specifically targeting ESG-integrated investments. These buyers understood sustainability value creation and were willing to pay for embedded capabilities.

Traditional Buyers with Growing ESG Awareness: Companies beginning their sustainability journeys who recognized the competitive advantages of acquiring established ESG capabilities rather than building them internally.

In the case study, the buyer analysis informed how Solid Hej Components positioned itself during the sale process. For strategic acquirers, the emphasis was on capability transfer and ESG objective achievement. For financial buyers, the focus was on proven value creation methodologies and competitive advantages. For traditional buyers, the story centred on operational excellence and risk mitigation.

8.1.3 Timeline Optimization for Maximum Impact

Research and practical experience demonstrated that ESG value creation followed predictable timeframes that could be optimized for exit preparation. Khan, Serafeim, and Yoon's (2016) materiality research showed that material ESG improvements typically required 12–24 months to demonstrate sustained results that buyers would recognize and value.

24–36 Months Before Exit: Foundation Building

The most impactful sustainability initiatives required 2–3 years to demonstrate sustained results and cultural integration. This timeline aligned with typical private equity holding periods while ensuring sufficient time for capability development:

Strategic Planning Integration: Incorporate sustainability into long-term strategic planning, ensuring ESG initiatives aligned with business strategy and market positioning. This reflected Yoon's (2024) finding that ESG creates shareholder value when focused on financially material issues with strong management execution.
System Implementation: Install measurement, monitoring, and management systems that would provide comprehensive data for exit documentation. The ESG Data Convergence Initiative framework provided standardized metrics that buyers increasingly recognized and valued.
Capability Development: Build internal expertise and establish governance structures that could operate independently after ownership transition. This included training programmes, certification processes, and leadership development initiatives.
Stakeholder Engagement: Develop strong relationships with customers, suppliers, employees, and community stakeholders that would advocate for the company during the sale process.

18–24 Months Before Exit: Performance Optimization

The second phase focused on optimizing sustainability performance and documenting business impact through third-party verification and benchmarking analysis:

Performance Acceleration: Implement quick-win initiatives that generated immediate results while building momentum for larger improvements. Focus on initiatives with clear ROI and measurable business impact.
Third-Party Validation: Obtain independent verification of sustainability claims through certifications, audits, and performance assessments. This external validation proved necessary for buyer confidence and premium justification.
Benchmarking Analysis: Compare performance against industry peers and best-in-class companies to demonstrate competitive positioning and identify additional improvement opportunities.
Case Study Development: Document success stories and lessons learned that could be transferred to buyer organizations or expanded across their portfolios.

12–18 Months Before Exit: Story Development

The final preparation phase focused on developing compelling narratives and positioning materials that would differentiate the company in competitive auction processes:

Table 8.2 Exit preparation timeline (12–18 months)

Phase	*Activities*	*Deliverables*
Months 12–18 Foundation	• ESG data systems implementation • Baseline metrics establishment • Governance structure set-up • Initial certification pursuit	• Data management platform • 3-year historical data • ESG governance charter • Relevant certifications
Months 6–12 Optimization	• Performance improvement initiatives • Third-party verification • Stakeholder engagement documentation • ESG narrative development	• Improved performance trends • Verified ESG data • Stakeholder testimonials • Investment memorandum content
Months 0–6 Execution	• Due diligence preparation • ESG story refinement • Management presentation training • Documentation finalization	• Due diligence dataroom • ESG presentation deck • Buyer-specific positioning • Supporting documentation

Impact Quantification: Calculate and verify the financial impact of sustainability initiatives using standardized methodologies that buyers could understand and trust.
Competitive Advantage Documentation: Demonstrate how ESG capabilities created barriers to entry, enabled premium pricing, or opened new market opportunities that competitors could not easily replicate.
Strategic Narrative Development: Create compelling stories connecting sustainability capabilities to business strategy, market positioning, and future growth potential in ways that resonated with different buyer types.
Management Team Preparation: Train leadership to effectively communicate sustainability value creation during buyer presentations and due diligence, ensuring consistent messaging and credible performance claims.

Common Questions Alex Fields

Q: How do you quantify the exit premium specifically attributable to ESG versus general operational improvements?
A: Buyer due diligence reports and bid rationale letters often quantify it explicitly. At Solid Hej Components, all six bidders mentioned sustainability in proposals, and the winner's analysis isolated €12–15 million premium for ESG infrastructure. We also had independent valuation analysis comparing our exit multiple to peer transactions without similar capabilities.
Q: What if buyers say they care about ESG but do not pay for it?
A: That means either the capabilities were not material enough to affect their business, or the story was not compelling. At Ridgeline Solutions, buyers competed specifically for circular economy capabilities because they faced customer demands they could not meet internally. The key is demonstrating strategic value, not just operational performance.

Q: How far in advance should you start preparing for an ESG-enhanced exit?
A: Ideally at acquisition. The best exits came from companies where we integrated ESG from day one, giving 3–5 years of documented performance. But even companies starting 18–24 months before exit achieved meaningful premiums through focused initiatives and strong documentation.

8.2 Five Value Creation Mechanisms That Buyers Recognize

8.2.1 Operational Excellence and Efficiency Gains

The most immediate and verifiable ESG value came from operational improvements that reduced costs while enhancing performance. Buyers could easily quantify these benefits and project them forward, making operational excellence claims credible and valuable.

Energy Efficiency and Resource Optimization: Solid Hej Components' broad energy efficiency and retrofits generated €234,000 annual savings that buyers could verify through utility bills and operational data. The sophisticated monitoring systems that enabled these savings represented transferable capabilities that buyers valued beyond the immediate cost reductions.
Waste Reduction and Circular Economy: Companies implementing circular economy principles often discovered revenue opportunities from waste streams while reducing disposal costs. Ridgeline Solutions' zero-waste-to-landfill achievement not only eliminated €89,000 annual disposal costs but created €2.1 million in new revenue from material recovery and sustainable product lines.
Quality Management and Process Excellence: ESG-driven quality improvements often reduced defects, rework, and customer complaints while improving satisfaction and loyalty. Summit Peak Facility Services' systematic quality management contributed to 96% customer retention rates that buyers recognized as competitive advantage worth premium pricing.

8.2.2 Risk Mitigation and Operational Resilience

Buyers increasingly valued ESG capabilities for risk mitigation, particularly as regulatory requirements expanded, and stakeholder expectations intensified. Companies with advanced ESG systems faced lower operational, regulatory, and reputational risks that affected insurance costs, financing terms, and stakeholder relationships.

Regulatory Compliance and Future-Proofing: Companies with strong ESG systems were typically 2–3 years ahead of regulatory requirements, creating competitive advantages that buyers valued. Solid Hej Components' advanced environmental management systems positioned them for emerging EU regulations that would burden competitors for years.

Stakeholder Relationship Strength: Strong employee, customer, supplier, and community relationships created operational resilience that reduced business continuity risks. Summit Peak Facility Services' 94% employee retention commitment post-acquisition reflected relationship quality that buyers recognized as valuable risk mitigation.

Reputation and Brand Protection: ESG excellence protected brand value and stakeholder trust that could take years to rebuild if damaged. Companies with verified sustainability performance faced lower reputational risks from activist campaigns, media scrutiny, or stakeholder criticism.

8.2.3 Market Access and Revenue Enhancement

Sustainability capabilities increasingly opened new market opportunities and enabled premium pricing that buyers could leverage across their operations or customer bases:

Customer Requirement Satisfaction: Major customers increasingly required supplier ESG credentials that could not be quickly developed. Ridgeline Solutions' sustainable packaging solutions opened access to customers that competitors without similar capabilities could not serve, creating €4.2 million in protected revenue that buyers valued highly.

Premium Market Positioning: Verified sustainability leadership enabled premium pricing in markets where customers valued environmental and social performance. Alpine Foods' organic certification and local sourcing credentials supported 15% average price premiums that buyers could maintain and potentially expand.

Brand Enhancement and Differentiation: Sustainability leadership created brand value and market differentiation that buyers could leverage for competitive advantage. Solid Hej Components' industry recognition as sustainability leader attracted customers and talent that competitors struggled to access.

8.2.4 Talent Advantages and Organizational Capability

In industries where talent quality determined competitive success, ESG capabilities created workforce advantages that buyers increasingly valued:

Employee Attraction and Retention: Summit Peak Facility Services' transformation from 47% to 12% annual turnover demonstrated that workplace culture investments created measurable financial value. The 94% employee retention commitment post-acquisition gave buyers confidence in operational continuity and reduced integration risks.

Skills and Capabilities: Companies with advanced ESG capabilities possessed workforce skills in sustainability management, stakeholder engagement, and system optimization that buyers could leverage across their operations. These capabilities represented intellectual capital that traditional operational improvements did not address.

Organizational Culture and Engagement: High-engagement cultures created performance advantages through innovation, problem-solving, and customer service excellence. Employee survey scores, retention rates, and satisfaction metrics provided verifiable evidence of cultural strength that buyers recognized as competitive advantage.

8.2.5 Technology and Innovation Platforms

Companies that integrated technology with sustainability often created innovation platforms that buyers valued beyond immediate operational benefits:

Digital Transformation Enablement: Solid Hej Components' IoT sensor networks and predictive analytics platforms enabled both environmental optimization and broader operational excellence. Buyers recognized these technology capabilities as intellectual property applicable across their organizations.
Innovation Pipeline and R&D: Sustainability challenges often drove innovation that created competitive advantages and new revenue opportunities. Ridgeline Solutions' sustainable materials database and design tools represented proprietary technology that buyers could license or expand across their product portfolios.
Industry Leadership and Thought Leadership: Companies recognized as sustainability innovators attracted partnership opportunities, customer collaboration, and market visibility that created strategic value beyond financial metrics. This leadership positioning often justified premium valuations from strategic buyers seeking to enhance their own market positions.

8.3 Case Studies: Premium Exits in Practice

8.3.1 Solid Hej Components: Strategic Premium for Sustainability Infrastructure

The Solid Hej Components exit provided the clearest example of sustainability value creation throughout Alex's career. Acquired for €52 million in 2019, the company was sold for €89 million in 2023 a 1.71× exit multiple that exceeded industry benchmarks by 23%.

ESG Value Creation Summary:

- Total ESG Investment: €596,000 over four years.
- Annual Value Creation: €456,000 (cost savings, revenue enhancement, risk reduction).
- ESG-Attributed Premium: €12–15 million of exit value.
- ROI on ESG Investment: 20× return over four-year holding period.

Buyer Rationale:

The strategic acquirer specifically cited Solid Hej's sustainability infrastructure as providing immediate value for their corporate ESG commitments. "Rather than building these capabilities from scratch which would have required 3–4 years and significant investment, we acquired a ready-made ESG leadership platform," explained the acquiring company's CEO in their bid rationale.

Competitive Dynamics:

All six final bidders specifically mentioned sustainability capabilities in their proposals, with the winning bid explicitly structured to preserve and expand ESG initiatives. The sustainability story became a differentiation factor that enabled premium pricing despite strong financial competition from multiple qualified buyers.

8.3.2 Ridgeline Solutions: Circular Economy Innovation Premium

Ridgeline Solutions' exit demonstrated how innovation-focused sustainability initiatives could create entirely new value categories that traditional competitors could not match.

ESG Innovation Summary:

- Circular Economy Implementation: Zero waste to landfill achieved within 18 months.
- Sustainable Product Development: 45% of revenue from sustainably designed packaging by exit.
- Customer Partnership Model: Joint innovation projects with eight major customers.
- Technology Platform: Proprietary sustainable materials database and design tools.

Exit Results:

- Sale Price: €67 million (acquired for €38 million three years earlier).
- Revenue Multiple: 2.1x (versus 1.6× industry average).
- ESG Premium Attribution: €8–12 million of additional value.
- Buyer Competition: Four strategic buyers competed specifically for sustainability capabilities.

The buyer, a multinational packaging corporation, was facing increasing customer demands for sustainable solutions but lacked internal capabilities to meet these requirements. Ridgeline's proven systems and customer relationships provided immediate market access that would have taken years to develop independently.

"We paid a premium to acquire three years of capability development," the buyer's integration director explained. "The alternative was spending that time building systems while losing market opportunities to competitors who already had sustainability solutions."

8.3.3 Summit Peak Facility Services: Social Impact and Employee Engagement Premium

Summit Peak Facility Services exemplified how social sustainability initiatives could create competitive advantages that buyers valued highly, particularly in service industries where talent quality directly impacted performance.

Social Sustainability Programme:

- Employee Turnover: Reduced from 47% to 12% annually (€600,000+ savings).
- Training and Development: 340 employees completed advanced skills programmes.
- Diversity and Inclusion: Leadership diversity increased from 23% to 52%.
- Community Engagement: Local partnership programmes in all operating regions.

Exit Performance:

- Sale Multiple: 8.9× EBITDA (versus 7.2× sector average).
- Employee Retention: 94% of personnel committed to stay post-acquisition.
- Customer Advocacy: 12 major customers provided buyer references citing service quality and relationship strength.
- Social Impact Premium: €4–6 million attributed to workforce advantages.

The acquiring company, expanding into new geographic markets, recognized that Summit Peak's employee engagement and community relationships would accelerate their expansion timeline while reducing integration risks. The 94% employee retention commitment de-risked the acquisition and preserved the customer relationships that drove Summit Peak's premium market position.

8.3.4 Technology-Enabled Sustainability: Advanced Manufacturing Case

A speciality chemicals manufacturer in Alex's portfolio demonstrated how technology-enabled sustainability could create intellectual property and competitive advantages that commanded premium pricing.

Technology Integration:

- AI-Powered Optimization: 34% reduction in energy consumption through machine learning algorithms.

- Predictive Analytics: 67% reduction in waste through process optimization.
- IoT Monitoring: Real-time environmental performance across all facilities.
- Digital Twin Modelling: Virtual optimization reducing physical testing by 78%.

Intellectual Property Development:

- Patent Portfolio: Seven patents filed for sustainable manufacturing processes.
- Software Platform: Proprietary optimization algorithms licensed to customers.
- Industry Recognition: Four technology awards from industry associations.
- Research Partnerships: Collaborations with three leading universities.

Exit Valuation Impact:

- Technology Premium: 40% higher valuation multiple due to IP portfolio.
- Licensing Revenue: €2.3 million annual recurring revenue from technology licensing.
- Strategic Value: Buyer acquired technology platform for broader portfolio application.
- Innovation Pipeline: Five-year R&D roadmap supporting continued competitive advantages.

The buyer, a global chemicals corporation, valued the technology platform as much as the operating business, recognizing its potential for application across their international operations. The intellectual property created through sustainability challenges became valuable beyond the immediate environmental benefits.

Common Questions Alex Fields

Q: How do you prevent buyers from discounting ESG premiums during price negotiations?
A: Third-party verification and buyer competition. At Solid Hej, having six bidders all citing sustainability created market validation. Independent valuation analysis comparing our multiple to peer transactions provided objective evidence. And detailed financial impact quantification made value concrete rather than aspirational.
Q: What if the buyer plans to reduce ESG investments post-acquisition?
A: That signals they do not understand the value creation mechanisms. At Summit Peak, we educated buyers that employee engagement drove customer retention which generated premium pricing. Buyers who understood that causation were willing to commit to continued investment. Those who saw ESG as a cost to cut were not the right buyers.

Q: Can you achieve exit premiums in industries not typically associated with sustainability?
A: Absolutely. Summit Peak was facilities management—not glamorous. But service quality depended on employee engagement, which created measurable financial value. Every industry has material ESG factors. The key is connecting them to business fundamentals that buyers care about.

8.4 Implementation Framework for Exit Optimization

8.4.1 Phase 1: Acquisition and Initial Assessment (Months 1–6)

Based on analysis of successful exits, Alex developed a comprehensive framework that private equity firms could use to systematically optimize sustainability value creation for exit positioning:

ESG Due Diligence Integration: Conduct comprehensive sustainability assessment during acquisition process, identifying both risks and value creation opportunities. This aligned with Kengelbach et al.'s (2024) finding that 75% of professionals uncovered material ESG issues during deals when systematic assessment was conducted.
Baseline Establishment: Document current sustainability performance using standardized metrics from the ESG Data Convergence Initiative, enabling accurate progress measurement and benchmarking analysis.
Quick Win Identification: Identify immediate improvement opportunities that could generate results within 6–12 months, building momentum and credibility for larger initiatives.
Stakeholder Mapping: Assess relationships with employees, customers, suppliers, and community stakeholders to understand engagement opportunities and potential resistance.

8.4.2 Phase 2: Value Creation Implementation (Months 6–24)

Material ESG Focus: Concentrate resources on sustainability factors with clear business relevance, following materiality frameworks developed by Khan, Serafeim, and Yoon (2016) showing that only material factors drive performance improvements.
System Integration: Build sustainability considerations into core business processes rather than creating separate ESG functions, ensuring operational integration and cultural embedding that survives ownership transitions.
Capability Development: Invest in technology, training, and governance structures that would create lasting competitive advantages and demonstrate sophistication to buyers during due diligence.
Performance Optimization: Implement improvement initiatives that generated measurable business value while building track records that could be verified by buyers through operational data and third-party assessments.

8.4.3 Phase 3: Exit Preparation (Months 24–36)

Story Development: Create compelling narratives that translated sustainability achievements into business language resonating with different buyer audiences—strategic acquirers, financial buyers, and traditional buyers with growing ESG awareness.
Documentation and Verification: Obtain third-party validation of sustainability claims through certifications, audits, and independent performance assessments that provided credibility during buyer due diligence.
Market Positioning: Research potential buyers and customize sustainability messaging to align with their strategic objectives and ESG commitments, ensuring relevance to specific buyer motivations.
Management Preparation: Train leadership teams to effectively communicate sustainability value creation and future potential during buyer presentations and due diligence processes, ensuring consistent messaging across all stakeholder interactions.

8.4.4 Success Metrics and Benchmarking

To ensure systematic optimization, Alex's framework included specific success metrics that predicted exit value enhancement based on analysis of previous successful exits.

Financial Performance Indicators:

- ESG ROI: Target 3:1 return on sustainability investments
- Cost Savings: Annual operational cost reduction of 5–15% from efficiency improvements
- Revenue Enhancement: New revenue from sustainability-driven opportunities
- Risk Reduction: Quantified reduction in insurance, compliance, and operational risks

Operational Excellence Metrics:

- Energy Efficiency: 15–30% improvement in energy intensity
- Waste Reduction: 20–40% decrease in waste generation
- Employee Engagement: Top quartile satisfaction and retention rates
- Customer Satisfaction: Industry-leading scores with sustainability-focused customers

Strategic Positioning Indicators:

- Market Recognition: Industry awards and certifications demonstrating leadership

- Thought Leadership: Conference presentations and best-practice sharing
- Innovation Pipeline: Patent applications and R&D partnerships
- Stakeholder Advocacy: Customer and employee references supporting sustainability claims

8.5 The Art of Sustainability Storytelling

8.5.1 Financial Buyer Messaging

The most successful exits combined strong operational performance with compelling narratives that helped buyers understand the strategic value of sustainability capabilities. This storytelling process required translating technical achievements into business language that resonated with different buyer audiences.

Private equity buyers focused primarily on value creation potential and competitive advantages that could be scaled across their portfolios:

Proven Value Creation Model: Demonstrate systematic approaches to ESG value creation that could be replicated in other portfolio companies. Solid Hej Components' methodology documentation enabled the buyer to apply similar approaches across their industrial holdings.
Competitive Differentiation: Show how sustainability capabilities created barriers to competition and enabled premium positioning. Ridgeline Solutions' proprietary sustainable materials database represented intellectual property that competitors could not easily replicate.
Operational Excellence: Highlight process improvements and efficiency gains that would continue generating value under new ownership. Summit Peak Facility Services' systematic employee engagement approach was embedded in operational processes rather than dependent on specific leadership.
Market Positioning: Demonstrate how ESG capabilities opened new market opportunities and strengthened customer relationships. Alpine Foods' organic certification and local sourcing credentials provided access to premium market segments that competitors without similar capabilities could not serve.

8.5.2 Strategic Buyer Messaging

Corporate acquirers typically emphasized how sustainability capabilities would accelerate their own ESG objectives and strategic initiatives:

Capability Acceleration: Show how acquiring proven sustainability systems would advance buyer ESG timelines by 3–4 years. The winning bidder for Solid Hej Components calculated that building equivalent capabilities internally would require significant time and investment.
Integration Synergies: Identify opportunities to expand sustainability practices across buyer operations and supply chains. Ridgeline Solutions' circular economy expertise could be applied across the buyer's international manufacturing network.

Market Access Enhancement: Demonstrate how combined sustainability capabilities would open new market opportunities. Summit Peak Facility Services' employee engagement methodologies could help the buyer improve retention and service quality across their geographic expansion.
Risk Mitigation: Highlight how ESG systems would reduce regulatory, operational, and reputational risks for the combined organization. Companies with advanced ESG capabilities faced lower future compliance costs as regulations expanded.
Regulatory Compliance Ready: Show preparation for current and anticipated ESG disclosure requirements. Solid Hej Components' advanced reporting systems positioned them 2–3 years ahead of emerging EU regulations that would burden competitors.

8.6 Future Trends in ESG Exit Value

8.6.1 Regulatory-Driven Value Creation

As Alex looked ahead to future exits, several trends were reshaping how sustainability influenced transaction value and buyer behaviour. Understanding these developments would be necessary for maximizing exit premiums in an evolving market.

Expanding disclosure requirements were creating new categories of value for companies with advanced ESG capabilities. The European Union's Corporate Sustainability Reporting Directive and Sustainable Finance Disclosure Regulation established comprehensive reporting requirements that advantaged companies with existing systems and data.

Companies like Solid Hej Components that had invested in advanced measurement and reporting systems found themselves 2–3 years ahead of competitors in regulatory compliance, creating competitive advantages that buyers increasingly valued as compliance deadlines approached.

8.6.2 Technology Integration and Digital Transformation

The convergence of sustainability and digital transformation was creating new value categories that combined operational efficiency with environmental performance. AI-powered optimization, IoT monitoring, and predictive analytics enabled companies to achieve sustainability improvements that were not possible through traditional approaches.

Buyers recognized these technology capabilities as intellectual property applicable across their organizations, often valuing the digital platforms as much as the immediate environmental benefits they generated. The speciality chemicals manufacturer's AI optimization algorithms commanded premium pricing because they could be licensed to customers or applied across the buyer's operations.

8.6.3 Climate Transition and Net Zero Commitments

Growing corporate commitments to net zero emissions were creating demand for companies with proven carbon reduction capabilities and climate adaptation strategies. Buyers facing aggressive decarbonization targets valued companies that could contribute immediately to their climate objectives rather than requiring years of capability development.

This trend particularly benefited companies in carbon-intensive industries that had achieved significant emissions reductions. Their documented approaches to decarbonization became valuable intellectual property that buyers could apply across their operations to accelerate progress toward climate commitments.

The Kerring Capital Partners annual meeting had evolved into a celebration of exit success rather than the tense justification sessions Alex remembered from early career. As Ivie Chen concluded her presentation on the Solid Hej Components exit and its implications for future deals, Jim Kerring rose with a question that captured the room's sentiment.

"You have convinced me about the exit advantages. But I want to understand the risks. What happens when the ESG momentum slows down or priorities change?"

Alex smiled. "That is exactly why we focus on business fundamentals rather than ESG trends. Companies that achieve genuine operational excellence, stakeholder engagement, and competitive positioning will create value regardless of how ESG terminology evolves. The sustainability advantage is not about marketing—it is about building better businesses."

The room reflected consensus. The evidence from multiple exits had demonstrated that ESG integration, when done systematically and with business discipline, consistently enhanced exit value through multiple mechanisms. The question was not whether sustainability created exit premiums—it was whether private equity firms could afford not to pursue these advantages.

As Ivie Chen noted in her closing remarks, "We are not just selling companies anymore—we are selling capabilities, relationships, and competitive advantages. Sustainability gives us all three."

ESG capabilities clearly enhanced exit value, but regulatory requirements now made sustainability integration mandatory rather than optional. Chapter 9 shows how to turn compliance requirements into competitive advantages, building on the exit value framework established here.

Chapter Summary

Core Insight

Systematic ESG implementation creates tangible exit value through five mechanisms: operational excellence (Solid Hej's €456K annual savings), risk mitigation (Summit Peak's 94% retention de-risking acquisition), market access (Ridgeline's €4.2M protected revenue), talent advantages (Summit Peak's 8.9×

vs 7.2× sector multiple), and technology platforms (chemicals company's 40% tech premium). Evidence shows 77% of M&A professionals observe higher valuations for ESG-mature companies (Kengelbach et al., 2024).

Critical Success Factors

- **Early preparation:** Begin exit preparation 24–36 months before sale with foundation building, performance optimization, and story development phases.
- **Quantified impact:** Solid Hej Components' €12–15M ESG-attributed premium documented through buyer due diligence reports and independent valuation analysis.
- **Third-party verification:** Certifications, audits, and independent assessments provide buyer confidence and premium justification.
- **Buyer-specific messaging:** Financial buyers seek proven value creation models; strategic buyers want capability acceleration and integration synergies.
- **Multiple buyer competition:** Six bidders for Solid Hej all citing sustainability created market validation that supported premium pricing.

Watch Out For

⚠ Starting exit preparation too late—best results require 3–5 years of documented performance.

⚠ Generic ESG claims without financial quantification fail to justify premium pricing.

⚠ Treating sustainability as compliance cost rather than strategic capability limits buyer interest.

⚠ Inadequate documentation making value attribution difficult during due diligence.

Tools You Can Use Now

- **Exit Preparation Timeline:** Three-phase framework (24–36 months foundation, 18–24 months optimization, 12–18 months story development).
- **Five Value Creation Mechanisms:** Operational excellence, risk mitigation, market access, talent advantages, technology platforms with specific examples.
- **Success Metrics Dashboard:** Financial indicators (ESG ROI 3:1 target), operational metrics (15–30% energy improvement), strategic positioning (industry recognition).
- **Buyer Messaging Matrix:** Customized value propositions for financial versus strategic acquirers.
- **Case Study Template:** Solid Hej/Ridgeline/Summit Peak models showing investment, annual value, exit premium attribution.

What's Next

Chapter 9 demonstrates how to turn regulatory compliance from burden to competitive advantage. Through systematic frameworks for navigating EU CSRD, SFDR, TCFD, and emerging ISSB standards, you will discover how companies like Solid Hej Components used regulatory preparedness to create 2–3-year competitive advantages that buyers recognized as valuable strategic positioning.

References

Alvarez & Marsal. (2024). ESG value creation opportunities for private capital in Southeast Asia and India survey 2024. Singapore Venture and Private Capital Association.

EY. (2024). How private equity can optimize ESG to maximize value creation. Ernst & Young Global Limited.

Kengelbach, J., Herfurth, J., Degen, D., Oberbracht, D., Fromholzer, F., & Schubert, J. (2024, April 18). The payoffs and pitfalls of ESG due diligence. Boston Consulting Group.

Khan, M., Serafeim, G., & Yoon, A. (2016). Corporate sustainability: First evidence on materiality. *The Accounting Review*, 91(6), 1697–1724. doi:10.2308/accr-51383.

Pedersen, L. H., Fitzgibbons, S., & Pomorski, L. (2021). Responsible investing: The ESG-efficient frontier. *Journal of Financial Economics, 142*(2), 572–597. doi:10.1016/j.jfineco.2020.11.004.

PwC. (2022). Global investor survey 2022. PricewaterhouseCoopers.

Shandal, R., & Entraygues, P. (2024). PE-backed companies stand out on ESG. Bain & Company Insights.

Yoon, A. (2024, February 7). Two factors that determine when ESG creates shareholder value. *Harvard Business Review*. https://hbr.org/2024/02/two-factors-that-determine-when-esg-creates-shareholder-value.

Part III

Navigating Complexity

9 Regulation Without Tears

Making Compliance Work for You

Regulation Without Tears

"We just received our third regulatory update this month."

Efe Iwinosa, compliance director at Solid Hej Components, stood at Alex Morgan's office door holding a stack of papers thick enough to serve as a doorstop. Her expression mixed frustration with resignation—a look Alex had seen frequently across portfolio companies as ESG regulations multiplied and evolved.

"The EU's new Corporate Sustainability Reporting Directive, updates to TCFD recommendations, and something called the International Sustainability Standards Board that apparently changes everything we thought we knew about ESG reporting," Ivie continued. "My team is spending 60% of their time just trying to understand what we are supposed to report, let alone actually preparing the reports."

Alex had heard similar complaints from compliance teams across the portfolio. What had started as a trickle of sustainability-related regulations in the early 2000s had become a flood by 2025. The European Union led with comprehensive frameworks like Sustainable Finance Disclosure Regulation (SFDR) and Corporate Sustainability Reporting Directive (CSRD). The United Kingdom implemented its own climate disclosure requirements. Asian markets developed green taxonomies and mandatory ESG reporting. Even the typically hands-off United States market was moving towards mandatory climate risk disclosure.

The regulatory complexity was real, but Alex had learned something important over 15 years of managing ESG compliance: companies that treated regulation as strategic intelligence rather than administrative burden consistently outperformed those that saw it only as cost and complexity.

"Let me show you something," Alex said, pulling up a presentation on Solid Hej Components' regulatory journey. "Two years ago, you were exactly where you are now, overwhelmed by requirements and wondering how to comply efficiently. Today, Solid Hej is ahead of most competitors on regulatory preparedness, and that advantage is worth real money at exit."

DOI: 10.4324/9781003625636-12

9.1 The Strategic Value of Regulatory Intelligence

9.1.1 From Compliance Burden to Competitive Advantage

The fundamental shift in thinking required treating regulatory development as market intelligence that revealed where industries were heading rather than just compliance obligations to be managed.

This strategic approach was supported by research from the Organisation for Economic Co-operation and Development (2020) showing that ESG regulation influenced capital allocation, competitive dynamics, and market access in ways that created advantages for early adopters. Companies that anticipated regulatory trends and built capabilities proactively found themselves positioned ahead of competitors when requirements became mandatory.

Early Adoption Benefits: Companies that started adopting Task Force on Climate-related Financial Disclosures (TCFD)-aligned reporting well before it became a legal requirement found themselves fully compliant when the regulations were finally enforced. In contrast, their competitors were left rushing to catch up. This early preparation delivered several key benefits as demonstrated by the case study:
Reduced Compliance Costs: Building systems gradually over years cost significantly less than rushing implementation to meet deadlines.
Superior Data Quality: Gradual implementation enabled system refinement and data quality improvement that rushed programmes could not achieve.
Strategic Positioning: Early compliance creates marketing advantages and customer confidence that competitors may not match.
Buyer Value at Exit: The acquiring company may value regulatory systems as avoided implementation costs—quantifiable value that could contribute to exit premium.

9.1.2 Regulatory Intelligence as Market Research

The most sophisticated firms learned to treat regulatory development as market research revealing future competitive dynamics and stakeholder expectations:

Customer Requirement Anticipation: Regulatory trends often preceded customer requirements by 18–24 months. Companies monitoring EU CSRD development could anticipate that major customers would soon require supplier ESG data, enabling proactive capability building.
Competitive Positioning: Early regulatory compliance created differentiation in procurement processes where buyers increasingly required ESG credentials. Companies that could not demonstrate strong ESG performance were being excluded from competitive processes regardless of price or quality advantages.
Investment Attraction: Institutional investors facing their own disclosure requirements increasingly required portfolio companies to provide ESG data. Companies with advanced reporting capabilities accessed capital more efficiently than those struggling with basic compliance.

9.1.3 Turning Requirements into Revenue Opportunities

Beyond defensive compliance, regulatory trends created revenue opportunities for companies positioned to benefit from market transformation.

Alpine Foods discovered that customer sustainability requirements driven by regulatory pressure created premium pricing opportunities. Retailers facing CSRD disclosure requirements needed suppliers who could provide verified sustainability data. Alpine's advanced measurement systems enabled them to command 8–12% price premiums from customers who valued regulatory preparedness.

Ridgeline Solutions found that circular economy regulations created demand for sustainable packaging solutions that competitors without relevant capabilities could not provide. The €4.2 million in new revenue from sustainable product lines was directly attributable to regulatory-driven market transformation.

Common Questions Alex Fields

Q: How do you keep up with constantly evolving regulations across multiple jurisdictions?

A: We do not try to track everything. Focus on regulations affecting your major markets and customers. For Solid Hej, that meant EU frameworks since 80% of customers were European. We subscribed to regulatory update services, joined industry associations, and assigned one person 20% time to monitor developments. It is intelligence gathering, not legal compliance.

Q: What if regulations conflict across different jurisdictions?

A: Comply with the most stringent requirement—it usually satisfies the others. Solid Hej's EU CSRD compliance covered UK TCFD and most customer-specific requirements. The "gold standard approach" reduces complexity while creating competitive advantages in all markets.

Q: How far ahead should you prepare for anticipated regulations?

A: Start when proposed rules enter consultation phase, typically 18–24 months before implementation. That timeline allows gradual capability building without rushing. We implemented ISSB frameworks while they were still drafts, giving us 2+ years' head start when they became market expectations.

9.2 Essential Frameworks Simplified

9.2.1 The Framework Proliferation Challenge

The proliferation of ESG frameworks created confusion for companies trying to understand which standards to follow and how to comply efficiently. Alex learned that most companies over-complicated their approach by trying to address every framework comprehensively instead of focusing on the requirements most relevant to their business.

This challenge was well-documented in research. Berg, Kölbel, and Rigobon (2022) revealed that about 56% of rating disparity came from measurement differences, 38% from scope, and 6% from weightings. Meanwhile, BNP Paribas Securities Services (2019) found that 65% of respondents were aligning investments with the UN Sustainable Development Goals, yet one-third cited technology limitations in analysing ESG data.

9.2.2 EU Sustainable Finance Disclosure Regulation: Practical Implementation

The EU's Sustainable Finance Disclosure Regulation exemplified both the complexity and opportunity of modern ESG regulation. While technically focused on financial services firms, SFDR's requirements cascaded to portfolio companies and created market pressure for enhanced sustainability disclosure.

In the Solid Hej Components case study, SFDR compliance became a competitive advantage when their strategic buyer—a company subject to Article 8 requirements—valued their existing ESG reporting systems at €180,000 in avoided implementation costs.

Simplified SFDR Implementation Framework:

Step 1: Classification Assessment: Determine which SFDR article applies to your fund strategy and investor base. Most traditional PE funds fall under Article 6 or 8, with Article 9 reserved for dedicated impact funds.
Step 2: Disclosure Preparation: Develop standardized ESG reporting templates that can satisfy both SFDR requirements and other regulatory frameworks simultaneously, reducing duplication of effort.
Step 3: Portfolio Integration: Implement portfolio company reporting systems that provide data needed for fund-level SFDR compliance without creating excessive administrative burden on operations teams.

Table 9.1 SFDR article classifications and requirements

Article	*Classification*	*Requirements*
Article 6	Standard Funds (No sustainability claims)	• Disclose how ESG risks are integrated • Principal adverse impact (PAI) statement • No specific sustainability objectives • Minimum transparency requirements
Article 8	Light Green (Promotes E/S characteristics)	• Must promote environmental or social characteristics • Disclose how characteristics are met • Report on PAIs • Portfolio company ESG disclosures • Regular monitoring and reporting
Article 9	Dark Green (Sustainable investment objective)	• Sustainable investment as core objective • Demonstrate positive impact • Do no significant harm (DNSH) principle • Comprehensive impact measurement • Detailed portfolio alignment reporting • Highest transparency standards

Step 4: Verification and Quality Control: Establish third-party verification processes for material metrics to ensure disclosure accuracy and credibility with investors and regulators.

The SFDR regime itself is also evolving. In November 2025, the European Commission proposed reforms intended to simplify SFDR disclosures and improve investor usability, explicitly responding to market feedback on complexity and cost (European Commission, 2025). For private equity managers, the practical lesson is to build compliance systems that are resilient to regulatory change: focus on governance controls, clear product claims, and evidence trails that can be adapted as SFDR requirements are refined.

9.2.3 TCFD Requirements: A Streamlined Approach to Climate Disclosure

The Task Force on Climate-related Financial Disclosures provided a structured framework for climate risk assessment and disclosure that had been adopted across multiple jurisdictions. While comprehensive, TCFD implementation could be streamlined by focusing on the most material climate risks and opportunities for each business.

The TCFD's influence on corporate reporting had been substantial. The framework's four pillars—governance, strategy, risk management, and metrics and targets—had become the global standard for climate-related disclosure, influencing national regulations from the UK to Hong Kong.

TCFD's Four Pillars Adapted for Private Equity:

Governance: Board and management oversight of climate-related risks and opportunities:

- Implementation: Include climate considerations in investment committee and board processes.
- Documentation: Clear policies and accountability structures for climate risk management.

Strategy: Climate impact on business strategy and financial planning:

- Implementation: Scenario analysis for portfolio companies in climate-sensitive sectors.
- Documentation: Strategic plans that address climate risks and opportunities.

Risk Management: Process for identifying, assessing, and managing climate risks:

- Implementation: Integration of climate factors into existing risk management frameworks.
- Documentation: Regular risk assessments and mitigation planning.

Metrics and Targets: Metrics and targets for climate risk and opportunity assessment:

- Implementation: Standardized carbon accounting and climate performance measurement.
- Documentation: Baseline establishment and improvement target setting.

At Summit Peak Facility Services, TCFD implementation revealed that climate adaptation investments could reduce business interruption risks by an estimated €340,000 annually while positioning the company for growth in climate-resilient service markets.

9.2.4 GRI Standards: Focusing on What Actually Matters

The Global Reporting Initiative Standards provided comprehensive frameworks for sustainability reporting but could overwhelm companies trying to implement every recommendation. Alex developed a materiality-focused approach that captured GRI's value without creating excessive reporting burden.

GRI Universal Standards (Foundation):

- GRI 2: General Disclosures providing organizational context.
- GRI 3: Material Topics identifying what matters most to the business.

GRI Topic Standards (Focused Selection):

- Implement only standards corresponding to material topics identified through stakeholder assessment.
- Solid Hej Components focused on GRI 302 (Energy), 305 (Emissions), 401 (Employment), and 403 (Occupational Health & Safety).
- This selective approach covered 85% of stakeholder priorities while requiring 40% less effort than comprehensive implementation.

"The breakthrough was recognizing that GRI does not require reporting on every topic," Ivie Chen explained. "We focused intensively on material issues rather than superficially covering everything. That focus created more useful information for stakeholders while reducing our reporting burden."

9.2.5 ISSB Standards: The Global Baseline Emerging

The International Sustainability Standards Board represented the most significant development in ESG regulation—the emergence of global baseline standards that could reduce fragmentation and compliance complexity.

IFRS S1: General Requirements for Sustainability Disclosure:

- Established baseline disclosure requirements applicable across jurisdictions.
- Focused on information material to investment decisions.
- Integrated with financial reporting frameworks.

IFRS S2: Climate-related Disclosures:

- Built on TCFD framework with enhanced specificity.
- Required Scope 1, 2, and 3 greenhouse gas emissions disclosure.
- Mandated climate scenario analysis for material exposures.

Solid Hej Components adopted ISSB standards during the consultation phase, positioning them 18 months ahead of market expectations when standards were finalized. This early adoption created competitive advantages in investor communications and customer relationships while simplifying compliance with multiple frameworks.

"ISSB was the convergence we had been waiting for," Alex explained. "Instead of managing ten different frameworks, we could focus on one comprehensive standard that satisfied most stakeholder requirements. That efficiency created real value."

9.3 Regional Variations and Multi-Jurisdictional Strategy

9.3.1 Understanding Regional Regulatory Approaches

While global frameworks provided standardization, significant regional variations persisted in regulatory philosophy, implementation timelines, and enforcement mechanisms. Companies operating internationally needed strategies for managing this complexity.

Research confirmed these regional differences. The Global Sustainable Investment Alliance (2021) documented varying ESG asset allocations across regions, reflecting different regulatory frameworks, investor preferences, and market structures.

European Union: Comprehensive Integration:

- Mandatory ESG disclosure for large companies through CSRD.
- Sustainable finance taxonomy affecting capital allocation decisions.
- Due diligence requirements for supply chain environmental and social impacts.
- Carbon border adjustments affecting international trade relationships.

United Kingdom: Climate-Focused Approach:

- Mandatory TCFD reporting for large companies and asset managers.
- Net-zero commitment integration into business planning requirements.

- Enhanced governance standards including board diversity and executive compensation disclosure.
- Sustainability-linked financing incentives through government programmes.

United States: Market-Driven Evolution:

- Securities and Exchange Commission climate disclosure rules creating mandatory reporting requirements.
- State-level initiatives driving regional compliance obligations.
- Investor pressure and litigation risk increasing ESG attention.
- Federal procurement requirements including sustainability criteria.

Asia-Pacific: Rapid Development:

- Singapore and Hong Kong green finance frameworks affecting capital market access.
- China's environmental information disclosure requirements for large companies.
- Japan's corporate governance reforms increasing ESG integration expectations.
- Australia's climate risk disclosure requirements for financial institutions.

9.3.2 *Compliance Efficiency Strategies*

The complexity of multi-jurisdictional compliance created both challenges and opportunities for portfolio companies operating internationally. Alex developed strategies for managing this complexity that turned regulatory burden into competitive advantage:

Gold Standard Approach: Companies that achieved compliance in the most demanding jurisdictions often found competitive advantages in markets with less stringent requirements. Solid Hej Components' EU-level environmental

Table 9.2 Integrated regulatory compliance framework

Framework	*Core Requirements*	*Integration Approach*
TCFD	• Governance • Strategy • Risk management • Metrics and targets Focus: Climate-related financial disclosures	Build foundation with climate scenario analysis, establish climate governance, integrate into existing risk management
CSRD/ESRS	• Double materiality assessment • Value chain reporting • All ESG topics (E, S, G) Focus: Comprehensive sustainability reporting	Leverage TCFD climate work, expand to full ESG, conduct double materiality, engage value chain
SFDR	• Fund-level classification (Articles 6/8/9) • PAI reporting • Portfolio company data Focus: Investment product transparency	Use ESRS disclosures from portfolio companies, aggregate for fund-level reporting, ensure consistent methodology

compliance provided advantages when expanding into Eastern European markets where competitors struggled with basic environmental management. **Early Adoption Benefits:** Anticipating regulatory convergence allowed companies to build capabilities once and apply them across multiple markets. Summit Peak Facility Services' TCFD implementation in the UK positioned them for expansion into EU markets where similar requirements were being phased in.

Solid Hej Components used Gold Standard Approach: EU CSRD compliance satisfied 85% of TCFD, GRI, and customer requirements, reducing costs by 60%.

9.3.3 Climate Risk Frameworks That Affect Valuation

Climate-related regulations increasingly affected asset valuations through both direct compliance costs and market positioning implications. Alex learned to incorporate these factors into investment analysis and portfolio management decisions.

Task Force on Climate-related Financial Disclosures research noted that climate risks could have material financial impacts through both physical risks (acute and chronic climate events) and transition risks (policy changes, technology shifts, market preferences).

Physical Risk Assessment: Regulations requiring climate risk disclosure forced companies to evaluate their exposure to extreme weather, sea-level rise, and other physical climate impacts. This assessment often revealed vulnerabilities that affected operational costs, insurance requirements, and asset values.
At Alpine Foods, mandatory climate risk assessment identified €2.3 million in potential flood damage to coastal facilities over 20 years. This analysis

Table 9.3 Compliance efficiency strategies

Strategy	*Description*	*Example*	*Benefits*
Gold Standard Approach	Comply with most stringent requirements globally	Implement EU CSRD standards across all operations	Simplifies multi-jurisdiction compliance, creates competitive advantages
Modular Framework	Build scalable systems that can be enhanced for different markets	Core ESG reporting plus jurisdiction-specific modules	Balances cost efficiency with local compliance
Anticipatory Implementation	Monitor regulatory development and implement before requirements	Early TCFD adoption based on consultation documents	Avoids rushed implementation, creates first-mover advantages
Strategic Selectivity	Focus compliance efforts on most important markets and stakeholders	Prioritize compliance in major customer and investor jurisdictions	Maximizes ROI on compliance investment

supported €340,000 in adaptation investments that reduced insurance costs while protecting operational continuity.

Transition Risk Evaluation: Carbon pricing, renewable energy requirements, and other climate policies created transition risks that affected competitive positioning and operational costs. Companies with early insights into these trends could build adaptation strategies that created competitive advantages.

Apex Industries' early analysis of potential carbon pricing in their markets led to energy efficiency investments that reduced exposure to future carbon costs by an estimated €180,000 annually while generating immediate operational savings.

Opportunity Identification: Climate regulations also created market opportunities for companies positioned to benefit from the transition to low-carbon economy. Portfolio companies with relevant capabilities could access growing markets and premium pricing.

Ridgeline Solutions' investment in low-carbon packaging solutions was initially driven by regulatory compliance but opened access to €4.2 million in new business from customers seeking to meet their own climate commitments.

Common Questions Alex Fields

Q: How do you balance compliance costs against limited resources?

A: Focus on material frameworks affecting your major stakeholders. Solid Hej prioritized EU regulations because 80% of customers and investors were European. We implemented one comprehensive system (CSRD) that satisfied multiple requirements rather than building separate programs for each framework. That focus reduced costs by 60% versus fragmented approach.

Q: What if our portfolio company operates in markets with conflicting regulations?

A: Conflicts are rarer than people think—most regulations converge around TCFD and GRI foundations. When genuine conflicts exist, comply with the more stringent requirement. It usually satisfies the less demanding one while creating competitive advantage. We have never encountered a situation where compliance in one market violated another market's requirements.

Q: How do you turn regulatory compliance into competitive advantage rather than just avoiding penalties?

A: Three ways: First, early compliance creates customer and investor confidence competitors cannot match. Second, regulatory intelligence reveals market trends before competitors recognize them. Third, compliance capabilities become saleable assets at exit—Solid Hej's systems were worth €180K to the buyer. Defensive compliance wastes that value.

9.4 The EU CSRD: Practical Implementation

9.4.1 Understanding CSRD Scope and Requirements

The European Union's Corporate Sustainability Reporting Directive represented the most comprehensive mandatory ESG reporting requirement implemented to date. As it affected 50,000+ companies starting 2024, the CSRD provided practical lessons in managing complex regulatory implementation.

The CSRD's scope and requirements represented an expansion from previous EU sustainability reporting requirements. The directive required companies to report on how sustainability matters affected their business (financial materiality) and how their activities impacted people and the environment (impact materiality), following a "double materiality" approach.

CSRD Implementation Timeline and Requirements

YEAR 1: PREPARATION PHASE:

- Gap analysis comparing existing reporting to CSRD requirements.
- Double materiality assessment identifying impact and financial materiality.
- Data system enhancement to collect required metrics.
- Third-party verification relationship establishment.

YEAR 2: IMPLEMENTATION PHASE:

- Full sustainability report preparation following CSRD format.
- Limited assurance from independent auditor.
- Integration with financial reporting processes and timelines.
- Stakeholder communication about enhanced disclosure.

Table 9.4 CSRD implementation timeline (2024–2028)

Year	*Companies Affected*	*Reporting Requirements*
2024	Large public-interest entities (>500 employees) already subject to NFRD	First reports published in 2025 for FY 2024 ESRS mandatory Double materiality assessment
2025	All large companies meeting 2 of 3 criteria:• >250 employees • >€50M revenue • >€25M total assets	First reports published in 2026 for FY 2025 Full ESRS compliance Value chain disclosures
2026	Listed SMEs (except micro-enterprises)	First reports published in 2027 for FY 2026 Proportionate requirements Simplified standards available
2028	Non-EU companies with: • EU revenue >€150M • At least one EU subsidiary/branch	First reports published in 2029 for FY 2028 Group-level reporting EU operations focus

YEAR 3: OPTIMIZATION PHASE:

- Continuous improvement based on stakeholder feedback.
- Advanced analytics and benchmarking capabilities.
- Integration of sustainability data into business decision-making.
- External recognition and competitive positioning.

9.4.2 Resource Requirements and Returns

Solid Hej Components invested €127,000 in CSRD implementation over 18 months, including external consulting (€45,000), data system enhancements (€38,000), staff training (€29,000), and third-party verification (€15,000).

However, the investment generated returns through improved operational efficiency, better risk management, and enhanced stakeholder relationships that more than offset the compliance costs. The systematic data collection revealed €234,000 in annual efficiency improvement opportunities that traditional analysis had missed.

9.4.3 Non-Financial Disclosure Strategies

The CSRD's emphasis on non-financial information required companies to develop new approaches to measuring and reporting qualitative factors like governance effectiveness, stakeholder relationships, and social impact.

Quantitative Backing for Qualitative Claims: Even non-financial disclosures benefited from quantitative support. Solid Hej Components' governance improvements were supported by board effectiveness surveys, meeting attendance records, and decision-making speed metrics.

Stakeholder Voice Integration: CSRD requirements for stakeholder engagement information encouraged companies to develop systematic approaches to gathering and incorporating stakeholder feedback into business decisions through advisory councils, satisfaction surveys, and collaborative planning forums.

Forward-Looking Information: Unlike traditional financial reporting focused on historical performance, CSRD encouraged disclosure of future plans, targets, and strategic approaches to sustainability challenges, creating accountability for improvement commitments.

Impact Pathway Documentation: Companies needed to explain not just what they were doing but how their actions created positive impacts for stakeholders and society, connecting activities to outcomes through logical causal chains.

9.4.4 Implementation Challenges and Solutions

The CSRD's comprehensive scope created implementation challenges that required systematic solutions and change management approaches:

Challenge: Data Availability and Quality: Many required metrics were not previously tracked or were tracked inconsistently. *Solution:* Phased implementation starting with available data and improving quality over time, with clear documentation of methodological changes and limitations.

Challenge: Double Materiality Assessment: The requirement to assess both impact materiality and financial materiality created analytical complexity. *Solution:* Structured stakeholder engagement processes combined with quantitative analysis to identify and prioritize material issues across both dimensions.

Challenge: Integration with Financial Reporting: Sustainability reporting needed to align with financial reporting timelines and quality standards. *Solution:* Integrated project management with finance teams leading overall coordination and sustainability teams providing technical expertise.

Challenge: Assurance and Verification: CSRD's requirement for limited assurance created new relationships and processes with external auditors. *Solution:* Early engagement with audit firms, pilot testing of assurance processes, and comprehensive documentation of data sources and methodologies.

9.5 Mastering Regulatory Complexity

9.5.1 Building Integrated Compliance Systems

"We need a system that works for every regulation, not just today's requirements."

This request came from Penelope Day, CFO of Apex Industries, during a portfolio company best-practices session on regulatory compliance. Her team had successfully implemented CSRD reporting but was struggling with overlapping requirements from TCFD, customer-specific ESG questionnaires, and emerging regulations in their international markets.

The solution required developing integrated compliance approaches that satisfied multiple requirements efficiently while remaining flexible enough to adapt to regulatory evolution.

9.5.2 Data Accuracy and Consistency: Practical Systems That Work

The foundation of effective regulatory compliance was reliable data systems that could provide accurate, consistent information across different reporting frameworks and time periods.

Research emphasized the importance of data quality in ESG reporting. Berg, Kölbel, and Rigobon (2022) noted that measurement differences account for the majority of ESG rating divergence, while the OECD (2020) called for improved disclosure standards and harmonization in ESG measurement to build investor confidence.

Integrated Data Management Architecture:

Single Source of Truth: All regulatory reporting drew from the same underlying data systems, eliminating discrepancies between different reports and reducing maintenance requirements.

Automated Collection: Material metrics were collected automatically from operational systems where possible, reducing manual input errors and administrative burden.
Quality Control Processes: Systematic verification procedures ensured data accuracy before it entered regulatory reports, including automated checks for outliers and manual review of changes.
Historical Tracking: Comprehensive historical data enabled trend analysis and ensured consistency in methodological approaches over time.

At Apex Industries, this integrated approach reduced regulatory reporting preparation time from 40 hours monthly to 32 hours monthly while improving data accuracy and stakeholder confidence.

9.5.3 Multiple Standards Compliance Without Duplication

The proliferation of ESG standards created opportunities for efficient compliance through strategic framework selection and implementation approaches that satisfied multiple requirements simultaneously.

Framework Mapping Analysis: Identify overlapping requirements across different frameworks to avoid duplication. Most frameworks converged around similar core metrics despite different presentation formats.
Core Plus Modular Architecture: Build comprehensive core system satisfying the most demanding requirements, then add lightweight modules for framework-specific elements. Solid Hej Components' CSRD system satisfied 85% of TCFD, GRI, and customer requirements with minimal additional work.
Automated Report Generation: Technology platforms could generate different report formats from single data source, reducing preparation time and ensuring consistency across stakeholders.
Regular Framework Review: Annual assessment of which frameworks remained relevant based on stakeholder requirements, eliminating unnecessary reporting burden as priorities evolved.

9.6 Future-Proofing Your Compliance Strategy

9.6.1 Anticipating Regulatory Evolution

Looking forward, Alex anticipated several trends that would continue reshaping ESG regulatory requirements and create new challenges and opportunities for portfolio companies:

Expanded Scope Requirements: Regulations would increasingly require disclosure beyond direct operations to include supply chain impacts, financed emissions, and full value chain assessment. Companies building supplier data collection capabilities early would face lower implementation costs when requirements expanded.

Enhanced Verification Standards: Third-party assurance requirements would evolve from limited to reasonable assurance, requiring more rigorous data collection and verification processes. Companies with strong data quality systems would transition efficiently while competitors struggled.

Technology-Enabled Disclosure: Real-time reporting and continuous disclosure would supplement annual reports, requiring technology infrastructure that could provide current performance data on demand.

Stakeholder-Centric Requirements: Regulations would increasingly require evidence of genuine stakeholder engagement rather than just disclosure, rewarding companies with authentic relationship management approaches.

9.6.2 Building Adaptive Compliance Infrastructure

The rapid pace of regulatory evolution required compliance systems that could adapt to changing requirements without complete rebuilding:

Modular System Architecture: Build compliance systems with modular components that could be updated independently as regulations evolved, avoiding monolithic systems that required complete redesign when requirements changed.

Technology Platform Selection: Choose platforms with regular updates and strong vendor support rather than custom-built systems that might become obsolete. Cloud-based solutions typically provided more agility than on-premise implementations.

Capability Over Compliance: Focus on building genuine sustainability capabilities rather than narrowly complying with current rules. Companies with authentic ESG performance could adapt reporting easily; those focused only on compliance struggled when requirements changed.

Continuous Learning Culture: Establish processes for monitoring regulatory development, evaluating implications, and implementing adaptations before deadlines created crisis situations.

As Ivie Chen reflected on Solid Hej Components' regulatory journey three years after that initial overwhelmed conversation, the transformation was remarkable. "We went from drowning in compliance to using regulatory intelligence as competitive advantage," she explained. "The turning point was recognizing that regulations reveal where markets are heading—they are strategic intelligence, not administrative burden."

Alex smiled. "The biggest opportunity is turning regulatory intelligence into market intelligence. The companies that understand where regulation is headed can position themselves to benefit from changes that hurt their competitors. That is the ultimate regulatory advantage."

Regulatory frameworks provide the rules of the game, but success depends on winning hearts and minds across stakeholder groups. Chapter 10 reveals how to build genuine commitment rather than mere compliance, scaling ESG excellence across entire portfolios through systematic knowledge sharing and capability building.

Chapter Summary

Core Insight

Regulatory compliance transforms from burden to competitive advantage when treated as strategic intelligence revealing market evolution. Solid Hej Components' early TCFD adoption (two years pre-mandate) created €180K buyer value at exit, demonstrating that regulatory preparedness generates tangible financial returns beyond avoiding penalties.

Critical Success Factors

- **Early adoption benefits:** Building capabilities 18–24 months before mandates reduces costs by 60% while creating competitive advantages in customer and investor relationships.
- **Gold standard approach:** Complying with most stringent requirements (EU CSRD) typically satisfies less demanding frameworks, simplifying multi-jurisdiction compliance.
- **Framework convergence:** ISSB standards provide global baseline covering 85% of TCFD, GRI, and SFDR requirements, enabling efficiency through single comprehensive system.
- **Integrated data architecture:** Single source of truth generating multiple report formats reduces Apex Industries' preparation time from 40 to 32 hours monthly.
- **Materiality focus:** GRI selective implementation covering only material topics reduces effort by 40% while improving information usefulness.

Watch Out For

⚠ Trying to comply with every framework comprehensively instead of focusing on stakeholder-relevant requirements wastes resources.

⚠ Waiting for final regulations before starting preparation creates rushed implementation and higher costs.

⚠ Building separate systems for each framework rather than integrated architecture multiplies administrative burden.

⚠ Treating compliance as legal obligation rather than market intelligence misses strategic opportunities.

Tools You Can Use Now

- **Regulatory Intelligence Framework:** Flowchart converting regulatory development into market intelligence, strategic positioning, and competitive advantage.
- **Framework Convergence Map:** Venn diagram showing ISSB baseline satisfying majority of SFDR, TCFD, and GRI requirements.
- **CSRD Implementation Roadmap:** Three-year timeline with preparation, implementation, and optimization phases.
- **Compliance Efficiency Matrix:** Four strategies (gold standard, modular, anticipatory, selective) with examples and benefits.
- **Multi-Jurisdictional Strategy:** Regional variations (EU, UK, US, Asia-Pacific) with specific compliance approaches.

What's Next

Chapter 10 demonstrates how to scale ESG excellence across entire portfolios through systematic knowledge sharing and capability building. You will discover how Kerring Capital Partners' fund-level integration strategy generated 8.2% higher IRR through network effects, cross-portfolio learning systems, and operational synergies that amplified individual company improvements into portfolio-wide competitive advantages.

References

Berg, F., Kölbel, J., & Rigobon, R. (2022). Aggregate confusion: The divergence of ESG ratings. *Review of Finance*, 26 (6), 1315–1344. doi:10.1093/rof/rfac037.

BNP Paribas Securities Services. (2019). ESG Global Survey 2019: Investor perspectives. BNP Paribas.

European Commission (2025). Commission proposes improvements to SFDR (21 November).

European Commission (2025). Commission simplifies transparency rules for sustainable financial products (20 November).

European Commission. (2022). Corporate Sustainability Reporting Directive (CSRD). Official Journal of the European Union.

European Union. (2019). Sustainable Finance Disclosure Regulation (SFDR). EU 2019/2088.

Global Reporting Initiative. (2021). GRI Standards. GRI.

Global Sustainable Investment Alliance. (2021). Global Sustainable Investment Review 2020. GSIA. https://www.gsi-alliance.org/wp-content/uploads/2021/08/GSIR-20201.pdf.

International Sustainability Standards Board. (2023). IFRS S1 General Requirements for Disclosure of Sustainability-related Financial Information. ISSB.

International Sustainability Standards Board. (2023). IFRS S2 Climate-related Disclosures. ISSB.

Organisation for Economic Co-operation and Development. (2020). ESG investing: Practices, progress and challenges. OECD Publishing. doi:10.1787/b4f71091-en.

Task Force on Climate-related Financial Disclosures. (2017). Recommendations of the Task Force on Climate-related Financial Disclosures. TCFD.

10 Portfolio-Level Optimization

Scaling ESG Excellence

Portfolio-Level Optimization

"We are missing the forest for the trees."

Alex Morgan's observation during Kerring Capital Partners' annual portfolio review captured a realization that had been building over months of analysing ESG performance across their investments. While individual companies like Solid Hej Components, Alpine Foods, and Summit Peak Facility Services had achieved impressive sustainability results, the firm was not systematically leveraging learnings, resources, or relationships across the portfolio.

"Look at this pattern," Alex continued, advancing to a slide showing ESG initiatives across 12 portfolio companies. "Summit Peak Facility Services spent six months developing an employee engagement programme that reduced turnover by 35%. Three months later, Precision Peak Manufacturing started from scratch on a nearly identical challenge. Meanwhile, both companies were independently negotiating with the same sustainability consulting firm, paying higher rates than we could achieve through portfolio-level procurement."

Jim Kerring, the firm's managing partner, leaned forward with interest. "What are you suggesting?"

"That we are treating ESG as 12 separate company initiatives when we should be building one integrated portfolio capability," Alex replied. "The evidence suggests that portfolio-level ESG integration creates value beyond individual company improvements. Companies that share learnings implement faster, avoid mistakes, and achieve better results. Vendors offer better pricing for portfolio-wide relationships. And when we go to market for exits, having multiple ESG-integrated companies creates credibility that benefits all of them."

This insight would transform how Kerring Capital Partners approached portfolio management, resource allocation, and value creation planning. Instead of discrete company strategies, they would develop fund-level ESG capabilities that enhanced performance across all investments while positioning the fund competitively for future fundraising and Limited Partner relations.

Research supported this integrated approach. Bain & Company (2022) found that private equity firms with systematic ESG integration achieved 8% higher IRRs than those without, while McKinsey & Company (2020) analysis showed

DOI: 10.4324/9781003625636-13

that portfolio-level ESG capabilities often created value exceeding the sum of individual company improvements.

Industry analysis published in late 2025 reinforces the shift described in this chapter: operational alpha increasingly depends on institutionalized value-creation capabilities rather than bespoke interventions. KPMG's October 2025 paper on value creation in private equity argues that leading firms are formalizing operating models built around proprietary data, scenario simulation, outside-in intelligence, and functional expertise (KPMG, 2025). For portfolio-level ESG execution, this supports a practical conclusion: scalability depends on systems and capabilities that reduce marginal effort per asset while improving consistency and accountability.

By creating network effects where each company's improvements amplified others, Kerring Capital Partners was discovering that systematic portfolio optimization represented ESG integration's next frontier—moving from company-level operational improvements to fund-level strategic advantages.

10.1 Fund-Level ESG Integration Strategy

10.1.1 From Company-Specific to Portfolio-Wide Approach

The evolution from company-specific to portfolio-wide ESG strategy required fundamental changes in how Alex approached investment management. Instead of treating sustainability as a company-level operational issue, it became a fund-level competitive capability that differentiated Kerring Capital Partners in LP fundraising, deal sourcing, and exit positioning.

The most successful portfolio optimization strategies Alex observed were those that built systematic capabilities rather than ad hoc responses to individual company needs. This approach reflected research showing that private equity firms with dedicated ESG resources and processes consistently outperformed those with ad hoc approaches.

Fund-Level ESG Infrastructure:

Dedicated Expertise: Kerring Capital Partners hired Ivie Chen as Director of ESG Integration, reporting directly to the managing partner rather than being embedded in individual deal teams. This structure ensured ESG considerations influenced fund strategy alongside company-specific implementation.

Ivie's responsibilities included developing portfolio-wide ESG frameworks, coordinating knowledge sharing across companies, managing relationships with sustainability service providers, and positioning the fund's ESG capabilities for LP communications and competitive differentiation.

Standardized Assessment Frameworks: The fund developed consistent ESG assessment approaches that could be deployed across all investments while maintaining sector-specific flexibility. These frameworks included due diligence checklists, materiality assessment methodologies, performance measurement systems, and exit preparation protocols.

Standardization enabled efficiency through shared tools and training while ensuring quality and comparability across portfolio companies. Companies could benchmark performance against portfolio peers, identify best practices, and access proven implementation approaches rather than reinventing methodologies.

Portfolio-Wide Technology Platforms: Rather than each company implementing separate ESG data management systems, Kerring Capital Partners deployed an integrated platform that aggregated performance across all investments while providing company-specific dashboards and analytics.

This technology investment of €125,000 annually enabled portfolio management efficiencies estimated at €450,000 in reduced consulting costs, accelerated implementation timelines, and improved decision-making quality.

10.1.2 Creating Network Effects through Knowledge Sharing

The most valuable aspect of portfolio-level ESG integration was the network effect created through systematic knowledge sharing and collaborative problem-solving.

Structured Learning Systems:

Rather than hoping that good ideas would spread naturally, Alex developed formal systems for capturing, developing, and disseminating best practices across the portfolio.

Best Practice Development Process:

Step 1: Success Identification: Systematic monitoring of ESG initiatives across portfolio companies to identify high-impact successes and lessons learned through quarterly reviews and annual benchmarking.

Step 2: Documentation and Analysis: Detailed documentation of successful approaches including implementation steps, resource requirements, results achieved, and lessons learned through case study development.

Step 3: Adaptation Framework Development: Analysis of how successful practices could be modified for different industry contexts, company sizes, and organizational cultures through pilot testing.

Step 4: Knowledge Dissemination: Structured communication of best practices to relevant portfolio companies through peer networks, training programmes, and implementation guides.

Step 5: Implementation Support: Provision of technical assistance and resources to companies adopting proven practices, accelerating implementation and improving success rates.

Step 6: Performance Monitoring: Tracking of results from knowledge transfer initiatives to verify value creation and identify continuous improvement opportunities.

10.1.3 Summit Peak Facility Services Case: Systematic Knowledge Transfer

When Summit Peak Facility Services successfully reduced employee turnover from 47% to 12% (a 35-percentage-point reduction) through comprehensive ESG-driven employee engagement programmes, Kerring Capital Partners systematically transferred this knowledge across service sector portfolio companies.

Transfer Process:

1. Summit Peak Facility Services documented their employee engagement methodology including assessment tools, programme design, implementation approach, and measurement systems in comprehensive playbook format.
2. Kerring Capital Partners convened service company HR leaders to review the approach and discuss adaptation requirements for their specific contexts and organizational cultures.
3. Three portfolio companies piloted adapted programmes with Summit Peak Facility Services providing implementation mentoring and troubleshooting support through regular check-ins.
4. Results from pilot implementations informed refinement of the approach for broader rollout, incorporating lessons about what worked across different contexts.
5. Four additional service companies implemented customized employee engagement programmes using the proven framework with ongoing support and monitoring.

Transfer Results:

- Average employee turnover reduction of 38% across implementing companies.
- Estimated annual savings of €840,000 from reduced recruitment and training costs.
- Improved customer satisfaction scores averaging 23% increase.
- Enhanced employer brand supporting talent acquisition in competitive labour markets.

Summit Peak Facility Services adopted Alpine Foods' customer advisory panel approach, while Solid Hej Components implemented similar supplier partnership programmes, demonstrating how authentic ESG practices transferred across different business models when properly adapted.

Common Questions Alex Fields

Q: How do you prevent knowledge sharing from becoming just more meetings without value?

A: Make it concrete and action oriented. Summit Peak Facility's knowledge transfer was not about sharing philosophy—it was documented playbooks, implementation mentoring, and results tracking. We measured success by adoption rates and performance improvements, not by meeting attendance. If knowledge sharing does not generate measurable results within six months, we kill it.

Q: What if companies resist sharing practices because they see portfolio peers as competitors?

A: That is a fund culture issue, not an ESG issue. We made clear that competitive advantage comes from execution excellence, not information hoarding. Companies that shared generously got first access to learnings from others. Those that held back found themselves isolated. The incentives aligned quickly once people saw the benefits.

Q: How do you adapt practices across different industries and company sizes?

A: Focus on principles rather than specifics. Summit Peak Facility's employee engagement approach was about systematic feedback, responsive action, and recognition systems—applicable anywhere. The specific survey questions, programme designs, and communication formats varied by context. We transferred the methodology, not the implementation details.

10.2 Operational Synergies and Resource Optimization

10.2.1 Collaborative Procurement and Vendor Management

Portfolio-level ESG integration created opportunities for operational synergies and resource optimization that individual companies could not achieve independently.

Consolidated Service Procurement:

Kerring Capital Partners negotiated portfolio-wide relationships with key sustainability service providers, achieving 25–40% cost savings compared to company-specific arrangements while ensuring service quality and consistency.

ESG Data Management Platform: Rather than each company licensing separate software, the portfolio-wide platform cost €125,000 annually versus €780,000 for 12 individual licenses—an 84% cost reduction while providing superior analytics and benchmarking capabilities.

Carbon Accounting Services: Consolidated contract with specialized provider reduced per-company cost from €35,000 to €18,000 annually while standardizing methodologies and enabling portfolio-level carbon footprint reporting.

Third-Party Verification: Portfolio relationship with assurance provider reduced audit costs by 30% while improving quality through reviewer familiarity with portfolio standards and expectations.
Sustainability Consulting: Framework agreement providing portfolio companies with discounted access to specialized expertise for complex challenges like circular economy implementation or supply chain sustainability programmes.

10.2.2 Joint Initiatives and Collaborative Projects

Beyond procurement efficiencies, portfolio companies collaborated on sustainability initiatives that created mutual benefits and competitive advantages.

Supply Chain Sustainability Programme:

Five manufacturing portfolio companies with overlapping supplier bases developed joint supplier sustainability programme that created value through collective action.

Programme Components:

- Shared supplier assessment framework and audit protocols.
- Collaborative capacity building and training for suppliers.
- Joint sustainability requirements and performance standards.
- Coordinated improvement initiatives and best practice sharing.
- Collective purchasing power for sustainable materials.

Programme Results:

- Supplier sustainability performance improved 34% on average across participating suppliers.
- Shared programme costs 60% less than individual company initiatives.
- Enhanced supply chain resilience through supplier relationship strengthening.
- Competitive advantage in customer relationships citing supply chain sustainability.

Renewable Energy Procurement:

Three companies with operations in similar geographic regions collaborated on renewable energy procurement, achieving pricing and contract terms that individual companies could not negotiate.

Collaborative Procurement Benefits:

- 15% lower energy costs through consolidated purchasing volume.
- Improved contract terms including price stability and long-term supply security.

- Enhanced sustainability credentials through verified renewable energy sourcing.
- Reduced procurement complexity and administrative burden.

10.2.3 Technology Platform Leverage

The portfolio-wide technology platform created value beyond cost savings through advanced analytics, benchmarking capabilities, and decision support that individual systems could not provide.

Cross-Portfolio Analytics:

- Identification of performance patterns and best practices across portfolio.
- Benchmarking enabling companies to assess relative performance and improvement opportunities.
- Predictive modelling based on portfolio-wide data rather than company-specific information.
- Early warning systems identifying emerging issues before they became problems.

Efficiency and Automation:

- Automated data collection reducing manual effort by 67% compared to spreadsheet-based approaches.
- Standardized reporting templates satisfying multiple stakeholder requirements.
- Real-time dashboards providing current performance visibility to management and investors.
- Integration with financial systems enabling comprehensive performance assessment.

At Alpine Foods, the integrated platform revealed energy consumption patterns that manual analysis had missed, leading to €67,000 in additional annual savings through targeted efficiency improvements.

10.3 Competitive Positioning and Market Differentiation

10.3.1 LP Fundraising Advantage

Portfolio-level ESG integration created competitive advantages in limited partner fundraising that individual company successes alone could not provide.

By 2024, the Institutional Limited Partners Association reported that 67% of LPs required specific ESG reporting from their general partners, and 84% considered ESG factors when making allocation decisions. This was not ideological pressure—it reflected recognition that ESG factors materially affected investment performance.

Kerring Capital Partners 2023 Fundraising Evolution

"Our latest fundraising was completely different from previous rounds," Alex recounted. "Where we used to spend 80% of LP meetings discussing track record and investment strategy, we now spend 40% on ESG integration methodology, stakeholder engagement frameworks, and sustainability performance measurement."

LPs were asking increasingly sophisticated questions that required systematic portfolio-level approaches rather than company-specific anecdotes:

- How do you identify material ESG factors for different industries?
- What is your approach to portfolio company capability building?
- How do you measure ESG impact and attribute it to financial performance?
- What systems ensure ESG integration throughout the investment lifecycle?
- How do ESG capabilities affect exit valuations and buyer interest?

Fund Performance Evidence

Kerring Capital Partners' current fund achieved 8.2% higher IRR compared to the previous fund, demonstrating the financial value of systematic ESG integration. This performance differential proved compelling to LPs evaluating allocation decisions.

The portfolio-wide approach created credibility that individual success stories could not match. Rather than cherry-picking one or two ESG successes, the firm could demonstrate systematic integration across all investments with consistent methodologies and measurable results.

10.3.2 Deal Sourcing Differentiation

ESG capabilities created competitive advantages in deal sourcing as investment bankers and business owners increasingly preferred buyers with sophisticated sustainability approaches.

Seller Preference Factors:

Capability Recognition: Sellers with strong ESG practices wanted buyers who would recognize and preserve their sustainability achievements rather than viewing them as costs to cut. Kerring Capital Partners' portfolio-wide ESG integration demonstrated commitment that resonated with sustainability-conscious sellers.

Value Maximization: Investment bankers increasingly understood that ESG capabilities created exit value premiums, making sustainability-sophisticated buyers more attractive than those treating ESG as compliance burden. Kerring Capital Partners' track record of ESG-enhanced exits provided compelling evidence.

Cultural Fit: Family-owned businesses and founder-led companies often valued sustainability for intrinsic reasons beyond financial returns. Kerring Capital Partners' authentic ESG commitment created cultural alignment that differentiated them from purely financial buyers.
Employee Continuity: Sellers concerned about employee welfare post-sale found confidence in Kerring Capital Partners' demonstrated commitment to workforce development and engagement across their portfolio.

At Alpine Foods, the family owners specifically cited Kerring Capital Partners' ESG track record as determining factor in selecting them over a higher financial bid. "The extra €2 million they offered was not worth risking the sustainability practices we had spent decades building," explained the founding family.

10.3.3 Industry Leadership and Thought Leadership

Portfolio-level ESG excellence created opportunities for industry leadership that enhanced competitive positioning and stakeholder relationships.

Industry Association Engagement

Kerring Capital Partners' systematic approach enabled active participation in private equity industry ESG initiatives, contributing to standard development and best practice sharing. This engagement created visibility, credibility, and early insights into emerging requirements.

Ivie Chen served on the Institutional Limited Partners Association ESG working group, providing input on emerging disclosure standards while gaining advance knowledge of LP expectation evolution. This involvement positioned Kerring Capital Partners at the forefront of industry developments.

Thought Leadership Platform

The firm's portfolio-wide results enabled credible thought leadership through conference presentations, research publications, and media engagement. Unlike firms with one or two ESG success stories, Kerring Capital Partners could demonstrate systematic integration with statistical validation.

Alex's conference presentations on portfolio-level ESG optimization attracted both LP interest and deal flow from sustainability-focused sellers. The firm's reputation as ESG leader created competitive advantages that compounded over time.

Academic and Research Collaboration

Partnership with universities and research institutions on ESG methodology development created access to cutting-edge thinking while validating the firm's approaches through academic rigour. These collaborations produced case studies, research papers, and teaching materials that enhanced reputation while generating actionable insights.

Common Questions Alex Fields

Q: How do you demonstrate portfolio-level ESG impact to LPs without revealing sensitive company information?

A: Aggregate data and anonymized case studies. We show portfolio-average improvements (23% EBITDA margin increase, 34% customer satisfaction improvement) without identifying specific companies. For detailed examples, we get company permission or use disguised names. LPs understand confidentiality requirements—they want evidence of systematic approach, not company-specific details.

Q: Does portfolio-level focus take resources away from individual company needs?

A: It is multiplicative, not competitive. Summit Peak Facility's employee engagement programme cost €180K to develop. Seven other companies implemented adapted versions for €40K each because they leveraged Summit Peak Facility's learning. Total portfolio investment was €460K versus €1.26M if each built independently. We spent less while achieving better results.

Q: How do you maintain portfolio-level coordination without creating bureaucracy?

A: Focus on high-value activities with clear ROI. We do not coordinate everything—just areas where collaboration creates measurable advantages. Quarterly CEO forums, specialized working groups on specific challenges, and digital knowledge repositories enable connection without excessive meetings. If an initiative requires more than 4 hours monthly per company, it needs strong justification.

10.4 Performance Measurement and Value Attribution

10.4.1 Portfolio-Level Metrics Framework

Measuring portfolio-level ESG impact required frameworks that aggregated individual company performance while identifying synergies and network effects that created additional value.

Aggregate Performance Indicators

PORTFOLIO-WIDE IMPROVEMENTS:

- Average EBITDA margin improvement: 23% over holding period.
- Average customer satisfaction increase: 34%.
- Average employee engagement improvement: 41%.

- Average energy efficiency gain: 27%.
- Average carbon footprint reduction: 31%.

SYNERGY VALUE QUANTIFICATION:

Knowledge Transfer Value: €840,000 annual savings from Summit Peak Facility Services employee engagement programme transfer, calculated as cost avoided versus independent development.
Procurement Efficiency: €655,000 annual savings from consolidated vendor relationships, measured as difference between portfolio pricing and company-specific alternatives.
Technology Platform ROI: €325,000 annual value from analytics and automation that individual systems could not provide, quantified through time savings and performance improvements.
Joint Initiative Benefits: €780,000 annual value from collaborative supply chain and renewable energy programmes, calculated as benefits exceeding what individual companies could achieve.
Total Portfolio Synergy Value: €2.6 million annually beyond individual company improvements—representing 15% of total ESG value creation attributable specifically to portfolio-level integration.

10.4.2 Fund-Level ROI Analysis

Kerring Capital Partners conducted comprehensive analysis of ESG investment and returns at both company and portfolio levels to validate the business case for systematic integration.

Fund-Level ESG Investment (Three-Year Period):

- Portfolio company ESG initiatives: €4.8 million.
- Fund-level infrastructure and resources: €950,000.
- Total ESG investment: €5.75 million.

Fund-Level ESG Returns (Annual):

- Company-specific value creation: €8.2 million annually.
- Portfolio synergy value: €2.6 million annually.
- Total annual value: €10.8 million.

Fund-Level ESG ROI:

- 3-year ROI: 188% (€5.75M investment generating €10.8M annual returns).
- IRR differential: 8.2% higher than previous fund without systematic ESG integration.
- Exit multiple premium: 1.3× average across ESG-integrated companies.

This portfolio-level analysis demonstrated that ESG integration generated returns justifying resource allocation while creating competitive advantages in fundraising, deal sourcing, and exit positioning.

10.4.3 Attribution Methodology

Distinguishing ESG value creation from other performance improvements required rigorous attribution methodologies that could withstand LP scrutiny and academic review.

Controlled Comparison Approach

Kerring Capital Partners compared ESG-integrated companies against portfolio companies from previous funds with similar characteristics but without systematic sustainability integration. This before–after comparison controlled for industry effects, market conditions, and general operational improvement capabilities.

Regression Analysis

Statistical analysis of ESG performance metrics against financial outcomes across 47 portfolio companies over the most recent eight years (where ESG integration was systematic) revealed significant correlations between sustainability integration and returns. Companies in the top quartile of ESG integration achieved 8.9 percentage points higher IRR than bottom quartile peers.

Buyer Verification

Exit processes provided external validation of ESG value attribution. Buyer due diligence reports and bid rationale letters explicitly quantified premiums attributed to sustainability capabilities, providing independent confirmation of value creation claims.

At Solid Hej Components, the winning buyer's analysis isolated €12–15 million of exit premium specifically attributable to ESG infrastructure—tangible market validation of sustainability value that no internal analysis could provide.

10.5 Scaling Best Practices and Continuous Improvement

10.5.1 Systematic Capability Building

Portfolio-level ESG excellence required systematic approaches to building capabilities across investment teams, portfolio company management, and operational personnel.

Investment Team ESG Training

All investment professionals completed comprehensive ESG training covering materiality assessment, due diligence integration, value creation planning, and exit positioning. This training ensured that sustainability considerations were embedded in investment processes rather than treated as specialist function.

Annual ESG Module Updates:

- Regulatory developments and compliance requirements.
- Emerging best practices and methodology improvements.
- Portfolio performance analysis and lessons learned.
- Industry trend assessment and strategic implications.

Portfolio Company Leadership Development

Kerring Capital Partners developed CEO and CFO sustainability leadership programmes that built capability for driving ESG integration within their organizations. This investment in human capital created lasting value that persisted beyond ownership periods.

Leadership Programme Components:

- Strategic ESG integration and business case development.
- Stakeholder engagement and relationship management.
- Performance measurement and continuous improvement.
- Communication and storytelling for various audiences.

Operational Personnel Training

Front-line managers and operational staff received role-specific ESG training enabling them to implement sustainability initiatives effectively within their functional areas.

Table 10.1 Stakeholder mapping matrix (portfolio level)

Quadrant	*Stakeholder Type*	*Engagement Strategy*
High Interest High Influence (Manage Closely)	• Board members • Key investors/LPs • Senior management • Major customers	• Regular one-on-one meetings • Strategic input solicitation • Early involvement in decisions • Detailed progress reporting
High Interest Low Influence (Keep Informed)	• Employees • Local community • Industry associations • NGOs	• Regular updates • Feedback channels • Transparency • Responsive communication
Low Interest High Influence (Keep Satisfied)	• Regulators • Financial institutions • Industry analysts • Rating agencies	• Meet requirements • Proactive compliance • Professional relationships • Periodic updates
Low Interest Low Influence (Monitor)	• General public • Distant suppliers • Peripheral competitors	• General communications • Monitor for changes • Minimal direct engagement

Functional Training Modules:

- Operations: Energy efficiency, waste reduction, safety excellence.
- Sales: Sustainability value propositions and customer engagement.
- HR: Employee engagement, development, and retention.
- Finance: ESG financial analysis and investment evaluation.
- R&D: Sustainable innovation and competitive advantage.

10.5.2 *Performance Review and Learning Systems*

Continuous improvement required systematic processes for evaluating performance, identifying lessons, and implementing refinements across the portfolio.

Quarterly Portfolio Reviews

Regular assessment of ESG performance across all portfolio companies enabled identification of trends, challenges, and opportunities requiring attention or resource allocation.

Review Process:

- Performance data analysis and benchmarking.
- Challenge identification and problem-solving.
- Best practice sharing and knowledge transfer.
- Resource allocation and priority setting.
- Stakeholder feedback integration.

Annual Strategy Sessions

Comprehensive annual reviews brought together investment team, portfolio company leaders, and external experts to assess ESG strategy effectiveness and plan future priorities.

Strategy Session Outcomes:

- ESG methodology refinements based on lessons learned.
- Resource allocation decisions for upcoming year.
- Priority initiatives and capability building focus.
- External relationship development and partnership opportunities.
- Competitive positioning and differentiation strategies.

10.5.3 *External Benchmark and Validation*

Portfolio-level performance required external validation through industry benchmarking, third-party assessment, and stakeholder feedback to ensure credibility and identify improvement opportunities.

Industry Benchmarking

Participation in industry benchmarking initiatives enabled Kerring Capital Partners to assess portfolio performance against peers while contributing to industry knowledge development.

The firm's portfolio performance placed them in the top quartile of PE firms for ESG integration maturity and financial performance attribution, providing external validation of their systematic approach.

Third-Party Assessment

Independent evaluation by ESG rating agencies and assessment firms provided objective performance feedback and stakeholder credibility. Kerring Capital Partners achieved high scores across major ESG assessment frameworks, supporting LP communications and competitive positioning.

LP Feedback Integration

Systematic collection and analysis of LP feedback on ESG reporting, performance, and strategy informed continuous improvement of fund-level capabilities and communication approaches.

LP satisfaction surveys showed 94% agreement that Kerring Capital Partners' ESG integration created value, with 87% rating the firm as best-in-class among their PE relationships for sustainability capabilities.

10.6 Future Evolution of Portfolio-Level Integration

10.6.1 Predictive Analytics and AI

Looking forward, Alex anticipated that technology would enable more sophisticated portfolio optimization through predictive analytics and artificial intelligence applications.

Pattern Recognition Across Portfolio

Machine learning algorithms could analyse performance data across all portfolio companies to identify patterns and success factors that human analysis might miss. These insights could inform investment decisions, value creation planning, and resource allocation with unprecedented precision.

Predictive Modelling

AI-powered models could forecast which ESG initiatives would generate highest returns for specific company contexts based on historical portfolio data and industry benchmarks. This capability would enable more efficient resource allocation and faster implementation.

Real-Time Optimization

Advanced analytics could provide real-time recommendations for portfolio-level resource allocation, identifying where additional investment or support would generate highest marginal returns across the portfolio.

10.6.2 Ecosystem Development and Partnership Networks

Portfolio-level integration would evolve towards broader ecosystem development, creating networks that extended beyond the fund to include suppliers, customers, service providers, and industry partners.

Industry Collaboration

Multiple PE firms collaborating on ESG methodology development, best-practice sharing, and industry standard advancement could accelerate innovation while reducing individual firm costs of capability development.

Supply Chain Integration

Portfolio-wide supply chain sustainability programmes could create value through collective action that individual companies could not achieve, particularly in industries with concentrated supplier bases serving multiple portfolio companies.

Technology Platform Evolution

Industry-wide technology platforms aggregating ESG data across multiple PE firms and thousands of portfolio companies could enable sophisticated benchmarking and analytics that fund-specific systems could not provide.

As the Kerring Capital Partners' annual portfolio review concluded, the transformation from company-specific to portfolio-wide ESG strategy had fundamentally changed how the firm created value, competed for deals, and positioned itself with limited partners.

"Three years ago, we treated ESG as 12 separate company initiatives," Alex reflected in the closing presentation. "Today, we have built a portfolio-level competitive capability that amplifies individual company improvements while creating synergies that none of them could achieve independently. The result is 8.2% higher IRR and exit multiples averaging 1.3× above our previous fund."

Jim Kerring smiled. "The question is no longer whether ESG creates value. The question is how to continue building on these advantages as competition intensifies and stakeholder expectations evolve."

"That is exactly the right question," Alex replied. "And the answer lies in maintaining our focus on business fundamentals while staying ahead of regulatory developments, technology innovations, and market evolution. Portfolio-level integration gives us systematic capabilities that competitors cannot easily replicate—sustainable competitive advantages in the truest sense."

The portfolio optimization journey demonstrated that ESG integration's ultimate value came not from individual company improvements alone, but from systematic approaches that created network effects, operational synergies, and strategic positioning advantages. Firms that mastered portfolio-level integration would increasingly outperform those treating sustainability as company-specific operational initiative.

As Kerring Capital Partners had discovered, the path from ESG compliance to competitive advantage ran through systematic portfolio integration—building capabilities, sharing knowledge, and creating synergies that transformed sustainability from cost centre to value driver at the fund level.

Chapter Summary

Core Insight

Portfolio-level ESG integration creates value exceeding individual company improvements through network effects, operational synergies, and strategic positioning. Kerring Capital Partners' fund-level approach generated 8.2% higher IRR compared to previous fund, with €2.6M annual synergy value (24% of total ESG value creation) attributable specifically to portfolio-level coordination beyond company-specific initiatives.

Critical Success Factors

- **Fund-level infrastructure:** Dedicated ESG director, standardized frameworks, and portfolio-wide technology platform (€125K annual investment generating €450K value through efficiency).
- **Systematic knowledge transfer:** Summit Peak Facility Services employee engagement programme transferred to seven companies generating €840K annual savings versus independent development.
- **Procurement optimization:** Consolidated vendor relationships achieving 25–40% cost savings (€655K annually) while improving service quality and consistency.
- **Performance measurement:** Portfolio-level metrics showing 23% EBITDA improvement, 34% customer satisfaction increase, 41% employee engagement gains across all companies.
- **LP competitive advantage:** 67% of LPs require ESG reporting, 84% consider ESG in allocations—systematic integration creates fundraising differentiation.

Watch Out For

⚠ Treating ESG as 12 separate initiatives instead of one integrated portfolio capability wastes synergy opportunities.
⚠ Knowledge hoarding by companies viewing portfolio peers as competitors undermines network effects.
⚠ Excessive coordination creating bureaucracy rather than value—focus only on high-ROI collaborative activities.
⚠ Inadequate attribution methodology making it difficult to demonstrate portfolio-level value to LPs.

Tools You Can Use Now

- **Knowledge Transfer Framework:** Six-step process (success identification, documentation, adaptation, dissemination, support, monitoring) with Summit Peak Facility Services case example.
- **Synergy Value Framework:** Three categories (procurement efficiency, joint initiatives, technology leverage) generating €2.6M annual portfolio value.
- **Performance Attribution Model:** Controlled comparison, regression analysis, and buyer verification methodologies isolating ESG value.
- **Best Practice Development System:** Structured approach to capturing, refining, and scaling successful initiatives across portfolio.
- **Fund-Level ROI Calculator:** Investment (€5.75M) versus returns (€10.8M annually) with 188% one-year payback (€10.8M annual returns versus €5.75M cumulative investment) and 8.2% IRR differential.

What's Next

Chapter 11 demonstrates how technology transforms ESG integration from administrative burden to strategic capability through artificial intelligence, IoT monitoring, blockchain verification, and digital engagement platforms. You will discover practical approaches to technology selection, implementation, and optimization across different organisational contexts, with frameworks that show how digital tools enhance sustainability performance while reducing compliance costs and improving stakeholder engagement.

References

Bain & Company. (2022). Global Private Equity Report 2022: ESG integration and value creation. Bain & Company.

Institutional Limited Partners Association. (2024). ESG considerations for limited partners: A best practice guide. ILPA.

KPMG (2025). Value Creation in Private Equity (Paper/Report, 28 October).

McKinsey & Company. (2020). Does ESG really matter—and why? How environmental, social, and governance factors create value. McKinsey Quarterly.

11 Technology and Digital Transformation for ESG Excellence

The Technology Revolution in ESG

"We are spending more time collecting data than actually improving performance."

Marcus Weber's frustration echoed across the conference room at Apex Industries. As Head of Operations, he had watched his team's administrative burden multiply as ESG requirements expanded. What had started as quarterly sustainability reporting now consumed 40 hours monthly across multiple spreadsheets, manual data collection processes, and stakeholder communication efforts.

"Look at this," Marcus continued, pulling up a spreadsheet showing energy consumption data. "We have sensors on every major piece of equipment, but someone still walks around with a clipboard every week recording readings. Then we manually enter data into spreadsheets, aggregate it for monthly reports, and by the time we identify problems, we have lost weeks of potential savings."

Alex Morgan had seen this pattern across portfolio companies: organizations drowning in ESG data collection while missing opportunities that technology could unlock. The challenge was not lack of commitment or resources; it was approaching sustainability measurement and management with 20th-century tools in a 21st-century business environment.

Research supported the technology imperative. McKinsey & Company (2023) found that companies leveraging advanced analytics and automation for ESG management achieved 40% lower compliance costs while identifying 30% more value creation opportunities than those relying on manual processes. The technology gap was becoming a competitive advantage gap.

"What if we could automate most of this data collection and get real-time insights instead of month-old reports?" Alex proposed. "The technology exists—IoT sensors, automated data aggregation, predictive analytics that identifies optimization opportunities before they become problems. The question is not whether to invest in technology, but how to do it strategically."

Over the following months, Apex Industries would implement an integrated ESG technology platform that transformed their approach from reactive compliance to proactive performance management. The results would demonstrate that technology was not just an efficiency tool—it was an enabler of sustainability excellence that manual processes could never achieve.

DOI: 10.4324/9781003625636-14

11.1 The Strategic Technology Framework

11.1.1 Technology as Competitive Advantage

The fundamental insight was that ESG technology investments created competitive advantages beyond operational efficiency. Companies with superior data collection, analysis, and optimization capabilities could identify opportunities faster, implement improvements more effectively, and demonstrate performance more credibly than competitors relying on traditional approaches.

Four Strategic Technology Roles:

Data Foundation: Technology provided reliable, consistent, and timely data that enabled evidence-based decision-making rather than intuition or periodic assessments. Automated data collection reduced errors while improving coverage and frequency.
Performance Optimization: Advanced analytics identified patterns and opportunities that human analysis might miss, enabling continuous improvement rather than episodic initiatives. Predictive modelling allowed proactive management instead of reactive responses.
Stakeholder Engagement: Digital platforms enabled more effective communication and collaboration with employees, customers, suppliers, and community stakeholders, strengthening relationships while reducing administrative burden.
Competitive Differentiation: Technology sophistication signalled organizational maturity and capability to customers, investors, and potential acquirers, creating intangible value beyond operational benefits.

11.1.2 Scalable Technology Approaches

Alex learned that effective ESG technology implementation required matching sophistication to organizational capabilities and resources. Companies that over-invested in complex systems before building basic competencies often wasted resources, while those that under-invested found themselves competitively disadvantaged.

Table 11.1 ESG technology maturity framework by company size

Company Size	*Basic Stage*	*Intermediate*	*Advanced*
Small (<€50M revenue)	Spreadsheets Manual tracking €5–15K	Cloud platforms Basic automation €15–50K	Integrated systems Basic analytics €50–100K
Medium (€50–250M)	Basic software Semi-automated €50–100K	ERP integration Dashboards €100–250K	Advanced analytics IoT sensors €250–500K
Large (>€250M)	Enterprise systems Automated collection €200–500K	Full integration Real-time analytics €500K–1M	AI/ML platforms Predictive analytics €1M+

Small Company Solutions (<€50M revenue):

- Cloud-based platforms requiring minimal IT infrastructure.
- Mobile applications enabling field data collection.
- Integrated spreadsheet tools with automation capabilities.
- Subscription-based services with operational expense models.
- **Investment Range:** €15,000–40,000 annually.
- **Expected Benefits:** 50–60% administrative time reduction, improved data quality.

Medium Company Solutions (€50–250M revenue):

- Enterprise platforms integrating ESG with financial systems.
- IoT sensors providing real-time environmental monitoring.
- Advanced analytics with dashboards and reporting automation.
- Custom integration with existing business systems.
- **Investment Range:** €50,000–150,000 annually.
- **Expected Benefits:** 60–70% efficiency improvement, predictive insights, stakeholder engagement enhancement.

Large Company Solutions (>€250M revenue):

- Comprehensive platforms with AI-powered optimization.
- Distributed data architecture for multi-site operations.
- Advanced predictive analytics and scenario modelling.
- Blockchain verification for supply chain transparency.
- **Investment Range:** €100,000–300,000 annually.
- **Expected Benefits:** Industry leadership positioning, significant performance improvement, innovation platform development.

Common Questions Alex Fields

Q: How do you justify technology investments when ROI is uncertain?

A: Start with quick wins that generate measurable returns. At Solid Hej Components, we began with energy monitoring IoT sensors costing €12,000 that identified €45,000 in annual savings within three months. That success funded broader platform investment. Pilot projects with clear business cases build credibility for larger initiatives.

Q: What if our company lacks technical expertise to implement sophisticated ESG technology?

A: Choose vendor-supported cloud platforms rather than custom development. Alpine Foods had one part-time IT person but successfully implemented comprehensive ESG management through Software-as-a-Service platform with vendor training and support. Technical sophistication should be in the platform, not necessarily in your team.

Q: How do you prevent technology from becoming "shelfware" that nobody uses?

A: Change management matters more than technical capabilities. We ensure executive sponsorship, comprehensive training, clear performance incentives, and continuous support. At Summit Peak Services, management compensation included technology adoption metrics—usage went from 40% to 95% within six months. Accountability drives adoption.

A further scaling driver is the expanding scope of decision-useful sustainability information beyond climate into nature-related risk. In October 2025, the ISSB publicly discussed how the TNFD framework may inform its work on biodiversity, ecosystems, and ecosystem services disclosures (IFRS Foundation, 2025). TNFD also noted in November 2025 that ISSB has signalled an intention to pursue new or modified disclosure requirements to meet investor information needs on nature-related risks and opportunities (TNFD, 2025). For private equity, this points to increased use of geospatial data, traceability, and verification tools where nature dependencies or impacts are material (IFRS Foundation, 2025; TNFD, 2025)

11.2 Artificial Intelligence and Machine Learning Applications

11.2.1 Predictive Analytics for Performance Optimization

AI-powered predictive analytics enabled organizations to anticipate problems and identify opportunities before they became apparent through traditional monitoring, creating proactive rather than reactive sustainability management.

Table 11.2 AI applications in ESG management

Application	*Use Cases*	*Value Delivered*
Predictive Analytics	• Energy consumption forecasting • Maintenance prediction • Quality issue detection • Risk early warnings	15–25% efficiency gains Proactive problem solving Cost avoidance Improved planning
Supply Chain Intelligence	• Supplier risk monitoring • ESG compliance tracking • Alternative sourcing identification • Carbon footprint optimization	Enhanced visibility Risk mitigation 10–20% emissions reduction Supplier performance
Stakeholder Sentiment	• Employee engagement analysis • Customer feedback processing • Social media monitoring • Reputation tracking	Real-time insights Early issue detection Improved response Trend identification
Reporting Automation	• Data aggregation • Report generation • Compliance checking • Multi-framework mapping	80% time savings Error reduction Consistent quality Faster closing

Energy Consumption Optimization

Solid Hej Components implemented machine learning algorithms that analysed energy consumption patterns across their manufacturing facilities, identifying optimization opportunities that manual analysis had missed.

Optimization Results:

- 15% additional energy savings beyond traditional efficiency improvements.
- €92,000 annual value from AI-identified opportunities.
- Predictive maintenance reducing equipment downtime by 23%.
- Real-time optimization adjusting operations based on energy pricing and demand.

The AI system learned from historical data and continuously refined recommendations as new patterns emerged. What had required quarterly engineering reviews now happened automatically, with human oversight focused on strategic decisions rather than routine optimization.

11.2.2 Supply Chain Risk Assessment and Management

Machine learning algorithms analysed supplier performance data, risk indicators, and sustainability metrics to identify optimization opportunities and potential issues before they disrupted operations.

Assessment Capabilities:

- Automated scoring and ranking of supplier sustainability performance.
- Risk assessment based on geographic, industry, and operational factors.
- Performance trend analysis identifying improvement or deterioration patterns.
- Benchmarking against industry standards and best practices.

Development Applications:

- Personalized improvement recommendations based on supplier characteristics.
- Training programme optimization based on individual supplier needs.
- Collaboration opportunity identification for joint sustainability initiatives.
- Progress monitoring and recognition programmes encouraging continuous improvement.

At Ridgeline Solutions, AI-powered supplier assessment identified three high-risk suppliers before issues affected operations, enabling proactive engagement that prevented €340,000 in potential disruptions while improving sustainability performance across the supply chain.

11.2.3 Stakeholder Sentiment Analysis

Natural language processing algorithms analysed social media posts, news coverage, and stakeholder communications to assess sentiment and identify emerging issues, providing early warning of potential problems and insights into stakeholder expectations.

Monitoring Capabilities:

- Real-time sentiment tracking across social media and news sources.
- Issue identification and escalation based on sentiment trends.
- Competitive analysis comparing stakeholder perception across industry peers.
- Trend analysis identifying emerging stakeholder concerns.

Engagement Optimization:

- Communication strategy optimization based on stakeholder response patterns.
- Timing and channel optimization for maximum engagement.
- Content personalization based on stakeholder interests.
- Relationship quality assessment and improvement recommendations.

Summit Peak Services' sentiment analysis revealed employee concerns about career development opportunities three months before they affected retention metrics, enabling proactive intervention that prevented turnover spike and maintained the 12% annual rate that had become competitive advantage.

11.3 Internet of Things and Real-Time Monitoring

11.3.1 Environmental Performance Monitoring

IoT sensors and connected devices enabled real-time monitoring of environmental performance across facilities and operations, providing data for immediate optimization and long-term strategic planning.

Solid Hej Components IoT Implementation:

The wind turbine manufacturer deployed comprehensive sensor networks across their production facilities, transforming environmental management from periodic assessment to continuous optimization.

Sensor Network Components:

- Energy consumption monitoring on all major equipment (250+ sensors).
- Water usage tracking across production processes (45 sensors).

- Waste generation monitoring at source points (38 sensors).
- Air-quality sensors monitoring emissions (12 sensors).
- Temperature and humidity sensors optimizing HVAC (67 sensors).

Implementation Results:

- Real-time visibility enabling immediate response to anomalies.
- €89,000 annual savings from optimization opportunities identified through continuous monitoring.
- Automated alerts preventing equipment failures and efficiency losses.
- Historical data enabling trend analysis and strategic planning.
- Regulatory compliance documentation automatically generated from sensor data.

"The transformation was remarkable," explained Solid Hej's operations director. "We went from monthly energy reports telling us what happened weeks ago to real-time dashboards showing current performance and recommending immediate actions. Problems that used to cost thousands before we discovered them now trigger alerts within minutes."

11.3.2 Workplace Safety and Employee Wellbeing

IoT applications extended beyond environmental monitoring to workplace safety and employee wellbeing, creating healthier work environments while reducing incident risks and insurance costs.

Safety Monitoring Systems:

- Wearable devices tracking worker location and environmental exposure.
- Air-quality sensors monitoring indoor environmental quality.
- Ergonomic sensors identifying repetitive strain risk patterns.
- Environmental sensors detecting hazardous conditions.
- Emergency alert systems enabling rapid response to incidents.

Wellbeing Applications:

- Occupancy sensors optimizing workspace utilization and comfort.
- Lighting systems adjusting based on natural light and occupancy.
- Temperature control optimizing comfort and energy efficiency.
- Acoustic monitoring ensuring appropriate noise levels.
- Stress indicator monitoring through environmental quality assessment.

At Apex Industries, workplace safety IoT implementation reduced recordable incidents by 47% while improving employee satisfaction scores by 12 percentage points through demonstrable commitment to worker wellbeing.

11.3.3 Asset Performance and Maintenance Optimization

IoT sensors enabled predictive maintenance approaches that reduced downtime while improving energy efficiency and equipment lifespan, creating operational and sustainability benefits simultaneously.

Predictive Maintenance Benefits:

- 30–40% reduction in unplanned downtime.
- 15–25% improvement in equipment energy efficiency.
- 20–30% extension of asset useful life.
- Reduced maintenance costs through optimized scheduling.
- Improved safety through proactive hazard identification.

The technology investment typically achieved 18–24-month payback through operational benefits alone, with sustainability improvements representing additional value that buyers recognized at exit.

Common Questions Alex Fields

Q: Is IoT implementation too expensive for smaller companies?
A: Not with modern cloud-connected sensors. Alpine Foods deployed 45 energy monitoring sensors for €18,000 total—€400 per sensor including installation and cloud platform access. The system identified €67,000 annual savings within first year. Technology costs have dropped 70% over five years, making it accessible to companies of all sizes.
Q: How do you prevent IoT data overload where you have more information than you can act on?
A: Focus on actionable metrics with automated alerts. We configure systems to flag only anomalies requiring attention—consumption spikes, efficiency drops, safety concerns. Solid Hej's 400+ sensors generate maybe 5–10 alerts daily that actually need human response. Everything else runs automatically in the background.
Q: What about cybersecurity risks from connected devices?
A: Valid concern requiring systematic management. We use industrial-grade IoT platforms with enterprise security, segregated networks isolating IoT from business systems, regular security audits, and vendor security assessments. Security is non-negotiable, but manageable with proper architecture and vendor selection.

11.4 Blockchain and Verification Technologies

11.4.1 Supply Chain Transparency and Traceability

Blockchain technology enabled transparent and verifiable tracking of products and materials through complex supply chains, creating credibility for sustainability claims while identifying risk and improvement opportunities.

Ridgeline Solutions Blockchain Implementation:

The sustainable packaging manufacturer implemented blockchain-based supply chain tracking to verify claims about recycled content and sustainable sourcing, creating competitive advantage through credible transparency.

Implementation Components:

- Digital product passports tracking material provenance.
- Supplier verification system ensuring sustainability credentials.
- Quality and safety data immutably recorded at each supply chain stage.
- Customer access portal providing transparency and verification.
- Integration with certification bodies and auditing organizations.

Business Results:

- Premium pricing of 8–12% based on verified sustainability claims.
- New customer wins requiring supply chain transparency (€2.1M annual revenue).
- Reduced audit costs through automated compliance verification.
- Enhanced brand reputation through demonstrable transparency.
- Competitive differentiation in markets where greenwashing concerns existed.

11.4.2 Carbon Credit and Offset Verification

Blockchain applications enabled transparent tracking and verification of carbon credits and environmental offsets, creating confidence in climate commitments while preventing double-counting and fraud.

Verification Benefits:

- Immutable record of carbon credit generation and retirement.
- Prevention of double-counting across different reporting frameworks.
- Transparent audit trail for regulatory compliance and stakeholder confidence.
- Automated matching of offsets to specific emissions sources.
- Real-time visibility into carbon neutrality progress.

11.4.3 Circular Economy and Waste Stream Tracking

Blockchain enabled tracking of materials through circular economy loops, verifying recycling claims and identifying opportunities for waste stream monetization.

Circular Economy Applications:

- Material composition tracking enabling efficient recycling.
- Waste stream origin verification ensuring quality and safety.

- Product life-cycle management from manufacture through disposal.
- Secondary market facilitation for reused or recycled materials.
- Performance data informing product design improvements.

Ridgeline Solutions's circular economy blockchain implementation created €890,000 annual revenue from waste streams previously considered disposal costs, demonstrating how technology could transform sustainability from cost centre to profit generator.

11.5 Digital Stakeholder Engagement Platforms

11.5.1 Employee Engagement and Communication

Digital platforms enabled more effective and continuous employee engagement around sustainability initiatives, replacing periodic surveys with real-time feedback and communication.

Summit Peak Services Digital Engagement

The facilities management company implemented comprehensive digital employee engagement platform that transformed workplace culture and retention.

Platform Capabilities:

- Mobile applications enabling convenient employee participation and feedback.
- Gamification elements encouraging participation and sustainability behaviours.
- Recognition and reward systems celebrating sustainability achievements.
- Training and development platforms building sustainability knowledge.
- Anonymous feedback enabling honest communication and problem identification.

Implementation Benefits:

- Participation rates increased from 42% (annual surveys) to 87% (continuous engagement).
- Real-time feedback enabling rapid response to employee concerns.
- €230,000 annual savings from employee-suggested improvements.
- Employee satisfaction increased from 52% to 89%.
- Turnover reduced from 47% to 12% annually.

"The platform gave employees voice and visibility they never had before," explained Summit Peak's HR director. "Within three months, we received over 400 improvement suggestions, implemented 60% of them, and saw immediate engagement improvement. Employees knew their input mattered because they saw action."

11.5.2 Customer Collaboration and Partnership

Digital platforms facilitated deeper customer collaboration on sustainability initiatives, creating shared value and competitive advantages that traditional relationship management could not achieve.

Collaboration Tools:

- Joint goal setting and progress tracking systems.
- Shared sustainability reporting and transparency platforms.
- Innovation collaboration tools enabling joint product development.
- Communication platforms facilitating regular interaction and feedback.
- Performance dashboards providing real-time visibility.

Partnership Benefits:

- Stronger customer relationships through shared sustainability objectives.
- Innovation opportunities through collaborative problem-solving.
- Market differentiation through demonstrated partnership capabilities.
- Revenue enhancement through premium positioning and value-added services.

Alpine Foods' customer collaboration platform enabled joint sustainability initiatives with eight major customers, generating €340,000 annual revenue from premium products developed through collaborative innovation while strengthening relationships that supported 96% retention rate.

11.5.3 Community and Investor Engagement

Technology platforms enabled more systematic and effective engagement with community stakeholders and investors, building trust through transparency while reducing administrative burden.

Engagement Applications:

- Community feedback and communication platforms.
- Public sustainability reporting portals providing transparent performance data.
- Partnership and collaboration tools facilitating joint initiatives.
- Issue tracking and resolution systems ensuring responsive stakeholder service.
- Investor reporting platforms automating ESG disclosure.

Solid Hej Components' public sustainability dashboard received 12,000 annual visits from stakeholders seeking information, while automated investor reporting reduced disclosure preparation time by 65% compared to manual processes.

11.6 Technology Selection and Implementation

11.6.1 Vendor Evaluation Framework

Selecting appropriate technology vendors required systematic evaluation beyond feature comparisons to assess long-term partnership potential and implementation success factors.

Critical Evaluation Criteria

FUNCTIONALITY AND INTEGRATION:

- Core capabilities meeting current requirements and future growth.
- Integration with existing business systems (ERP, financial, operational).
- Customization capabilities for company-specific needs.
- Mobile accessibility and user experience quality.
- Reporting and analytics functionality.

VENDOR STABILITY AND SUPPORT:

- Financial stability and long-term viability assessment.
- Customer reference checks and satisfaction evaluation.
- Implementation support quality and responsiveness.
- Training and change management services availability.
- Product roadmap and innovation commitment.

SECURITY AND COMPLIANCE:

- Data security and privacy protections.
- Regulatory compliance capabilities (CSRD, TCFD, GRI, ISSB).
- Audit trail and verification features.
- Disaster recovery and business continuity capabilities.
- Industry certifications and third-party security assessments.

TOTAL COST OF OWNERSHIP:

- Licence or subscription costs.
- Implementation and customization expenses.
- Training and change management investment.
- Ongoing support and maintenance fees.
- Integration and data migration costs.

11.6.2 Implementation Success Factors

Technology implementation success depended more on change management and user adoption than technical capabilities. Organizations that invested adequately in training and stakeholder engagement achieved significantly better results.

Critical Success Elements:

Executive Sponsorship: Visible leadership commitment and resource allocation signalling organizational priority rather than IT project, ensuring adoption and sustained use.
Comprehensive Training: Role-specific training ensuring all users understood capabilities relevant to their responsibilities, with ongoing support rather than one-time event.
Phased Rollout: Incremental implementation enabling learning and refinement rather than big-bang approach that overwhelmed users and risked failure.
Change Champions: Internal advocates supporting peers through adoption challenges, providing peer-to-peer assistance that supplemented formal training.
Performance Incentives: Integration of technology adoption into performance management and compensation, ensuring accountability and sustained use.
Continuous Improvement: Regular user feedback collection and system refinement based on actual usage patterns rather than assuming initial configuration was optimal.

At Apex Industries, systematic change management resulted in 95% user adoption within six months versus industry average of 60% for enterprise technology implementations, demonstrating that people factors determined technology success more than technical factors.

Common Questions Alex Fields

Q: Should we build custom ESG technology or buy commercial platforms?
A: Buy unless you have unique requirements that commercial platforms cannot address. Custom development costs 3–5× more and takes 2–3 years longer than platform implementation. Solid Hej considered custom but chose commercial platform, going live in four months for €85K versus estimated €400K and 18 months for custom development. Your competitive advantage is execution, not technology ownership.
Q: How do you ensure technology actually gets used rather than becoming "shelfware"?
A: Three things: executive sponsorship making it strategic priority, comprehensive training ensuring competence and confidence, and performance incentives creating accountability. At Summit Peak, we included platform usage in manager scorecards—adoption went from 40% to 95%. Technology without accountability is just expensive software.
Q: What is the typical ROI timeline for ESG technology investments?
A: 18–24 months for comprehensive platforms through efficiency gains, faster for targeted applications. Solid Hej's IoT sensors paid back in eight months through energy savings. The key is starting with quick wins that build credibility for broader investment. Do not wait for three-year business cases—find opportunities with 12–18 month returns and expand from success.

11.7 Future Technology Trends and Opportunities

11.7.1 Advanced AI and Autonomous Optimization

Looking forward, AI systems would evolve towards autonomous optimization of sustainability performance with minimal human intervention, creating step-change improvements in efficiency and effectiveness.

Predictive Sustainability Analytics:

- Climate risk assessment and adaptation planning based on predictive modelling.
- Supply chain disruption prediction enabling proactive risk management.
- Stakeholder sentiment prediction facilitating relationship management.
- Market trend prediction informing strategic planning.

Autonomous Optimization Systems:

- Self-learning algorithms continuously improving performance.
- Automated decision-making within defined parameters.
- Real-time optimization across multiple variables simultaneously.
- Adaptive systems responding to changing conditions automatically.

11.7.2 Extended Reality and Digital Twin Applications

Virtual and augmented reality technologies would enable new approaches to training, facility design, and stakeholder engagement that enhanced sustainability outcomes.

Digital Twin Applications:

- Virtual facility models enabling optimization before physical changes.
- Scenario testing reducing risk and improving decision quality.
- Training simulations building capabilities without operational risk.
- Stakeholder visualization improving communication and engagement.

Extended Reality Benefits:

- Remote collaboration reducing travel-related emissions.
- Enhanced training effectiveness through immersive experiences.
- Improved design quality through virtual prototyping.
- Stakeholder engagement through compelling visualization.

11.7.3 Quantum Computing and Complex Modelling

As quantum computing matured, it would enable complex sustainability modelling that classical computers could not achieve, revolutionizing climate risk assessment, supply chain optimization, and material science.

Potential Applications:

- Climate modelling with unprecedented accuracy and granularity.
- Supply chain optimization across millions of variables.
- Material science discovery accelerating sustainable innovation.
- Financial modelling integrating sustainability factors comprehensively.

While quantum applications remained mostly future potential, forward-thinking organizations would position themselves to leverage these capabilities as they matured, creating competitive advantages through early adoption.

As Marcus Weber reflected on Apex Industries' technology transformation two years after that initial frustrating conversation, the change was remarkable. "We went from 120 hours monthly on data collection to 32 hours focused on strategic improvements. The technology did not just make us more efficient—it made us better at sustainability by freeing time and mental energy for actual problem-solving."

Alex smiled. "That is the entire point. Technology should not be the strategy—it should enable the strategy by removing barriers and creating capabilities that manual processes never could. The companies winning on sustainability are those using technology to amplify human judgment rather than replace it."

Technology transformed ESG from compliance burden to strategic capability, but ultimate success required winning hearts and minds across stakeholder groups. Chapter 12 provides the comprehensive playbook for putting all these pieces together—from due diligence through exit—into systematic approach that any firm can adapt to their context and objectives.

Chapter Summary

Core Insight

Technology transforms ESG from administrative burden to strategic capability by automating data collection, enabling predictive analytics, and facilitating stakeholder engagement. Solid Hej Components' €45,000 annual technology investment generated €135,000 value through automated optimization (€67K), predictive analytics (€45K), and stakeholder engagement (€23K), demonstrating 3:1 ROI while reducing administrative time 73%.

Critical Success Factors

- **Scalable approaches:** Match technology sophistication to organizational capabilities—small companies (€15–40K/year cloud platforms), medium (€50–150K enterprise systems), large (€100–300K AI-powered solutions).

- **Quick win strategy:** Solid Hej's IoT sensors (€12K investment) identified €45K annual savings in three months, building credibility for broader platform investment.
- **Change management priority:** Summit Peak's systematic adoption approach (executive sponsorship, comprehensive training, performance incentives) achieved 95% usage versus 60% industry average.
- **AI applications:** Predictive analytics, supply chain intelligence, and sentiment analysis enable proactive rather than reactive sustainability management.
- **IoT monitoring:** Real-time environmental, safety, and performance data enables immediate optimization—Solid Hej's 400+ sensors generate only 5–10 actionable alerts daily.

Watch Out For

⚠ Over-investing in complex systems before building basic competencies wastes resources and risks failure.
⚠ Treating technology as strategy rather than enabler misses the point—human judgment remains critical.
⚠ Inadequate change management causes "shelfware" problem where platforms go unused despite investment.
⚠ Custom development costing 3–5× more and taking 2–3 years longer than commercial platform implementation.

Tools You Can Use Now

- **Technology Maturity Matrix:** Company size and ESG maturity framework guiding appropriate technology selection and investment levels.
- **AI Applications Framework:** Predictive analytics, supply chain intelligence, stakeholder sentiment analysis with specific use cases.
- **IoT Implementation Model:** Solid Hej's 400+ sensor network generating €89K annual savings through real-time optimization.
- **Vendor Evaluation Framework:** Functionality, support, security, and cost criteria for systematic vendor assessment.
- **Change Management Checklist:** Executive sponsorship, training, phased rollout, champions, incentives, continuous improvement.

What's Next

Chapter 12 synthesizes all frameworks from Chapters 1–11 into a comprehensive sustainable PE playbook, providing step-by-step implementation roadmap from initial assessment through portfolio-wide optimization. The capstone chapter distils key lessons into actionable guidance that firms at any stage of ESG journey can adapt to their specific context and objectives.

References

IFRS Foundation. (2025). ISSB Update October 2025 (28 October).

McKinsey & Company. (2023). The ESG premium: New perspectives on value and performance. McKinsey Quarterly.

Taskforce on Nature-related Financial Disclosures (TNFD). (2025). TNFD welcomes ISSB decision on nature-related standard setting drawing on TNFD framework (7 November).

12 The Sustainable PE Playbook

Lessons from the Field

The Sustainable PE Playbook

"We have learned a lot over the past five years, but I am not sure we have a system that others could replicate."

The observation came from Kenyon Iken, CEO of Precision Peak Manufacturing, during the final session of Alex Morgan's sustainability leadership programme. Representatives from 12 portfolio companies had gathered to share experiences, discuss challenges, and extract lessons learned from their ESG integration journeys.

Around the table sat executives whose companies had transformed their sustainability performance, often dramatically. Building on the Solid Hej Components methodology detailed in Chapter 3, they had achieved measurable improvement in sustainability performance while generating superior financial returns. Summit Peak Services had implemented the employee engagement strategies from Chapter 6, reducing turnover from 47% to 12% annually. Ridgeline Solutions had applied the circular economy principles from Chapter 8, creating €2.1 million in new revenue streams. Alpine Foods had scaled the stakeholder value creation approaches from Chapter 6 across three new geographic markets.

But as Alex listened to the discussion, a pattern emerged. Each company had developed effective approaches through trial and error, learning from mistakes, and adapting to their unique circumstances. While the results were impressive, the knowledge remained largely tacit embedded in relationships, processes, and organizational culture rather than documented in transferable systems.

The portfolio-wide results validated systematic ESG integration: companies implementing comprehensive sustainability programmes achieved average company-level IRR improvements of 3.8 percentage points (with the fund-level differential reaching 8.2% relative to the previous Kerring fund). Yet, capturing that success in a replicable framework remained elusive.

"That is exactly why we are here," Alex responded. "To extract the systematic approaches from your individual experiences and create a playbook that new portfolio companies can follow. Not a rigid template, but a flexible framework that guides implementation while allowing adaptation to specific contexts."

DOI: 10.4324/9781003625636-15

12.1 Comprehensive Assessment and Gap Analysis

12.1.1 Current State Assessment Framework

The sustainable PE journey began with comprehensive assessment of current ESG performance, capabilities, and positioning relative to stakeholders, competitors, and best practices. This assessment provided the baseline for improvement planning and performance measurement.

Performance Assessment

Systematic evaluation of environmental, social, and governance performance using material metrics frameworks developed in Chapter 7. The assessment applied lessons learned from Solid Hej Components' energy efficiency breakthrough and Summit Peak Services' employee engagement transformation.

Performance Assessment Components:

- **Environmental:** Energy efficiency, waste management, emissions, resource consumption benchmarked against industry standards.
- **Social:** Employee satisfaction, turnover, safety performance, customer satisfaction, community relationships assessed through surveys and data analysis.
- **Governance:** Board composition, risk management systems, ethics programmes, stakeholder engagement mechanisms evaluated for effectiveness.
- **Overall:** Integration assessment determining how sustainability was embedded in business operations versus treated as separate function.

Table 12.1 Comprehensive assessment and baseline establishment

Assessment Area	*Key Questions*	*Outputs*
Current State	• What ESG data exists? • What systems are in place? • What's the compliance status? • What initiatives are underway?	• Data inventory • System assessment • Compliance scorecard • Initiative mapping
Performance Gaps	• Where do we stand vs peers? • What are material risks? • What are quick win opportunities? • What requires long-term investment?	• Benchmark comparison • Risk heat map • Opportunity matrix • Investment roadmap
Stakeholder Expectations	• What do investors expect? • What do customers demand? • What do employees value? • What does the community need?	• Stakeholder map • Expectations register • Materiality assessment • Engagement plan
Value Creation Potential	• Where can we drive EBITDA? • What enhances revenue? • What reduces risk? • What supports exit multiple?	• Value driver tree • Financial impact model • Risk-adjusted returns • Exit positioning strategy

Capability Assessment

Evaluation of organizational capabilities for sustainability management including systems, skills, governance structures, and stakeholder relationships, drawing on culture embedding strategies proven successful in Chapter 6.

Capability Assessment Elements:

- **Systems:** Data collection, performance monitoring, reporting infrastructure assessed for maturity and effectiveness.
- **Skills:** Sustainability knowledge, stakeholder engagement capabilities, continuous improvement competencies evaluated across organization.
- **Governance:** Board oversight, management accountability, cross-functional integration mechanisms reviewed for robustness.
- **Stakeholder Relationships:** Employee, customer, supplier, community relationship quality assessed as foundation for value creation.

Risk Assessment

Identification of ESG-related risks that could affect business performance including regulatory, operational, reputational, and market risks, incorporating climate scenario analysis approaches from Chapter 5.

Risk Assessment Categories:

- **Regulatory Risks:** Current compliance status and preparedness for emerging requirements like CSRD assessed.
- **Operational Risks:** Supply chain vulnerabilities, resource availability, workplace safety issues identified.
- **Reputational Risks:** Stakeholder perception, media exposure, activist concerns evaluated.
- **Market Risks:** Customer requirement evolution, competitor positioning, investor expectations analysed.

Opportunity Assessment

ESG-driven value creation opportunities including cost reduction, revenue enhancement, risk mitigation, and competitive positioning, leveraging portfolio optimization strategies from Chapter 10.

Opportunity Categories:

- **Operational Efficiency:** Energy, waste, resource optimization opportunities quantified.

- **Revenue Enhancement:** Premium positioning, new market access, customer partnership opportunities identified.
- **Risk Mitigation:** Regulatory preparedness, stakeholder relationship, operational resilience benefits assessed.
- **Competitive Positioning:** Differentiation, thought leadership, talent attraction advantages evaluated.

12.1.2 Alpine Foods Comprehensive Assessment Example

Alpine Foods' comprehensive assessment revealed how systematic evaluation could identify hidden value creation opportunities that traditional due diligence missed. The assessment applied lessons from multiple portfolio successes to identify material factors and improvement priorities.

Performance Assessment Results:

- **Environmental:** Strong local sourcing (78% within 200km) and organic certification (67% of products) but moderate energy efficiency compared to leaders.
- **Social:** Excellent employee retention (8% versus 22% industry average) but limited formal development programmes constraining innovation.
- **Governance:** Strong family values requiring formal board-level sustainability oversight mechanisms, committee structures, and reporting lines.
- **Overall:** Foundation of authentic sustainability practices requiring systematic enhancement and scalability.

Capability Assessment Findings:

- **Systems:** Basic sustainability tracking lacking integrated management systems and real-time monitoring.
- **Skills:** Strong operational expertise but limited formal sustainability knowledge and best practice awareness.
- **Governance:** Board-level sustainability oversight mechanisms, committee structures, and reporting lines that embed ESG accountability into decision-making.

Risk and Opportunity Analysis:

- **Regulatory Risk:** Growing disclosure requirements requiring enhanced reporting and verification systems.
- **Market Opportunity:** Premium positioning potential through verified sustainability leadership and competitive differentiation.
- **Operational Efficiency:** €280,000+ annual cost reduction potential through energy and waste optimization identified.
- **Revenue Enhancement:** €340,000+ potential through premium pricing and customer collaboration on sustainability initiatives.

Common Questions Alex Fields

Q: How long should the comprehensive assessment take?
A: 4–6 weeks for thorough assessment. Week 1–2: data collection and stakeholder interviews. Week 3–4: external analysis and benchmarking. Week 5–6: synthesis and prioritization. Alpine Foods took six weeks; Summit Peak Services managed in four because they had better existing data. Do not rush—comprehensive assessment prevents expensive mistakes later.
Q: Should we use external consultants or internal teams for assessment?
A: Combination works best. External consultants bring objectivity and benchmarking insights; internal teams provide context and relationship knowledge. We typically use consultants for framework and analysis, internal teams for data collection and stakeholder engagement. Costs 30–40% less than fully outsourced while building internal capability.
Q: How do you prioritize improvements when assessment reveals many opportunities?
A: Materiality and feasibility matrix. Plot opportunities by business impact (revenue, cost, risk) and implementation difficulty. Start with high-impact, low-difficulty quick wins that build credibility. Then tackle high-impact, high-difficulty strategic initiatives. Ignore low-impact regardless of difficulty—focus resources where they create value.

This prioritization discipline mirrors the direction of operating-model research in private equity. KPMG's 2025 value creation paper argues that repeatable performance depends on institutionalised capabilities—data infrastructure, functional expertise, and embedded governance—rather than ad hoc interventions (KPMG, 2025). In sustainability terms, assessment frameworks become most valuable when they translate directly into resourced plans, measurable milestones, and accountable execution.

12.2 Implementation Roadmap Development

12.2.1 Three-Phase Implementation Strategy

Alex's experience demonstrated that successful ESG integration required phased approaches balancing quick wins, strategic initiatives, and transformational goals. Companies attempting comprehensive transformation without building capabilities and stakeholder support experienced significantly higher failure rates.

Phase 1: Quick Wins (0–6 Months)

Quick win initiatives generated immediate results while building momentum and stakeholder confidence for larger transformations. These initiatives typically required minimal investment and leveraged existing organizational capabilities.

Table 12.2 Phased implementation roadmap

Phase	*Timeline*	*Investment*	*Key Milestones*
Foundation	Months 0–6	€150–300K	• Baseline established • Quick wins delivered • Governance set up • Team onboarded • Systems selected
Build	Months 6–18	€300–700K	• Systems implemented • Training complete • Metrics tracked • Early results visible • Stakeholders engaged
Scale	Months 18–36	€200–500K	• Full deployment • Performance improvement • Certifications achieved • Culture embedded • Value documented
Optimize	Months 36+	€100–300K/year	• Continuous improvement • Industry leadership • Innovation pipeline • Exit ready • Premium validated

QUICK WIN CHARACTERISTICS:

- High-impact, low-cost, short timeline (2–4 months).
- Aligned with existing business priorities and pain points.
- Visible results building credibility and support.
- Minimal organizational disruption or resistance.
- Foundation for larger strategic initiatives.

ALPINE FOODS QUICK WIN EXAMPLES:

- LED lighting retrofit: €45,000 investment, €67,000 annual savings, four-week implementation.
- Employee recognition programme: €23,000 investment, €89,000 turnover reduction, six-week launch.
- Supplier communication enhancement: €12,000 investment, €156,000 quality gains, eight-week rollout.
- Customer sustainability communication: €34,000 investment, €234,000 premium pricing, three-month programme.

Phase 2: Strategic Initiatives (6–24 Months)

Strategic initiatives required more substantial investment and longer timeframes but created competitive advantages and sustained performance improvements that quick wins could not achieve.

STRATEGIC INITIATIVE CHARACTERISTICS:

- Medium-high investment, medium-high impact, 12–18-month timeline.
- Systematic capability building and process improvement.

- Integration with business strategy and operations.
- Stakeholder engagement and relationship development.
- Measurable business impact and competitive differentiation.

STRATEGIC INITIATIVE EXAMPLES:

- Energy management systems: Comprehensive monitoring and optimization infrastructure.
- Employee engagement programmes: Systematic feedback, development, and retention initiatives.
- Customer partnership development: Collaborative innovation and shared value creation.
- Supply chain sustainability: Supplier assessment, development, and collaboration programmes.
- ISO certification: Environmental management system certification and verification.

Phase 3: Transformational Goals (18–36 Months)

Transformational initiatives created industry leadership and competitive moats that sustained advantages beyond ownership periods, requiring sustained commitment and sophisticated execution.

TRANSFORMATIONAL CHARACTERISTICS:

- High investment, transformational impact, 24–36-month timeline.
- Industry leadership positioning and thought leadership.
- Competitive advantages difficult for competitors to replicate.
- Buyer value recognition at exit through premium multiples.
- Sustained benefits beyond ownership period.

TRANSFORMATIONAL EXAMPLES:

- Circular economy implementation: Zero waste to landfill achievement.
- Carbon neutrality: Net zero operations through efficiency and offsets.
- Industry leadership: Best practice development and thought leadership.
- Technology platform: AI-powered optimization and innovation capabilities.
- Ecosystem development: Industry collaboration and partnership networks.

12.2.2 Resource Allocation and Investment Planning

Effective implementation required systematic resource allocation balancing financial investment, management attention, and organizational capacity across multiple initiatives simultaneously.

Financial Investment Framework

YEAR 1: FOUNDATION BUILDING (€100–200K TYPICAL RANGE):

- Quick wins and pilot projects: 40% of budget
- Assessment and planning: 20% of budget
- Capability building and training: 20% of budget
- Technology and systems: 20% of budget

YEAR 2: STRATEGIC SCALING (€150–300K TYPICAL RANGE):

- Strategic initiative implementation: 50% of budget
- Capability expansion: 25% of budget
- Technology enhancement: 15% of budget
- External verification: 10% of budget

YEAR 3 ONWARDS: TRANSFORMATION AND EXIT PREP (€200–500K SCALE PHASE; €100–300K/YEAR ONGOING OPTIMIZATION):

- Transformational initiatives: 40% of budget
- Exit documentation and positioning: 25% of budget
- Continuous improvement: 20% of budget
- Thought leadership: 15% of budget

Management Attention Allocation

Beyond financial resources, successful implementation required appropriate management attention and leadership commitment throughout the journey.

CEO/LEADERSHIP TIME:

- Year 1: 15–20% time on ESG strategy and stakeholder engagement.
- Year 2: 10–15% time on strategic initiative oversight and relationships.
- Year 3: 10% time on exit positioning and competitive differentiation.

FUNCTIONAL LEADERSHIP TIME:

- Operations: 20–25% on efficiency and operational excellence initiatives.
- HR: 25–30% on employee engagement and culture development.
- Sales/Marketing: 15–20% on customer partnerships and positioning.
- Finance: 10–15% on ROI measurement and exit value documentation.

12.2.3 Success Metrics and Milestones

Clear success metrics and milestones enabled progress tracking, course correction, and stakeholder communication throughout the implementation journey.

Financial Metrics:

- ESG investment ROI: Target 3:1 return within two years.
- Cost savings: 5–15% operational cost reduction annually.
- Revenue enhancement: 5–10% premium pricing or new revenue.
- Exit multiple premium: 10–20% above comparable transactions.

Operational Metrics:

- Energy efficiency: 15–30% improvement over baseline.
- Waste reduction: 20–40% decrease in waste generation.
- Safety performance: 30–50% reduction in incident rates.
- Quality improvement: 20–30% defect reduction.

Stakeholder Metrics:

- Employee engagement: Top quartile industry scores (>85%).
- Customer satisfaction: Industry-leading retention (>90%).
- Supplier performance: 30–50% sustainability improvement.
- Community support: Positive stakeholder sentiment (>80%).

Competitive Positioning:

- Industry recognition: Awards, certifications, thought leadership.
- Market share gains: Premium segment expansion.
- Talent attraction: Reduced recruitment time and improved candidate quality.
- Investor interest: LP allocation and competitive fundraising.

12.3 Stakeholder Engagement and Communication Strategy

12.3.1 Comprehensive Stakeholder Approach

Successful ESG integration required systematic engagement with all material stakeholder groups using approaches tailored to their interests, influence levels, and relationship quality.

Employee Engagement Programmes:

- Training and development building sustainability knowledge and capabilities.
- Recognition and reward systems celebrating achievements and innovation.
- Participation opportunities enabling contribution and co-creation.
- Communication systems providing transparent updates and feedback channels.
- Career development opportunities in sustainability leadership roles.

Customer Partnership Development:

- Collaborative sustainability initiatives creating shared value.
- Joint goal-setting and progress tracking strengthening relationships.
- Innovation partnerships developing sustainable products and services.
- Communication platforms facilitating regular interaction and feedback.
- Premium positioning based on verified sustainability leadership.

Supplier Development Programmes:

- Capacity building supporting supplier sustainability improvement.
- Collaborative initiatives creating mutual value and competitive advantages.
- Performance tracking and recognition encouraging continuous improvement.
- Training and development enabling capability enhancement.
- Partnership opportunities for innovation and market development.

Community Relations:

- Proactive engagement building social licence to operate.
- Local hiring and economic development initiatives.
- Environmental stewardship and community investment programmes.
- Transparent communication addressing concerns and sharing progress.
- Partnership development on shared community priorities.

Investor Communication:

- Regular reporting demonstrating sustainability value creation.
- Strategic dialogue on ESG integration approach and results.
- Performance benchmarking against portfolio peers and industry standards.
- Exit value documentation quantifying ESG contributions.
- Thought leadership positioning fund as ESG integration leader.

12.3.2 Communication Best Practices

Effective communication transformed sustainability from technical initiative to shared organizational purpose, building commitment and ownership across stakeholder groups.

Multi-Channel Approach:

- Leadership communication providing strategic context and commitment demonstration.
- Peer-to-peer sharing building credibility through employee champions and success stories.

- Data-driven updates demonstrating progress and celebrating successes quantitatively.
- External validation reinforcing achievements through recognition and awards.
- Stakeholder feedback integration showing responsiveness and continuous improvement.

Resistance Management:

- Understanding before persuading through systematic listening and empathy.
- Addressing legitimate concerns through collaborative problem-solving rather than dismissal.
- Building on existing values connecting sustainability to organizational culture.
- Demonstrating personal relevance showing individual benefits and contributions.
- Creating positive experiences generating personal investment and support.

Summit Peak Services' communication transformation illustrated best practices in action. Rather than top-down sustainability mandates, they framed initiatives as solutions to business challenges employees already cared about—customer satisfaction, workplace culture, operational efficiency. This approach converted initial sceptics into champions who drove adoption throughout the organization.

Common Questions Alex Fields

Q: How do you maintain momentum when initial enthusiasm fades?
A: Systematic reinforcement through measurement, recognition, and storytelling. Summit Peak tracked engagement weekly, celebrated wins monthly, and tied sustainability to performance reviews quarterly. When something becomes how we measure success rather than extra programme, momentum sustains itself. The key is integration, not inspiration.
Q: What if employees view ESG as a management fad that will pass?
A: Consistent action over time builds credibility that words cannot. At Precision Peak, we made ESG a board agenda item every quarter for three years, included metrics in everyone's performance reviews, and tied executive compensation to results. When people see sustained commitment through resource allocation and accountability, scepticism fades.
Q: How do you communicate ESG value to stakeholders sceptical about sustainability?
A: Focus on business outcomes, not ESG labels. We do not talk about "employee engagement programmes"—we discuss turnover cost reduction and productivity improvement. We do not mention "circular economy"—we highlight revenue from waste streams. Frame sustainability in language stakeholders already understand and care about.

12.4 Training and Capability Building

12.4.1 Tiered Training Approach

Systematic capability building required training programmes tailored to different organizational levels and functional roles, ensuring everyone understood their contribution to sustainability success.

Executive Development:

- Advanced training on sustainability strategy and business value creation.
- Stakeholder management and engagement best practices.
- Financial analysis and ROI evaluation for sustainability investments.
- Industry trends and competitive positioning in sustainability leadership.
- Board reporting and governance oversight of ESG performance.

Management Training:

- Sustainability implementation and team leadership development.
- Performance management including ESG metrics and accountability.
- Change management and employee engagement strategies.
- Cross-functional collaboration and integration approaches.
- Continuous improvement methodologies and problem-solving techniques.

Employee Education:

- Sustainability importance and business relevance understanding.
- Individual contribution opportunities and impact awareness.
- Organizational goals and progress transparency.
- Tools and resources for personal and professional sustainability development.
- Recognition and reward systems celebrating achievements and innovation.

Specialist Development:

- Advanced technical training for sustainability professionals.
- Data management and analytics capabilities development.
- Stakeholder engagement and communication expertise building.
- Compliance and regulatory knowledge enhancement.
- Industry certification and professional development support.

12.4.2 Training Content Customization

Training content required customization for different industries, functional areas, and organizational contexts to ensure relevance and effectiveness.

Industry-Specific Content:

- Manufacturing: Operational efficiency and environmental management focus.
- Consumer goods: Brand positioning and customer engagement emphasis.
- Healthcare: Patient safety and community health impacts priority.
- Technology: Data privacy, employee retention, and innovation attention.
- Financial services: Governance, transparency, and stakeholder trust importance.

Role-Based Learning:

- Operations: Efficiency, waste reduction, and safety improvement techniques.
- Sales: Sustainability value propositions and customer engagement approaches.
- Human Resources: Employee engagement, development, and workplace culture strategies.
- Finance: ESG financial analysis and investment decision-making integration.
- R&D: Sustainable innovation and competitive advantage development.

Alpine Foods customized training for their food manufacturing context, emphasizing local sourcing, organic certification, and community relationships relevant to their business model and stakeholder priorities. This customization generated higher engagement and faster implementation than generic sustainability training would have achieved.

12.5 Technology Platform Selection and Implementation

12.5.1 Technology Decision Framework

Technology selection required systematic evaluation balancing functionality, cost, implementation complexity, and organizational readiness using frameworks developed in Chapter 11.

Technology Readiness Assessment:

Question 1: What is the organization's current ESG data maturity?

- Basic capabilities → Start with simple, proven cloud-based technologies.
- Intermediate capabilities → Implement integrated platforms with growth potential.
- Advanced capabilities → Deploy cutting-edge solutions for competitive advantage.

Question 2: What are the resource constraints?

- Limited budget → Cloud-based solutions with operational expense models.
- Limited technical expertise → Vendor-supported platforms with comprehensive training.

- Limited time → Pre-configured solutions with rapid deployment capabilities.

Question 3: What are the strategic priorities?

- Efficiency focus → Automation and analytics for operational improvement.
- Stakeholder focus → Engagement and communication platforms.
- Competitive focus → Advanced capabilities creating differentiation.

Vendor Evaluation Criteria:

- Functionality and integration with existing systems.
- Vendor stability and long-term support commitment.
- Implementation support quality and responsiveness.
- Training and change management services availability.
- Cost structure and scalability matching growth trajectory.

12.5.2 Implementation Approach

Technology implementation success depended on systematic change management and user adoption strategies rather than just technical deployment.

Critical Implementation Elements:

- Executive sponsorship demonstrating strategic priority.
- Comprehensive training ensuring competence and confidence.
- Phased rollout enabling learning and refinement.
- Change champions providing peer support and troubleshooting.
- Performance incentives creating accountability and sustained use.
- Continuous improvement based on user feedback and usage patterns.

Apex Industries' technology implementation illustrated best practices, achieving 95% user adoption within six months through systematic change management that treated technology as business transformation rather than IT project.

12.6 Continuous Improvement and Learning Systems

12.6.1 Performance Review and Refinement

Sustained excellence required systematic processes for evaluating performance, identifying lessons, and implementing refinements across the organization and portfolio.

Quarterly Performance Reviews:

- Performance data analysis against targets and benchmarks.
- Challenge identification and collaborative problem-solving.
- Best practice sharing and knowledge transfer across portfolio.

- Resource allocation adjustments based on results and priorities.
- Stakeholder feedback integration and response planning.

Annual Strategy Sessions:

- Comprehensive ESG strategy effectiveness assessment.
- External environment analysis including regulatory and competitive evolution.
- Capability development planning for upcoming year.
- Priority initiative selection and resource allocation.
- Long-term goal setting and exit value positioning.

Continuous Learning Culture:

- Regular stakeholder feedback collection and responsive action.
- Experimentation encouragement with rapid learning from failures.
- Cross-functional collaboration fostering innovation and improvement.
- External best-practice monitoring and selective adoption.
- Documentation of lessons learned and knowledge sharing.

12.6.2 Portfolio-Level Learning Systems

Kerring Capital Partners developed systematic approaches for capturing and disseminating learning across portfolio companies, amplifying individual successes into portfolio-wide capabilities as detailed in Chapter 10.

Knowledge Transfer Mechanisms:

- Quarterly portfolio company forums sharing experiences and solutions.
- Digital knowledge repositories documenting best practices and lessons.
- Peer mentoring programmes connecting companies facing similar challenges.
- Cross-portfolio working groups addressing common issues.
- Annual sustainability summit celebrating achievements and fostering collaboration.

The Summit Peak Services employee engagement methodology transferred to seven portfolio companies generated €840,000 annual savings versus independent development, demonstrating how systematic knowledge sharing created portfolio-level value exceeding individual company improvements.

12.7 Exit Preparation and Value Realization

12.7.1 Systematic Exit Value Documentation

The ultimate test of ESG integration success was value realization at exit through systematic documentation and buyer education using approaches from Chapter 8.

Capability Documentation:

- Environmental management system effectiveness and competitive advantages.
- Employee engagement excellence and talent retention capabilities.
- Customer relationship strength and loyalty drivers.
- Community partnership value and social license benefits.
- Governance system maturity and risk management sophistication.

Financial Impact Quantification:

- Direct cost savings with detailed attribution and verification.
- Revenue enhancement with customer testimony and market evidence.
- Risk reduction value with insurance cost savings and incident reduction.
- Market positioning advantages with premium pricing evidence.
- Operational excellence capabilities with third-party benchmarking.

Buyer Education Strategy:

- Early ESG capability communication during auction preparation.
- Detailed documentation for due diligence teams with verification.
- Management presentations positioning sustainability as strategic asset.
- Stakeholder introduction facilitating relationship transfer.
- Post-acquisition support offering ensuring continuity and value capture.

12.7.2 Exit Success Examples

Solid Hej Components' €12–15 million ESG-attributed premium, Ridgeline Solutions' circular economy innovation value, and Summit Peak Services' workforce advantage premium demonstrated how systematic documentation and buyer education captured sustainability value at exit.

The common elements across successful exits were:

- Early preparation starting 18–24 months before exit.
- Third-party verification providing buyer confidence.
- Financial quantification making value tangible and defensible.
- Buyer-specific messaging addressing strategic priorities.
- Competitive auction dynamics validating ESG value through multiple bidders.

As the portfolio company leadership programme concluded, Alex reflected on the journey from individual company successes to systematic portfolio-wide capability. "Five years ago, we were experimenting with ESG integration at a handful of companies. Today, we have a replicable playbook that generates superior returns while building better businesses."

Kenyon Iken nodded. "The playbook is invaluable, but what strikes me most is the mindset shift. We stopped thinking about ESG as compliance requirement and started seeing it as competitive advantage. That fundamental reframing drove everything else."

"Exactly right," Alex replied. "The playbook provides the how, but success requires believing in the why. Companies that view sustainability as opportunity rather than obligation consistently outperform those treating it as necessary evil. The evidence is overwhelming—ESG integration, done systematically and with business discipline, creates sustainable competitive advantages that persist beyond ownership periods."

Jim Kerring, Kerring Capital Partners' Managing Partner, stood to offer closing thoughts. "What you have all accomplished demonstrates that sustainable private equity is not just possible—it is profitable. Our fund's 8.2% IRR improvement and 1.3x exit multiple premium compared to previous funds validates the business case. But more importantly, you have proven that we can build better businesses while generating superior returns. That is the future."

The sustainable PE playbook provided frameworks, tools, and methodologies for systematic ESG integration. But ultimate success required authentic commitment to stakeholder value creation, disciplined execution, and willingness to learn and adapt. Companies and funds that embraced this approach were not just doing well—they were doing good while doing well, creating value for all stakeholders rather than extracting it from some to benefit others.

As Alex had learned through dozens of investments across multiple industries and contexts: ESG integration was not about sacrifice or trade-offs between financial and sustainability performance. When done systematically with business discipline, it amplified financial returns precisely because it created genuine competitive advantages through operational excellence, stakeholder relationships, and strategic positioning that traditional approaches could not replicate.

The future of private equity belonged to firms and investors who understood this fundamental truth and built systematic capabilities to execute on it consistently across their portfolios. The playbook provided the roadmap—the journey required commitment, discipline, and belief that doing right and doing well were not just compatible but mutually reinforcing.

Chapter Summary

Core Insight

Systematic ESG integration across the investment life cycle creates sustainable competitive advantages generating superior returns. Kerring Capital Partners' portfolio companies achieved 67% average sustainability improvement, 3.8 percentage points IRR enhancement, and 1.3× exit multiple premium through replicable frameworks balancing quick wins (0–6 months), strategic initiatives (6–24 months), and transformational goals (18–36 months).

Critical Success Factors

- **Comprehensive assessment:** 4–6-week baseline evaluation (performance, capabilities, risks, opportunities) identifies material factors and improvement priorities before implementation.
- **Three-phase roadmap:** Quick wins building momentum (€100–200K Year 1), strategic initiatives creating advantages (€150–300K Year 2), transformational goals establishing leadership (€100–250K Year 3).
- **Systematic capability building:** Tiered training (executive development, management training, employee education, specialist development) with industry and role customization.
- **Portfolio learning systems:** Knowledge transfer mechanisms (quarterly forums, digital repositories, peer mentoring) generating €840K savings from Summit Peak Services methodology transfer.
- **Exit value documentation:** Systematic capability and financial impact quantification with third-party verification capturing premiums (Solid Hej €12–15M, Ridgeline €8–12M, Summit Peak €4–6M).

Watch Out For

⚠ Attempting comprehensive transformation without building capabilities through quick wins risks failure and stakeholder resistance.

⚠ Generic training content without industry and role customization wastes resources and reduces effectiveness.

⚠ Inadequate change management in technology implementation creates "shelfware" despite significant investment.

⚠ Late exit preparation (<12 months) prevents value documentation and buyer education necessary for premium capture.

Tools You Can Use Now

- **Assessment Framework:** Four-quadrant evaluation (performance, capabilities, risks, opportunities) with Alpine Foods detailed example.
- **Three-Phase Roadmap:** Timeline with investment levels, activities, and success metrics for Quick Wins, Strategic Initiatives, Transformational Goals.
- **Resource Allocation Model:** Financial investment and management attention allocation across three-year implementation with typical ranges.
- **Stakeholder Engagement Matrix:** Comprehensive approaches for employees, customers, suppliers, community, investors with communication best practices.
- **Training Framework:** Tiered approach (executive, management, employee, specialist) with industry-specific and role-based customization.
- **Exit Value Playbook:** Documentation, quantification, and buyer education strategies with success examples and premium attribution.

What's Next

This concluding chapter synthesizes the book's frameworks into practical guidance firms can immediately apply regardless of their current ESG maturity. The journey from compliance to competitive advantage requires commitment, discipline, and systematic execution—but the evidence is clear: ESG integration done right generates superior returns while building better businesses. The playbook provides the roadmap; success requires authentic belief that stakeholder value creation and shareholder returns are mutually reinforcing rather than competing objectives.

References

KPMG (2025). Value Creation in Private Equity (28 October).

13 Conclusion

The Future of Sustainable Private Equity

13.1 The Transformation Is Complete

As we finish writing this book, it is clear that the private equity world has fundamentally shifted beneath our feet. The question isn't whether ESG will become important—that battle was fought and won years ago. The real question now is whether your firm will be among the winners who figured this out early, or the stragglers still wondering what happened to their deal flow.

We keep having the same conversation with those who misunderstand ESG and what it represents. They are missing the fundamental shift in how value gets created in modern private equity. They are still thinking about ESG as something you bolt onto a traditional investment process, rather than recognizing it as the investment process.

13.2 Our Shared Vision: Where We Go from Here

Looking ahead, we see several critical developments that will shape the future of sustainable private equity. First, regulatory frameworks are moving towards simplification and higher decision-usefulness rather than indefinite expansion. The European Commission's November 2025 SFDR reform proposal explicitly targets complexity and usability, signalling that sustainability disclosures will be judged increasingly on credibility and governance rather than volume (European Commission, 2025). Second, sustainability reporting standards are being refined in response to implementation experience. In December 2025, EFRAG published technical advice and draft simplified ESRS materials aimed at reducing burden while maintaining materiality discipline (EFRAG, 2025). Third, market expectations are broadening beyond climate into nature-related risk. The ISSB discussed TNFD alignment in October 2025 and TNFD reported in November 2025 that ISSB intends to pursue nature-related disclosure requirements to meet investor needs (IFRS Foundation, 2025; TNFD, 2025). Together, these developments reinforce the central message of this book: sustainable private equity advantage will be determined by execution quality, governance, and systems that make sustainability measurable and investable.

DOI: 10.4324/9781003625636-16

13.2.1 The Integration Imperative

ESG considerations are rapidly moving from separate workstreams to integral components of investment decision-making. The firms that treat sustainability as a bolt-on exercise will find themselves at an increasing disadvantage compared to those that embed these considerations throughout their investment processes.

This integration requires new skills, new systems, and new ways of thinking about value creation. The firms that invest in building these capabilities now will establish competitive advantages that become increasingly difficult for peers to replicate.

13.2.2 The Data Revolution

Real-time data collection and AI-powered analytics will make comprehensive impact measurement cost-effective for middle-market transactions. This measurement sophistication will enable better decision-making, more effective stakeholder communication, and clearer demonstration of value creation through sustainability practices.

13.2.3 Stakeholder Capitalism Mainstreams

The concept of optimising for all stakeholders rather than shareholders alone will become standard practice in private equity, driven by both regulatory requirements and competitive dynamics. Companies that successfully balance stakeholder interests will outperform those that optimise for single constituencies.

This shift will require new analytical frameworks, governance structures, and performance metrics that private equity firms are only beginning to develop.

13.2.4 Technology Transforms Implementation

Artificial intelligence, blockchain, and other emerging technologies will revolutionize ESG data collection, analysis, and verification. Real-time sustainability monitoring will become as routine as financial reporting. Predictive analytics will identify ESG risks and opportunities before they affect business performance.

These technological capabilities will enable private equity firms to manage ESG factors with the same sophistication and precision they currently apply to financial analysis.

13.3 The Choice Before Us

As we conclude this book, private equity professionals face a clear choice. They can embrace the transformation to sustainable investing, developing the capabilities needed to thrive in an economy increasingly shaped by ESG factors. Or they can resist this evolution, hoping that traditional approaches will remain viable despite mounting evidence to the contrary.

13.4 Our Call to Action

We wrote this book because the private equity industry stands at an inflection point. The next decade will determine which firms build sustainable competitive advantages through ESG integration and which struggle to remain relevant in a transformed market.

The tools, frameworks, and methodologies presented in this book provide everything needed to begin this transformation. The case studies demonstrate what is possible when sustainability integration is implemented systematically and measured rigorously. The research evidence proves that ESG creates rather than destroys financial value when properly executed.

But reading about sustainable private equity is not sufficient. Implementation requires commitment, investment, and persistence through inevitable challenges and setbacks. It requires building new capabilities, developing different analytical approaches, and often having difficult conversations with sceptical colleagues and portfolio company management teams.

The reward for this effort is building competitive advantages that peers cannot easily replicate. Firms that master ESG integration will attract better deal flow, achieve superior portfolio company performance, and command premium valuations from limited partners who value sustainability expertise.

More importantly, they will contribute to building an economy that generates prosperity while addressing the environmental and social challenges that define our era. Private equity manages trillions in assets globally, providing these firms with both opportunity and responsibility to influence how business gets done across every sector of the economy.

Your transformation starts with three decisions:

This Week: Conduct the materiality assessment outlined in Chapter 7. Identify your 10–12 material ESG factors. This costs nothing but 4–6 hours of management time.
This Month: Implement one quick win from Chapter 6. Choose high-impact, low-cost initiatives (LED retrofits, employee surveys, supplier engagement) that build credibility for larger programmes.
This Quarter: Develop your three-year ESG roadmap using Chapter 12's framework. Balance quick wins, strategic initiatives, and transformational goals aligned with your hold period and exit timeline.

The playbook provides the how. Your commitment provides the why. Start now.

13.5 The Future Starts Now

Three forces will separate winners from laggards over the next five years:

The Technology Inflection: AI-powered ESG monitoring will make real-time sustainability management as routine as financial reporting. Firms building these capabilities now create 2–3-year competitive advantages.

The Regulatory Ratchet: EU CSRD, US SEC climate rules, and ISSB standards are converging towards mandatory disclosure. Companies prepared through early adoption will capture premium valuations while competitors' scramble.
The Stakeholder Revolution: Employees choose employers based on values. Customers select suppliers based on ESG credentials. Investors allocate capital to sustainable strategies. Stakeholder capitalism is not coming, it is here.

The sustainable private equity revolution is already here. But will your firm be among the leaders who shape this transformation or the laggards who struggle to adapt?

We hope this book provides the foundation you need to choose leadership.

The future of private equity is sustainable. The firms that recognize this first will build the competitive advantages that define industry leadership for the next generation.

The transformation starts with your next investment decision.

The future of sustainable private equity is being written today.

The firms that master this integration will create value that extends far beyond their portfolios, contributing to an economy that works for investors, stakeholders, and society as a whole. That is not just good business, it is essential for the future we all want to build.

References

European Commission. (2025). Commission proposes improvements to SFDR (21 November).

EFRAG. (2025). EFRAG provides its technical advice on draft simplified ESRS to the European Commission (3 December).

IFRS Foundation. (2025). ISSB Update October 2025 (28 October).

TNFD. (2025). TNFD welcomes ISSB decision on nature-related standard setting drawing on TNFD framework (7 November).

Glossary

AI (Artificial Intelligence)	Computer systems capable of performing tasks that typically require human intelligence, used in ESG contexts for predictive analytics, automated reporting, and optimization recommendations.
API (Application Programming Interface)	Software interfaces that allow different systems to communicate and share data automatically, crucial for integrating ESG data across multiple platforms.
AUM (Assets Under Management)	The total market value of investments that a private equity firm manages on behalf of limited partners, used as a measure of firm size and success.
Baseline Assessment	Initial measurement of a company's current ESG performance before implementing improvement initiatives, used to track progress over time.
B-Corp Certification	Certification for companies that meet rigorous standards of social and environmental performance, accountability, and transparency.
Benchmarking	Comparing a company's ESG performance against industry peers, best-in-class performers, or established standards to identify improvement opportunities.
Blockchain	Distributed ledger technology enabling supply chain traceability, impact verification, and transparent stakeholder communication systems.
Carbon Footprint	Total amount of greenhouse gases produced directly and indirectly by an organization, typically measured in carbon dioxide equivalent.

DOI: 10.4324/9781003625636-17

Carried Interest	Share of profits from investments that general partners receive as compensation, typically 20% of profits above a hurdle rate, commonly 8%.
Circular Economy	Economic model aimed at eliminating waste through the continual use of resources via reuse, sharing, repair, refurbishment, remanufacturing, and recycling.
CSR (Corporate Social Responsibility)	Business approach that contributes to sustainable development by delivering economic, social and environmental benefits for all stakeholders.
CSRD (Corporate Sustainability Reporting Directive)	EU regulation requiring large companies to report detailed information about sustainability matters and their impacts on people and the environment.
Data Analytics	Process of examining datasets to draw conclusions about the information they contain, used for ESG performance optimization and trend identification.
Digital Twin	Virtual model of a physical system used for optimization and testing, increasingly used for environmental performance modelling and improvement.
Double Materiality	Approach that considers both how sustainability issues affect the company (financial materiality) and how the company affects society and the environment (impact materiality).
Drawdown / Capital Call	Process by which a private equity fund requests committed capital from its limited partners to fund investments or pay expenses, typically called in instalments over the fund's investment period rather than at fund close.
Dry Powder	Amount of committed capital that has not yet been invested by a private equity fund.
Due Diligence	Comprehensive investigation and analysis of a potential investment, including ESG factors that could affect business performance and valuation.
EBITDA	Earnings before interest, taxes, depreciation, and amortization. Financial measure used to evaluate company operating performance, commonly used in private equity for valuation multiples.

ESG	Environmental, social, and governance. Framework for evaluating sustainability factors: environmental (climate, resources), social (people, communities), governance (leadership, ethics).
ESRS (European Sustainability Reporting Standards)	Detailed standards developed under CSRD specifying how companies should report on sustainability matters.
Exit Multiple	Ratio of exit value to initial investment, showing total return generated during the ownership period.
Fiduciary Duty	Legal obligation to act in the best interests of clients or beneficiaries, increasingly interpreted to include consideration of ESG risks and opportunities.
Fund Life	Typical lifespan of a private equity fund, usually ten years with possible extensions.
GP (General Partner)	Private equity firm that manages the fund and makes investment decisions, typically receiving management fees and carried interest.
GRI (Global Reporting Initiative)	International standards for sustainability reporting that help organizations understand and communicate their ESG impacts.
Greenwashing	Practice of making misleading claims about environmental benefits or sustainability performance to appear more environmentally responsible than actually warranted.
GHG Emissions	Gases that trap heat in the atmosphere and contribute to climate change, including carbon dioxide, methane, nitrous oxide, and fluorinated gases. In ESG reporting, emissions are categorised into Scope 1 (direct), Scope 2 (indirect from purchased energy), and Scope 3 (other indirect emissions across the value chain). See also Scope 1, 2, 3 Emissions.
Hurdle Rate	Minimum annual return that a private equity fund must generate for its limited partners before the general partner becomes entitled to carried interest, commonly set at 8% in industry practice. Also referred to as the preferred return.
Impact Investing	Investment approach that intentionally seeks to generate positive, measurable social and environmental impact alongside financial return.

IoT (Internet of Things)	Network of connected devices that collect and share data, used in ESG contexts for environmental monitoring and operational efficiency.
IRR (Internal Rate of Return)	Annualized effective compound return rate that makes the net present value of investment cash flows equal to zero. It is the key performance metric in private equity.
ISSB (International Sustainability Standards Board)	Global body developing baseline sustainability disclosure standards to create consistency across markets.
KPI (Key Performance Indicator)	Measurable values that demonstrate how effectively an organization is achieving key business objectives, including ESG targets.
LP (Limited Partner)	Investor in a private equity fund, typically pension funds, endowments, or wealthy individuals who provide capital but do not participate in management.
LBO (Leveraged Buyout)	Acquisition of a company using significant amounts of borrowed money to meet the cost of acquisition, common private equity strategy.
Machine Learning	Type of artificial intelligence that enables systems to automatically learn and improve from experience without being explicitly programmed.
Management Fee	Annual fee paid to general partners for managing the fund, typically 2% of committed capital.
Materiality Assessment	Process of identifying and prioritizing ESG issues that are most significant to business success and stakeholder concerns.
Money Multiple	Ratio of total cash distributions plus residual value returned to limited partners divided by total capital contributed, expressed as a multiple (e.g. 2.5x). Used alongside IRR as a headline performance metric in private equity. Also referred to as MoM or TVPI
Multiple Expansion	Increase in valuation multiple (e.g. price-to-earnings ratio) between acquisition and exit, often influenced by improved ESG performance.
Net Zero	Achieving balance between greenhouse gases emitted and removed from the atmosphere, often through emissions reduction and carbon offsetting.

NLP (Natural Language Processing)	AI technology that helps computers understand and interpret human language, used for analysing ESG reports and stakeholder feedback.
NPV (Net Present Value)	Difference between present value of cash inflows and outflows over a period of time, used in investment analysis.
Portfolio Company	Company owned by a private equity fund as part of its investment portfolio.
Predictive Analytics	Use of data, statistical algorithms, and machine learning techniques to identify the likelihood of future outcomes based on historical data.
PRI (Principles for Responsible Investment)	UN-supported network encouraging investors to incorporate ESG factors into investment decision-making.
ROI (Return on Investment)	Performance measure used to evaluate efficiency of an investment, calculated as (gain from investment minus cost of investment) divided by cost of investment.
SASB (Sustainability Accounting Standards Board)	Organization that develops industry-specific standards for disclosure of financially material sustainability information.
Scope 1, 2, 3 Emissions	Categories of greenhouse gas emissions: Scope 1 (direct emissions), Scope 2 (indirect from purchased energy), Scope 3 (other indirect emissions in value chain).
SDGs (Sustainable Development Goals)	17 global goals adopted by UN member countries to address worldwide challenges including poverty, inequality, climate change, and peace.
SFDR (Sustainable Finance Disclosure Regulation)	EU regulation requiring financial market participants to disclose how they integrate sustainability risks and consider adverse sustainability impacts.
Social License to Operate	Ongoing acceptance and approval of a business by local communities and stakeholders, crucial for operational success and expansion.
SRI (Socially Responsible Investing)	Investment discipline that considers environmental, social, and corporate governance criteria to generate long-term competitive financial returns and positive societal impact.
Stakeholder Engagement	Process of involving people who may be affected by business decisions or who can influence implementation of those decisions.

TCFD (Task Force on Climate-related Financial Disclosures)	Framework for organizations to disclose climate-related financial risks and opportunities in their financial filings.
Third-Party Verification	Independent assessment of ESG data and claims by external auditors or certification bodies to ensure accuracy and credibility.
Value Creation	Strategies and initiatives implemented during ownership period to improve company performance and increase enterprise value before exit.
Value Creation Plan	Detailed roadmap outlining specific initiatives, investments, and improvements to be implemented during the ownership period to enhance company value.
Vintage Year	Year in which a private equity fund makes its first investment, used for performance comparison.

Additional Reading Resources

This comprehensive reading list provides both academic rigour and practical application, supporting implementation of the frameworks and strategies outlined in your sustainability integration methodology.

Core Academic Foundations

Change Management and Organizational Development

- Cooperrider, D. L., & Srivastva, S. (1987). Appreciative inquiry in organizational life. *Research in Organizational Change and Development*, 1, 129–169.

  —Foundational framework for strengths-based organizational transformation
  —Essential for understanding culture change during ESG integration

- Cooperrider, D. L., & Whitney, D. (2005). *Appreciative inquiry: A positive revolution in change*. Berrett-Koehler Publishers.

  —Practical application of appreciative inquiry principles
  —Particularly relevant for stakeholder engagement strategies

- Kotter, J. P. (2012). Leading change. Harvard Business Review Press.

  —Eight-step process for transformational change
  —Critical for ESG implementation across portfolio companies

- Schein, E. H. (2010). *Organizational culture and leadership* (4th ed.). Jossey-Bass.

  —Comprehensive framework for understanding and changing organizational culture
  —Essential for embedding sustainability practices

Stakeholder Theory and Engagement

- Kujala, J., Sachs, S., Leinonen, H., Heikkinen, A., & Laude, D. (2022). Stakeholder engagement: Past, present, and future. *Business & Society*, 61 (5), 1136–1196.

DOI: 10.4324/9781003625636-18

—Contemporary academic framework for systematic stakeholder engagement
—Validates comprehensive stakeholder approach during acquisition integration

- Shleifer, A., & Summers, L. H. (1988). Breach of trust in hostile takeovers. In A. J. Auerbach (Ed.), *Corporate takeovers: Causes and consequences* (pp. 33–68). University of Chicago Press.

  —Theoretical foundation for stakeholder relationship management during acquisitions
  —Explains why explicit attention to trust-building is essential

Industry-Specific Research and Reports

Private Equity and ESG Integration

- A Simple Model. (2024). Post-acquisition work: The first 100 days.

  —Industry evidence: 90% of PE firms use systematic 100-day plans
  —Validates structured approach to early integration

- CFGI. (2021). Navigating those critical first 100 days of private equity ownership.

  —Professional services perspective on PE transformation
  —Practical guidance for systematic capability building

- Grant Thornton. (2024). PE finance transformation objectives for the first 100 days.

  —Focus on people, processes, and systems alignment
  —Industry validation for structured integration approaches

- Principles for Responsible Investment. (2023). Private equity: Responsible investment during the first 100 days. PRI Association.

  —Official guidance from leading responsible investment organization
  —Framework for ESG integration from acquisition to exit

Employee Engagement and Retention

- *Financier Worldwide*. (2022). M&A challenges: Employee engagement and retention. *Financier Worldwide*, December issue.

  —Cites MIT Sloan research: 34% average attrition in acquired companies vs 12% for hired employees
  —Critical data supporting focus on employee engagement during integration

- Edmans, A. (2012). The link between job satisfaction and firm value, with implications for corporate social responsibility. Academy of Management Perspectives, 26(4), 1–19.

  Academic evidence: "100 Best Companies to Work For in America" generated 2.3% to 3.8% higher stock returns per year than their peers (1984-2011).

Practitioner-Focused Resources

Essential Guides

- "Impact revolution: Private equity's new blueprint for success" by Bain & Company

  —Practical integration frameworks from real deal experience
  —Case studies with measurable financial and impact results

- "ESG investing: A practical guide for asset managers" by CFA Institute

  —Comprehensive ESG integration techniques
  —Risk management and performance measurement approaches
  —Regulatory compliance strategies

- "The sustainability advantage: Seven business case benefits of a triple bottom line" by Bob Willard

  —Quantified business benefits with ROI calculation methodologies
  —Change management strategies for sustainability transformation

Annual Industry Reports

- PwC Private Equity ESG Survey (Annual)

  —Benchmark data on ESG integration across PE industry
  —Emerging trends and regulatory developments
  —Best-practice examples from leading firms

- McKinsey Global Institute: "Where companies with a long-term view outperform their peers"

  —Evidence linking long-term thinking to financial outperformance
  —Strategic frameworks for sustainable value creation

- Preqin Private Equity ESG Report (Quarterly)

  —Market data on ESG-focused PE fundraising
  —LP perspectives on ESG integration requirements
  —Performance analysis of ESG-integrated funds

Regulatory and Standards Resources

Official Frameworks

- PRI Private Equity ESG Due Diligence Questionnaire

  —Standardized framework for ESG assessment in PE transactions
  —Sector-specific guidance and materiality considerations

- Network for Greening the Financial System. (2022). Progress report on bridging data gaps. NGFS Secretariat.

  —Guidance on ESG data collection and management systems
  —Emphasizes cultural embedding over external imposition

Sector-Specific Guidelines

- SASB Standards (Sustainability Accounting Standards Board)

  —Industry-specific ESG metrics and disclosure frameworks
  —Financial materiality focus aligned with investor needs

- TCFD Recommendations (Task Force on Climate-related Financial Disclosures)

  —Climate risk assessment and disclosure framework
  —Essential for climate-related due diligence and integration

Reading Path Recommendations

For New Practitioners

1. Start with Willard's "Sustainability advantage" for business case fundamentals
2. Read Kotter's "Leading change" for change management framework
3. Review PRI's "Private equity: Responsible investment" for industry context
4. Study annual PwC ESG Survey for current industry benchmarks

For Experienced PE Professionals

1. Focus on Cooperrider & Whitney for advanced stakeholder engagement
2. Review academic papers by Kujala et al. and Edmans for research validation
3. Study CFGI and Grant Thornton reports for implementation best practices
4. Monitor quarterly Preqin reports for market trends

For Portfolio Company Leadership

1 Heath & Heath's "Switch" for practical change implementation
2 Schein's "Organizational culture and leadership" for culture transformation
3 CFA Institute ESG guide for practical integration techniques
4 Industry-specific SASB standards for relevant metrics

Subject Index

A

A Simple Model (2024), 100-day plans, 99, acquisition, due diligence, 75–92; first 100 days, 60–63, 98–115; integration, 60–72; valuation, 4–6, 76–77, 140–148

Acronyms and Abbreviations, xx-xxi additional reading resources, 241–245

AI, see artificial intelligence

Alpine Foods, baseline assessment, 63, 121, 212; customer satisfaction, 73% to 89%, 103; customer sustainability communication, 214; ESG integration laboratory, 57–72; ESG Quick Start Programme, 101–103; family ownership, 100, 182; figures €114K invested, €546K annual, 379% ROI, 48, 103, 214; LED retrofit €45K invested, €67K savings, 214; local sourcing 78% within 200km, 63, 100, 120; Mediterranean speciality producer, 47–48, 57–72, 100; organic certification 67%, 63; reporting preparation time reduction 73%, 130; revenue growth 18%, 71, 120; supplier communication enhancement, 214; technology infrastructure, 66–67, 120–121, 198

Alvarez and Marsal (2024), 137, 156

Annan, Kofi, PRI invitation, 7–8, 18 antitrust law, 32

Apex Industries, automotive supplier, 118; CFO see Day, Penelope; CSRD reporting, 120, 132; energy cost overrun €180K, 119; ESG metrics reduction 127 to 12, 118, 123; Head of Operations see Weber, Marcus; IoT sensors, 198; material factors tier-1, tier-2, tier-3, 121; quality management, 120; reporting hours 40 to 32 monthly, 118, 124, 192, 206; skilled worker retention, 121; technology transformation, 196–211

Appreciative Inquiry, framework, 99, 116; Schein (2010), 99, 116, 117; Cooperrider and Srivastva (1987), 99, 117

Application Programming Interface, see API

API, definition, 232; ESG data integration, 121–122, 193, 199

Article 6 funds (SFDR), 162–163

Article 8 funds (SFDR), 162–163

Article 9 funds (SFDR), 162–163 artificial intelligence, definition, 232; AI document review, 66; AI energy savings (Solid Hej), 196; AI predictive maintenance (Solid Hej), 196; AI supplier risk (Ridgeline), 196; AI sustainability dashboards, 66, 193–195; applications in ESG management, 195; future autonomous optimization, 205; pattern recognition, 133; predictive analytics, 67, 133, 196; see also machine learning; natural language processing

Assets Under Management, see AUM

Atz, U., 65, 74, 119, 138 audit, see assurance; due diligence; third-party verification

AUM, definition, 232; growth 2014 to 2024, 4–5, 5; ESG-integrated PE funds, 141; private equity industry, 4–5; sustainable funds, 141

B

Bain and Company, Global Private Equity Report (2022), 191; PRI and Bain (2025) value creation in private markets, 13, 16; impact revolution recommendation, 243

Bassen, A., 21, 33 baseline assessment, definition, 232; Alpine Foods, 63, 120, 212; Solid Hej, 25, 38–39; Summit Peak, 47, 105–106; see also due diligence; materiality assessment
B-Corp certification, 236 benchmarking, definition, 232; Apex evolution, 131–132; industry, 90, 131; peer company, 130–131; portfolio-level, 181–183; see also performance measurement
Berg, F., 21–22, 33, 86–87, 96, 118, 136, 162, 175
Berg, Kölbel and Rigobon (2022), ESG ratings divergence, 21–22, 33, 86–87, 96, 118, 136, 160, 175 best-in-class assessment, 131, 191 biodiversity, 59, 195; see also nature-related disclosures; TNFD blockchain, definition, 232; ESG technology applications, 193, 199–201; Ridgeline circular economy, 200–201; supply chain traceability, 193, 203–204
BNP Paribas Securities Services (2019), 162, 175 board governance, Alpine sustainability committee, 68; capability assessment, 215; ESG accountability, 68, 212; reporting, 125; see also governance bottom quartile, ESG integration, 10, 188
Busch, T., 21, 33
Business Roundtable (2019), Statement on the Purpose of a Corporation, 19; 181 CEOs, 19 buyer education strategy, exit preparation, 228 buyer messaging, financial buyers, 150; strategic buyers, 152–153

C

capability assessment, Alpine Foods example, 211–212; framework, 215–216; governance, 212; see also baseline assessment capital access, ESG-driven, 40 carbon credit verification (blockchain), 204 carbon footprint, definition, 232; Alpine reduction, 120, 184; portfolio-level reduction 31%, 184; Solid Hej reduction 38%, 138; see also Scope 1, 2, 3 emissions
Carried Interest, definition, 233; hurdle rate, 237
CFA Institute, ESG investing guide, 243
CFGI (2021), post-acquisition first 100 days, 99, 117, 242 champion development, 108–109 change management, Appreciative Inquiry, 99, 107–108; cultural integration, 110–111; Kotter (2012), 117, 238; resistance management, 107–108; see also Cooperrider, D. L.
Chen, Ivie (Director of ESG Integration, Kerring Capital Partners), 19, 66, 137, 178; ILPA ESG working group, 185
Chief Executive Officer, see CEO; leadership
Chief Financial Officer, see CFO; Day, Penelope
Chief Human Resources Officer, see CHRO
CHRO, Acronyms list, xx circular economy, definition, 233; blockchain applications (Ridgeline), 200–201; principles, 142, 145; Ridgeline Solutions case, 143, 145, 159, 200–201; see also Ridgeline Solutions
Clark, C., 65, 74, 97, 119, 136, 195
Clark, G. L., Feiner and Viehs (2015), ESG and stock performance, 20, 33, 36, 53 climate change, see climate risk; nature-related disclosures; TCFD climate risk, Apex carbon cost reduction, 168; physical risk, 85, 165–166; scenario analysis, 85–87, 87; TCFD framework, 85, 95, 97, 157, 161–162, 173; transition risk, 85, 168 climate scenarios, NGFS, 85–87, 87; orderly transition, 86; disorderly transition, 86; hot house world, 86
Coastal Manufacturing, see Ridgeline Solutions collaborative renewable energy procurement, 182–183 commercial due diligence, 90–91
Common Questions (Alex Fields format), Ch.1, 12–13; Ch.2, 21–22; Ch.3, 41–42; Ch.4, 70–71; Ch.5, 83–84; Ch.6, 110; Ch.7, 131–132; Ch.8, 150–151; Ch.9, 173–174; Ch.10, 183; Ch.11, 194, 203; Ch.12, 219; Ch.13, 234 community engagement, Alpine community stakeholder group, 69; community relations assessment, 84; supplier development, 59 competitive advantage, ESG-driven differentiation, 91–92; market access, 145 compliance, early adoption benefits, 160–161; integrated systems, 169–170; see also regulation consumer goods sector, ESG materiality, 86, 89, 122

Cooperrider, D. L., and Srivastva (1987) Appreciative Inquiry, 99, 117; and Whitney (2005), 117, 241 core data repository, 131
Corporate Social Responsibility, see CSR
Corporate Sustainability Reporting Directive, see CSRD
CSR, definition, 237
CSRD, definition, 233; Apex implementation, 120, 132; implementation timeline, 167, 167; mandatory disclosure, 231; scope 50,0 + companies, 167; Solid Hej coverage 85%, 165; see also EU regulation cultural integration, Apex 95% adoption, 208; Cooperrider and Srivastva (1987), 99, 117; Schein (2010), 99, 116, 117; values alignment, 110–111 customer engagement, Alpine customer partnership forum, 69, 202; customer requirements, 91, 143; sustainability premium pricing 8–12%, 143, 200; see also stakeholder engagement customer satisfaction, Alpine, 73% to 89%, 103; Solid Hej, 78% to 94%, 128; Summit Peak, 67% to 94%, 106; see also stakeholder engagement

D

data analytics, definition, 233; cross-portfolio, 180; ESG decision-making, 121–125; portfolio-level synergies, 180; predictive, 67, 133–134, 188; real-time, 197–198; see also predictive analytics data collection hierarchy, 124; primary collection, 87; proxy measures, 122; secondary sources, 123 data privacy, GDPR considerations, 133, 226 data quality, Berg, Kölbel and Rigobon (2022), 21–22, 86–87; data quality scoring framework, 88; ESG measurement challenges, 86–87; primary collection, 87; rating agency divergence, 21–22, 86–87
Day, Penelope (CFO, Apex Industries), 119–120, 131–132, 171 deal sourcing, ESG-driven advantage, 92, 184–185 digital materiality assessment, 80, 80 digital twin, definition, 233; Helix Chemicals modelling, 147; future applications, 209 disclaimer (fictional companies), xiii
Double Materiality, definition, 233; CSRD requirement, 167–168; see also materiality assessment
Dry Powder, definition, 237
Due Diligence, definition, 233; commercial integration, 90–91; data collection, 80–82; ESG factors, 75–92; financial integration, 91; four-dimensional assessment, 76–77, 78; Helix Chemicals discovery, 75, 80–82, 95; management assessment, 91; operational integration, 91; PRI ESG DDQ, 241; strategic intelligence, 91–92; technologyenhanced, 79–80, 80; see also Helix Chemicals; materiality assessment

E

Earnings Before Interest, Taxes, Depreciation, and Amortization, see EBITDA
EBITDA, definition, 233; Alpine improvement, 71; multiples, 4–6, 140–148, 184, 189; Solid Hej, 38–39, 41–42; Summit Peak growth 22% annual, 106; Summit Peak margins 9% to 14%, 47; valuation, 4–6
Eccles, R. G., Ioannou and Serafeim (2014), high sustainability companies study, 10, 16, 19–20, 33, 35–37, 53, 96
'Edmans, A. (2012), employee satisfaction and firm value (100 Best Companies study), 240'
EFRAG, (2025a) draft simplified ESRS technical advice (3 December), 77, 96, 232, 231; (2025b) resource hub materials, 96 emerging markets, IFC business case, 6, 16, 138 employee engagement, Alpine 87% vs industry 64%, 84; engagement platforms, 67; portfolio improvement 41%, 184, 193; satisfaction surveys, 84; Solid Hej 67% to 89%, 128; Summit Peak 52% to 89%, 105–106, 201; sustainability scores >85% target, 217; Sull and Sull (2022), 118; turnover correlation, 39–40, 84 employee retention, Alpine 92% three-year, 64; Solid Hej, 39; Summit Peak €1.7M cost savings, 106; turnover reduction 47% to 12% (Summit Peak), 47, 106, 126, 143, 205
Entraygues, P., 138, 156 environmental, social, and governance, see ESG
ESG, definition, 233; Alpine integration laboratory, 57–72; data quality challenges, 86–87, 121–122; ESG Data Convergence Initiative, 140, 148; ESG integration frameworks, 60–72, 87; ESG

integration in practice, 57–72; ESG metrics, 118–136, 121; financial materiality, 76–77, 89, 118–119; framework proliferation, 118, 159–160; integration framework five-phase, 60–63, 72; investment thesis, 11–12; portfolio-level optimization, 174–191; quick wins, 99, 214; Quick Start Programme, 101–103; ratings divergence, 21–22, 86–87; sector materiality, 89, 121; technology applications, 192–207; valuation impact, 4–6; value creation mechanisms, 40, 7 mechanisms
ESG Quick Start Programme, Alpine Foods application, 101–103; Days 1–30 Assessment, 102; Days 31–60 Foundation, 102; Days 61–90 Momentum, 102; timeline, 102
ESRS, definition, 234; CSRD requirement, 169–170; EFRAG simplified ESRS (2025a), 77, 96, 228; mandatory, 169
EU regulation, CSRD, 157, 163, 167–168, 175; ESRS, 167–168; SFDR, 157, 162–163, 228; Sustainable Finance Disclosure Regulation, see SFDR; see also European Commission
European Commission, (2025a) Impact assessment SFDR review, 14, 16; (2025b) Proposal amending Regulation (EU) 2019/2088, 14, 16; (2025c) Commission proposes improvements to SFDR, 32, 117, 136, 173, 228, 231; (2025d) Commission simplifies transparency rules, 32, 136, 173; SFDR reform proposal (November 2025), 59, 101, 120, 163
European Sustainability Reporting Standards, see ESRS exit advantage, see exit preparation Exit Multiple, definition, 234; Kerring portfolio average 1.3×, 115, 184, 192, 190, 209, 225; Ridgeline 1.76 acquisition-to-sale, 145; Solid Hej 1.71×, 43, 144; Summit Peak 8.9×
EBITDA, 146, 155 exit preparation, buyer education strategy, 228; exit narratives, 140–146; exit story development, 138–139; ESG-driven value enhancement, 138; Phase 5 (months 18–36), 62–63; timeline, 141; sustainability premium, 137, 144–148 exit premium, ESG attribution, 8–12% (Ridgeline), 143, 159; Ridgeline €8–12M, 145, 224, 226; Solid Hej €12–15M, 137, 144, 185, 224, 226; Summit Peak €4–6M, 146, 224, 230
EY (2024) PE survey, 137, 139, 156

F
facility management, see Summit Peak
Facility Services family ownership, Alpine Foods, 100, 185
Feiner, A., 20, 33, 36, 53
Fiduciary Duty, definition, 238
Fields, Alex, see Common Questions financial buyers, see buyer messaging financial due diligence, 91 financial materiality, Khan, Serafeim and Yoon (2016), 11–12, 16, 76, 95, 96, 118, 136; SASB framework, 89, 95, 97, 241; see also materiality assessment
Financier Worldwide (2022), M&A challenges, 117, 242 first 100 days, Alpine Foods, 101–103; CFGI (2021), 99, 117; foundation elements, 99; framework, 98–115; Grant Thornton (2024), 117; PRI (2023), 98, 117, 239; quick wins, 99, 101–103, 217–218
Fitzgibbons, S., 26, 33, 137, 156 five mechanisms cultural integration, 110–111; measurement and accountability, 111; skills development, 110; stories and communication, 110–111; systems integration, 110; values alignment, 110
Foreword, xiv-xv; Ioannou, I., xv
Friede, Busch and Bassen (2015), ESG-CFP meta-analysis, 21, 33, 37, 53
Fund life, definition, 238 fund-level ESG infrastructure, 178–181 fund-level ROI, 188% one-year payback, 187, 194

G
GDPR, see data privacy
General Partner, see GP
Global Reporting Initiative, see GRI
Global Sustainable Investment Alliance (2021), 163, 175 governance, Alpine board sustainability committee, 68; capability assessment, 215; ESG accountability, 68, 212; see also board governance
GP, definition, 234; managing partner role, 175, 181; see also Kerring Capital Partners
Grant Thornton (2024), PE finance transformation, 117, 242
Greenfield, Monk and Rook (2026), 40, 53

Greenwashing, definition, 238
GRI, definition, 234; Solid Hej selective implementation 40% effort reduction, 164; Universal Standards, 164

H
Heath, C. and Heath, D. (2010), Switch, 241, 245
Helix Chemicals, due diligence €15M discovery, 75, 80–82, 95; environmental liability quantification, 81; methylene chloride mass balance analysis, 75, 81; €78M revenue, 75; €11.2M enterprise value contribution, 82; purchase price adjustment €12M / €3M escrow, 82; technology exit (Section 8.4.2), 148–149; 2.8× four-year return, 82, 149
HSBC, iii human capital, see employee engagement; talent attraction

I
IFC (2002), Developing value: business case in emerging markets, 6, 16, 138
IFRS Foundation (2025a), ISSB Update October 2025, 195, 208, 228, 235
Iken, Kenyon (CEO, Precision Peak Manufacturing), 98, 209, 229
ILPA (2024), ESG LP best practice guide, 183, 195
Impact Investing, definition, 234; see also SRI implementation framework, Phase 1 acquisition (months 1–4), 60, 148; Phase 2 investment committee, 60, 148; Phase 3 first 100 days (months 5–8), 61–62, 149; Phase 4 operational excellence (months 6–24), 62; Phase 5 exit preparation (months 18–36), 62–63 inflection point, private equity industry, 234
Institutional Limited Partners Association, see ILPA integrated reporting architecture, Alpine Foods, 131
Internal Rate of Return, see IRR
International Capital Market Association (ICMA), Sustainability-Linked Bond Principles, iii
International Finance Corporation, see IFC
International Sustainability Standards Board, see ISSB
Internet of Things, see IoT investor reporting, fund-level, 180–181; LP requirements, 129, 180; SFDR Articles, 162–163
Ioannou, I., 10, 16, 19–20, 33, 35–37, 53, 96, 173; Foreword, xv
IoT, definition, 234; Apex sensors, 198; environmental monitoring, 66, 121; safety wearables, 198; Solid Hej sensor network 412 sensors, 197–198, 207; Solid Hej IoT €12K investment / €45K savings, 194, 207; €89K annual savings, 202, 211
IRR, definition, 234; Bain (2022) ESG funds 8% uplift, 174, 191; EY (2024) advanced ESG funds 8 percentage points uplift, 139, 154; Kerring fund 8.2% improvement vs previous fund, 184, 184, 225; portfolio company average 3.8 percentage points uplift, 115, 184, 209; top vs bottom quartile 8.9 percentage points, 188
ISO 14001 certification, Alpine Foods, 64
ISSB, definition, 234; (2025a) ISSB Update October 2025, 195, 208, 228, 231; IFRS S1 General Requirements, 163; IFRS S2 Climate-related Disclosures, 163; Solid Hej early adoption 18 months ahead, 165; TNFD framework alignment, 199
Iwinosa, Efe (compliance director, Solid Hej Components), 159

J
just transition, see climate risk; ESG

K
Kengelbach, J. (2024), M&A dealmakers survey, 137, 148, 156
Kerring, Jim (managing partner, Kerring Capital Partners), 35, 44, 209, 229
Kerring Capital Partners, 47 investments 2010–2024, 35; firm structure, 4–6, 35–36, 175–176, 181; fund-level ESG infrastructure, 175–178; fund-level IRR 8.2% improvement, 181, 184, 225; LP fundraising advantage, 180–181; portfolio companies, see Alpine Foods; Apex Industries; Helix Chemicals; Precision Peak Manufacturing; Ridgeline Solutions; Riviera Specialty; Solid Hej Components; Summit Peak Facility Services; portfolio-level metrics, 186–187; portfolio-level optimization, 177–194
Khan, Serafeim and Yoon (2016), material ESG outperformance 4.2 percentage points, 11–12, 16, 76, 95, 96, 118, 136,

141, 148, 156 knowledge sharing networks, Kerring portfolio, 179–181
Kölbel, J., 21–22, 33, 86–87, 96, 118, 136, 162, 175
Kotter, J. P. (2012), Leading change, 117, 241
KPI, definition, 234; see also performance measurement
KPMG (2025), Value Creation in Private Equity, 175, 191, 213, 231
Kramer, M. R., 58, 74
Kravis, Henry, 7
Kujala et al. (2022), stakeholder engagement, 117, 241

L

Laude, D., 118
LBO, definition, 235; pioneers 1980s, 7
Leveraged Buyout, see LBO licence to operate, ESG and corporate licence, 40, 40
Limited Partner, see LP listening sessions, Precision Peak transformation, 100 local sourcing, Alpine Foods 78% within 200km, 63, 100, 121
LP, definition, 234; fundraising advantage, 183–184; ILPA (2024) best practice guide, 180, 191; LP survey 94% agreement (Kerring), 188; reporting requirements, 129, 183

M

machine learning, definition, 235; Solid Hej energy optimization, 196; see also artificial intelligence; predictive analytics management fee, definition, 239 managing partner, Jim Kerring (Kerring Capital Partners), 35, 175, 184 manufacturing sector, ESG materiality, 86, 89, 121; Kerring portfolio companies, 5, 182
Materiality Assessment, definition, 235; Apex Industries diagnostic, 120; double materiality, 167–168; financial materiality (Khan, Serafeim and Yoon 2016), 11–12, 16, 76, 95, 96, 118, 136; four-dimensional matrix, 76–77, 78; materiality-driven prioritization, 77; sector-specific frameworks, 89, 121; SASB framework, 89, 95, 97; tier-1 direct financial impact, 120; tier-2 medium-term, 120; tier-3 long-term, 121
McKinsey and Company, (2020) ESG portfolio capabilities, 174, 191; (2023a) Private markets turn to value creation through ESG, 136, 191; (2023b) ESG premium, 192, 208; Global Institute, 243
Mediterranean Foods, see Riviera Specialty
Meridian Manufacturing, see Precision Peak Manufacturing methylene chloride, Helix Chemicals discrepancy, 75, 81 metrics, see ESG; KPI; performance measurement
M&A integration, see acquisition; first 100 days
Mitchell, Tom, Ridgeline Solutions CEO, 6
Monk, A., 40, 53
Morningstar (2021), sustainable funds outperformance 71%, 65, 74
Morgan, Alex (protagonist; partner, Kerring Capital Partners), career arc, 3–15, 35–44, 57–72; Common Questions, see Common Questions; leadership at Kerring, 4–6, 35–37, 119, 174–175; sceptic-to-advocate transformation, 12–15, 35–37; Riviera Specialty crisis catalyst, 17–19, 23
Morgan Stanley (2025), Sustainable Signals: Corporates 2025, 33
Mueller, Hans (senior maintenance technician, Precision Peak Manufacturing), 100, 108–109 multiple expansion, definition, 235; ESG-driven, 14, 184, 189; exit multiples averaging 1.3× (Kerring), 115, 184, 192–193, 209, 225; see also Exit Multiple

N

Natural Language Processing, see NLP nature-related disclosures, biodiversity, 59, 195; ISSB and TNFD framework alignment, 195, 208; Nature Action 100 status report (October 2025), 59, 74; TNFD welcomes ISSB decision (November 2025), 195, 208, 228, 235
Nature Action 100 (2025), first status report, 59, 74
Net Present Value, see NPV
Net Zero, definition, 235; buyer demand, 154
Network for Greening the Financial System, see NGFS
NGFS, climate scenarios, 85–87, 87; (2022) Progress report on bridging data gaps, 97, 244
NLP, definition, 235; sentiment analysis, 80, 197; Summit Peak early career concern detection, 197; see also artificial intelligence

Nordic Components, see Solid Hej Components
NPV, definition, 239

O

OECD (2020), ESG investing report, 158, 171, 176 operational excellence, Alpine Foods Phase 4 (months 6–24), 62, 142; Helix Chemicals AI optimization 34% energy reduction, 146–147; Solid Hej 31% energy efficiency, 138; see also implementation framework

P

patents, Helix Chemicals seven sustainable manufacturing, 147; Ridgeline sustainable packaging portfolio, 27
Pedersen, Fitzgibbons and Pomorski (2021), greenium effect, 26, 33, 137, 156
Peninsula Services, see Summit Peak Facility Services performance measurement, 23% EBITDA improvement portfolio, 183, 190; 27% energy efficiency portfolio, 184; 31% carbon footprint reduction portfolio, 187; 34% customer satisfaction increase portfolio, 183, 190; 41% employee engagement portfolio, 183, 190; benchmarking, 90, 130–131; KPI definition, 234; portfolio-level framework, 183–184; quarterly reviews, 190, 222; sector-specific, 89; stakeholder metrics, 221
PFA Pension, iii
PE, see private equity
Pomorski, L., 26, 33, 137, 156
Porter and Kramer (2011), shared value, 58, 72, 74
Portfolio Company, definition, 235; named portfolio companies, see Alpine Foods; Apex Industries; Helix Chemicals; Precision Peak Manufacturing; Ridgeline Solutions; Riviera Specialty; Solid Hej Components; Summit Peak Facility Services portfolio-level optimization, annual strategy sessions, 187, 222; cross-portfolio analytics, 180; fund-level ESG infrastructure, 175–178; joint supplier programmes, 179; knowledge sharing networks, 176–178; LP fundraising advantage, 180–181; operational synergies, 178–180; portfolio-level metrics framework, 183–184; synergy value quantification, 184; technology platforms, 178–179
Precision Peak Manufacturing, boardroom courtroom, 98; CEO see Iken, Kenyon; cultural transformation, 98–115; ESG board agenda item, 219; first-100-days failure, 98–100; LED retrofit €52K invested, €74K savings, 100; listening sessions, 100; productivity drop 12%, 98; recovery, 99–115; senior maintenance technician see Mueller, Hans; strike vote, 98; turnover 34%, 98 predictive analytics, definition, 235; Alpine technology infrastructure, 67; Helix Chemicals waste reduction 67%, 149; portfolio-level, 188; Solid Hej maintenance downtime reduction 23%, 200; see also data analytics
PRI, definition, 235; PRI and Bain (2025) value creation, 13, 16; PRI ESG due diligence questionnaire, 241; PRI Private Equity Responsible Investment First 100 Days (2023), 98, 117, 239; six principles, 8; UN-supported network, 7–8, 18, 239
Principles for Responsible Investment, see PRI private equity, AUM growth 2014–2024, 4–5, 5; industry history (1980s LBOs), 7; industry size 2024, 4–5; inflection point, 230; market segmentation, 5
PwC, (2022) Global Investor Survey, 35, 53, 139, 154; Private Equity ESG Survey, 243

Q

quality management, Apex Industries, 121 quantum computing, future ESG applications, 209–210 quarterly portfolio reviews, 187, 226
Quick Start Programme, see ESG Quick Start Programme quick wins, Alpine Foods examples, 214; Phase 1 (0–6 months), 213–214; see also first 100 days

R

rating agencies (ESG), Berg, Kölbel and Rigobon (2022) correlation 0.54 vs 0.99, 21–22, 33, 86–87, 96, 118; measurement differences 56% of rating disparity, 22, 87, 118, 137
real-time data, see IoT; predictive analytics

regression analysis, 47 portfolio companies, 8 years, 188
regulation, compliance early adoption, 160–161; CSRD, 157, 163, 167–168, 175; ESRS, 167–168; EU SFDR, 157, 162–163, 228; framework proliferation, 161–162; integrated compliance systems, 169–170; ISSB, 157, 162–163, 199, 208; OECD (2020), 158, 169, 173; regulatory revenue opportunities, 159; TCFD, 85, 95, 97, 161–162, 173; TNFD, 195, 208; UK climate-focused approach, 163–164; US SEC climate rules, 133, 235 regulatory due diligence, 89–90 renewable energy procurement, collaborative, 182–183 reporting requirements, core data repository, 130; CSRD timeline, 167; multi-stakeholder, 128–129; SFDR Article classifications, 160–161, 160; stakeholder-specific outputs, 131 resistance management, five types, 107–108; champion development, 108–109; competence resistance, 107; priority resistance, 107; resource resistance, 107; trust resistance, 107; values resistance, 107
Responsible Investment, see PRI; SRI Return on Investment, see ROI revenue enhancement, Alpine Foods, 70;
Ridgeline circular economy €4.2M, 143, 161; sustainability premium pricing, 25, 145, 204
revenue multiple, see Exit Multiple
Ridgeline Solutions, blockchain digital product passports, 200; circular economy case, 143, 145, 159, 200–201; customer joint innovation projects, 145; exit €67M from €38M (Section 8.3.2), 147; ESG premium €8–12M, 145, 224, 230; new revenue from circular economy €2.1M, 142, 200; packaging manufacturer, 4–6, 27; patents around sustainable packaging, 27; revenue 45% from sustainable design, 145; sustainability premium pricing 8–12%, 204; zero-waste-to-landfill achievement, 144, 147
Rigobon, R., 21–22, 33, 86–87, 96, 118, 137, 160, 175
risk management, climate scenario analysis, 85–87, 87; ESG-driven, 11, 40; exit positioning, 138, 142–143; portfolio-level, 165–166; reputation and brand protection, 143; see also climate risk; due diligence
Riviera Specialty, case study Ch.2, 17–32; environmental crisis, 17–19, 23–24; industrial chemical blending and solvents, 17, 23; Alex's catalyst experience, 17–19, 23
Roberts, George, 7
ROI, definition, 235; Alpine Foods 379% first-year (Ch.3/Ch.12), 48, 103, 214; fund-level 188% one-year payback, 187, 191; Helix Chemicals 2.8× four-year, 82, 147; see also Exit Multiple; IRR
Rook, D., 40, 53

S

Sachs, S., 118
Santos, Maria (referenced in disclaimer p. xiii), xiii
SASB, definition, 235; (2018) materiality map, 97; industry-specific frameworks, 89, 95, 244 satellite imagery, due diligence, 75, 80, 94
Schein, E. H. (2010), Organizational culture and leadership, 99, 116, 117, 241
Scope 1, 2, 3 Emissions, definition, 240
SDGs, definition, 236; UN Sustainable Development Goals investor alignment 65%, 162
Securities and Exchange Commission, see US SEC climate disclosure rules
sector materiality, consumer goods, 86, 89, 121; healthcare, 86, 89; manufacturing, 86, 89, 121; technology, 86, 89
Serafeim, G., 10, 16, 19–20, 33, 35–37, 53, 76, 95, 96, 118, 136, 139, 148, 156
SFDR, definition, 236; Article 6 classification, 160–161; Article 8 classification, 160–161; Article 9 classification, 160–161; article classifications, 160; reform proposal (November 2025), 59, 101, 119, 161, 175, 228; Solid Hej avoided implementation costs €180K, 160, 168, 174
Shajari, S., and David, S. (2025), Bridging the silos of digitalization and sustainability, 29, 33
Shandal, R., 138, 156
Shleifer and Summers (1988), trust in hostile takeovers, 242
skilled worker retention, Apex Industries, 121

social factor analysis, 60, 76–77
Social Licence to Operate, definition, 240
Socially Responsible Investing, see SRI
Society for Human Resource Management (SHRM), 118
Solid Hej Components, AI energy savings €92K, 196; AI predictive maintenance 23% downtime reduction, 196; baseline assessment, 25, 38–39; compliance director see Iwinosa, Efe; customer satisfaction 78% to 94%, 128; employee engagement 67% to 89%, 129; energy efficiency 31%, 38, 127, 140; ESG investment €596K over four years, 25, 29, 41–42, 144; exit €52M acquired 2019, €89M sold 2023, 43, 146; exit premium €12–15M ESG attribution, 137, 144, 185, 224, 226; exit multiple 1.71×, 43, 144; GRI selective implementation, 162; IoT sensor network 412 sensors (250+ energy, 45 water, 38 waste, 12 air, 67 HVAC), 201–202, 207; IoT €12K investment, €45K savings, 194, 207; LED retrofit €178K investment, €67K savings, 38, 41; manufacturing waste reduction 45%, 128; methodology (Ch.3 case study), 38–44, 209; €456K annual operating cost savings, 25, 29, 38, 41; €1.095M annual value creation, 25, 29; ROI of ESG 20× return, 144; SFDR avoided implementation costs €180K, 162, 166, 172; six bidders at exit, 137, 147; supplier partnership programmes, 180; technical integration, 127–128; technology infrastructure, 189–207; technology investment €45K, €135K value, 211
Srivastva, S., 99, 117, 241
SRI, definition, 236; see also Impact Investing
stakeholder advisory mechanisms, Alpine Foods, 68–69
Stakeholder Engagement, definition, 236; community relations, 84; customer relationship analysis, 83; digital platforms, 201–202; employee evaluation, 83; engagement methods, 108, 105; engagement protocols, 105; five-point assessment, 77; Kujala et al. (2022), 117, 238; mapping matrix (Ch.6), 104; mapping matrix portfolio level (Ch.10), 186; messaging by function, 109–110; priority mapping, 84–85; regulatory relationship assessment, 84; resistance management, 107–108; six-step development, 176;
stakeholder value creation approach, 58–59; supply chain evaluation, 83–84; see also customer engagement; employee engagement stakeholder value creation, approach, 58–59; Section 6.2 case studies, 104–115; Summit Peak €1.7M cost savings, 106; Summit Peak €2.3M EBITDA contribution, 106; see also value creation
strategic acquirers, buyer messaging, 152–153; ESG commitments, 139; Solid Hej rationale, 147
strategic intelligence, due diligence as, 91–92
Sull and Sull (2022), toxic culture, 118
Summit Peak Facility Services, CEO challenge transformation, 47, 105–106; customer satisfaction 67% to 94%, 106; customer retention 78% to 96%, 106, 127, 143; digital employee engagement participation 42% to 87%, 201; EBITDA growth 22% annual, 106; employee engagement methodology transferred to seven companies, 180–181, 184, 223; employee engagement €840K annual savings, 177, 187, 223; employee satisfaction 52% to 89%, 105–106, 201; employee suggestions €230K, 201; exit case 8.9× EBITDA multiple, 146, 153; exit premium ESG attribution €4–6M, 146, 228, 226; facilities management company, 39, 47; leadership diversity 23% to 52%, 146; €31M revenue, 47; €1.7M annual cost savings, 106; €2.3M EBITDA contribution, 106; quality management 96% customer retention, 144; TCFD €340K business interruption reduction, 162; training 340 employees, 148; turnover 47% to 12%, 47, 106, 127, 143, 205
supplier development, Alpine Foods communication enhancement, 214; cross-portfolio sustainability programme, 177, 179; Helix Chemicals supplier risk, 196; Solid Hej partnership programmes, 180
supply chain, AI risk assessment, 196; blockchain traceability (Ridgeline), 203–204; due diligence evaluation,

83–84; sustainability programme, 179; transparency regulation, 94
Sustainability Accounting Standards Board, see SASB
Sustainability-Linked Bond Principles (ICMA), iii
sustainable funds, Morningstar (2021) outperformance 71%, 65, 74; Whelan et al. (2021) NYU Stern meta-analysis 58% positive ESG-financial link, 65, 74, 120, 138
Sustainable Development Goals, see SDGs
Sustainable Finance Disclosure Regulation, see SFDR

T
talent attraction, Summit Peak case, 39, 105–106; turnover reduction correlation, 39, 84
Task Force on Climate-related Financial Disclosures, see TCFD
Taskforce on Nature-related Financial Disclosures, see TNFD
TCFD, definition, 236; (2017) Recommendations, 95, 97, 136, 173, 244; climate risk framework, 85, 157, 163–164; four pillars (governance, strategy, risk management, metrics), 163–164; Summit Peak €340K business interruption reduction, 164 technology, ESG technology four strategic roles, 193; ESG technology maturity framework, 193; future trends, 209–210; large company solutions, 194; medium company solutions, 194; small company solutions, 194; vendor evaluation framework, 203, 222; see also AI; blockchain; IoT
Tesla, luxury pricing average $54,660 in 2020, 25
Third-Party Verification, definition, 236; cross-portfolio audit cost reduction 30%, 182
TNFD, (2025) welcomes ISSB decision, 199, 208, 228, 231; ISSB framework alignment, 195; nature-related disclosure framework, 195; see also nature-related disclosures
transition planning, see climate risk; net zero
trust building, 100, 107
turnover, Alpine 8% vs industry 22%, 84, 100; correlation with engagement, 39–40, 84; portfolio average 38% reduction, 177; reduction methodologies, 39, 177; Summit Peak 47% to 12%, 47, 106, 126, 143, 201; see also employee retention

U
UK climate-focused approach, 165–166
UN Global Compact (2004), Who Cares Wins, 7, 16
UN Sustainable Development Goals, see SDGs
United Nations Principles for Responsible Investment, see PRI
UNPRI, see PRI
Usmen, Emre, endorsements page, i
US SEC climate disclosure rules, 133, 235

V
Valencia headquarters, Alpine Foods, 57 valuation, EBITDA multiples, 4–6, 138– 148, 184, 189; ESG impact, 4–6; exit multiple, 4–6, 138–146; multiple expansion, 14; technology premium (Helix Chemicals), 147; see also Exit Multiple
Value Creation, definition, 236; ESG value creation evolution, 58, 59; ESG value creation mechanisms, 40; KPMG (2025), 175, 191, 213, 227; long-term, 13, 19–20; methodology transferability, 71–72; portfolio-level synergies, 184; seven mechanisms framework, 23–25, 40, 52; see also Khan, Serafeim and Yoon (2016); Porter and Kramer (2011)
Value Creation Plan, definition, 240
Van Holt, T., 65, 74, 119, 138 vendor evaluation, 203, 226
Viehs, M., 20, 33, 36, 53
Vintage Year, definition, 240

W
Walsh, Jennifer, see Day, Penelope waste reduction, Helix Chemicals predictive analytics 67%, 147; portfolio target 20–40%, 217; Ridgeline zero-waste-to-landfill, 142; Solid Hej manufacturing 45%, 129
water usage tracking, Solid Hej IoT sensors, 201

Weber, Marcus (Head of Operations, Apex Industries), 192, 210
Whelan, T., Atz, Van Holt and Clark (2021), NYU Stern meta-analysis 58% positive ESG-financial link, 65, 74, 120, 138
Whitney, D., 117, 241
Willard, B. (2012), The new sustainability advantage, 243

Y

Yoon, A., 11–12, 16, 76, 95, 96, 118, 136, 141–142, 148, 156

Z

Zala, Imade (Alpine Foods owner), 57, 65,
zero waste, Ridgeline achievement, 142, 147; Ridgeline circular economy 18 months, 147

Author Index

Secondary lookup of cited sources by author surname. Each entry gives the work's year, short identifier, and all page references where the work is cited in the book. Co-authored works appear under each author's surname (one entry per author for the same work).

A

A Simple Model, (2024) Post-acquisition work: the first 100 days, 99, 117, 242

Alvarez and Marsal, (2024) PE survey, 139, 156

Atz, U., Whelan, Atz, Van Holt and Clark (2021) NYU Stern meta-analysis, 65, 74, 119, 138

B

Bain and Company, (2022) Global Private Equity Report, 191; PRI and Bain (2025) value creation in private markets, 13, 16; Impact revolution (recommended reading), 243

Barton, D., and McKinsey Global Institute (2017) Measuring the economic impact of short-termism, 243

Bassen, A., Friede, Busch and Bassen (2015) ESG-CFP meta-analysis, 21, 33, 37, 53

Berg, F., Berg, Kölbel and Rigobon (2022) Aggregate confusion, 21–22, 33, 86–87, 96, 118, 136, 160, 175

BNP Paribas Securities Services, (2019) ESG global survey, 160, 175

Busch, T., Friede, Busch and Bassen (2015), 21, 33, 37, 53

C

CFA Institute, (2018) Guidance and case studies for ESG integration, 243

CFGI, (2021) Navigating those critical first 100 days, 99, 117, 242

Clark, C., Whelan, Atz, Van Holt and Clark (2021), 65, 74, 119, 138

Clark, G. L., Clark, Feiner and Viehs (2015) ESG and stock performance, 20, 33, 36, 53

Cooperrider, D. L., Cooperrider and Srivastva (1987) Appreciative inquiry, 99, 117, 238; Cooperrider and Whitney (2005), 241

D

David, S., Shajari and David (2025) Bridging the silos, 29, 33

E

Eccles, R. G., Eccles, Ioannou and Serafeim (2014) High sustainability companies, 10, 16, 19–20, 33, 35–37, 53, 96

Edmans, A., (2011) Does the stock market fully value intangibles?, 243

EFRAG, (2025a) Technical advice on draft simplified ESRS (3 December), 77, 96, 232, 231; (2025b) Draft Simplified ESRS resource hub, 96

Entraygues, P., Shandal and Entraygues (2024), 138, 156

European Commission, (2025a) Impact assessment SFDR review, 14, 16; (2025b) Proposal amending Regulation (EU) 2019/2088, 14, 16; (2025c) Commission proposes improvements to SFDR (21 November), 32, 117, 137, 173, 228, 231; (2025d) Commission simplifies transparency rules (20 November), 32, 137, 175

EY, (2024) PE ESG funds IRR analysis, 141, 156

F

Feiner, A., Clark, Feiner and Viehs (2015), 20, 33, 36, 53

Financier Worldwide, (2022) M&A challenges: employee engagement and retention, 117, 242

Fitzgibbons, S., Pedersen, Fitzgibbons and Pomorski (2021) greenium effect, 26, 33, 139, 156

Friede, G., Friede, Busch and Bassen (2015) ESG-CFP meta-analysis, 21, 33, 37, 53

G

Global Sustainable Investment Alliance, (2021) Global Sustainable Investment Review 2020, 163, 175

Godsall, J., Barton et al. (2017), 243

Grant Thornton, (2024) PE finance transformation, 117, 242

Greenfield, E., Greenfield, Monk and Rook (2026) ESG value creation in private equity, 40, 53

H

Heath, C., and Heath, D., (2010) Switch, 241, 245

I

IFC, (2002) Developing value: business case in emerging markets, 6, 16, 138

IFRS Foundation, (2025a, 28 October)

ISSB Update October 2025, 195, 208, 232, 235

ILPA, (2024) ESG considerations for limited partners, 180, 195

Ioannou, I., Eccles, Ioannou and Serafeim (2014), 10, 16, 19–20, 33, 35–37, 53, 96; Foreword, xv

K

Kengelbach, J., (2024) M&A dealmakers survey, 137, 148, 156

Khan, M., Khan, Serafeim and Yoon (2016) Corporate sustainability: first evidence on materiality, 11–12, 16, 76, 95, 96, 118, 136, 139, 148, 156

Kölbel, J., Berg, Kölbel and Rigobon (2022), 21–22, 33, 86–87, 96, 118, 136, 162, 175

Koller, T., Barton et al. (2017), 243

Kotter, J. P., (2012) Leading change, 118, 241

KPMG, (2025, 28 October) Value Creation in Private Equity, 175, 191, 217, 231

Kramer, M. R., Porter and Kramer (2011) Creating Shared Value, 58, 72, 74

Kravis, H., (historical reference), 7

Kujala, J., Kujala et al. (2022) Stakeholder engagement: past, present, and future, 118, 241

M

Manyika, J., Barton et al. (2017), 243

McKinsey and Company, (2020) ESG portfolio capabilities, 174, 191; (2023a) Private markets turn to value creation through ESG, 136, 191; (2023b) The ESG premium, 192, 212

Monk, A., Greenfield, Monk and Rook (2026), 40, 53

Morgan Stanley, (2025) Sustainable Signals: Corporates 2025, 33

Morningstar, (2021) Sustainable Funds Landscape Report, 65, 74

N

Nature Action 100, (2025) First status report (28 October), 59, 74

Network for Greening the Financial System, (2022) Progress report on bridging data gaps, 97, 241; NGFS Climate Scenarios, 85–87

O

OECD, (2020) ESG investing and climate transition, 158, 169, 176

P

Palter, R., Barton et al. (2017), 243

Pedersen, L. H., Pedersen, Fitzgibbons and

Pomorski (2021) Responsible investing: the ESG-efficient frontier, 26, 33, 139, 156

Pomorski, L., Pedersen, Fitzgibbons and

Pomorski (2021), 26, 33, 137, 156

Porter, M. E., Porter and Kramer (2011) Creating Shared Value, 58, 72, 74

Preqin, Private Equity ESG Report (quarterly issues), 243

PRI (Principles for Responsible Investment), PRI and Bain (2025) value creation, 13, 16; (2023) Private equity: responsible investment during the first

100 days, 98, 117, 239; PRI ESG Due Diligence Questionnaire, 244
PwC, (2022) Global Investor Survey, 35, 53, 139, 154; Private Equity ESG Survey (annual), 243

R
Rigobon, R., Berg, Kölbel and Rigobon (2022), 21–22, 33, 86–87, 96, 118, 136, 162, 175
Roberts, G., (historical reference), 7
Rook, D., Greenfield, Monk and Rook (2026), 40, 53

S
SASB, (2018) SASB Materiality Map, 89, 95, 97, 244
Schein, E. H., (2010) Organizational culture and leadership, 4th ed., 99, 116, 118, 241
Serafeim, G., Eccles, Ioannou and
Serafeim (2014), 10, 16, 19–20, 33, 35–37, 53, 96; Khan, Serafeim and Yoon (2016), 11–12, 16, 76, 95, 96, 118, 138, 139, 148, 156
Shajari, S., Shajari and David (2025), 29, 33
Shandal, R., Shandal and Entraygues (2024), 138, 156
Shleifer, A., Shleifer and Summers (1988) Breach of trust in hostile takeovers, 242
Society for Human Resource Management (SHRM), 118
Srivastva, S., Cooperrider and Srivastva (1987), 99, 117, 241
Summers, L. H., Shleifer and Summers (1988), 242
Sull, C., and Sull, D., (2022) Toxic culture is driving the Great Resignation, 118

T
Task Force on Climate-related Financial Disclosures (TCFD), (2017) Recommendations of the Task Force, 95, 97, 136, 173, 244
Taskforce on Nature-related Financial Disclosures (TNFD), (2025) TNFD welcomes ISSB decision (7 November), 199, 208, 228, 235

U
United Nations Global Compact, (2004) Who Cares Wins, 7, 16

V
Van Holt, T., Whelan, Atz, Van Holt and Clark (2021), 65, 74, 119, 138
Viehs, M., Clark, Feiner and Viehs (2015), 20, 33, 36, 53

W
Whelan, T., Whelan, Atz, Van Holt and Clark (2021) NYU Stern meta-analysis, 65, 74, 119, 138
Whitney, D., Cooperrider and Whitney (2005), 241
Willard, B., (2012) The new sustainability advantage, 10th anniversary ed., 243

Y
Yoon, A., Khan, Serafeim and Yoon (2016), 11–12, 16, 76, 95, 96, 118, 136, 141, 148, 154; (2024) Two factors that determine when ESG creates shareholder value, 140, 156

Z
Zoffer, J., Barton et al. (2017), 243

For Product Safety Concerns and Information please contact our EU representative GPSR@taylorandfrancis.com
Taylor & Francis Verlag GmbH, Kaufingerstraße 24, 80331 München, Germany

www.ingramcontent.com/pod-product-compliance
Ingram Content Group UK Ltd.
Pitfield, Milton Keynes, MK11 3LW, UK
UKHW020150200926
475702UK00016B/2632
9781041038375